"Paradigms Tossed"

Debunking Faulty Christian Beliefs

Contents

APPENDIXES

Acknowledgments

In almost all non-fictional literary works, there is a long list of contributors from whom the author has garnered invaluable research and/or insightful information. This book is no exception. Within the pages of "Paradigms Tossed" one will find the influences of such theological giants as Erich Sauer, J. Dwight Pentecost, Norman Geisler, Robert Thieme, Dr. Louis Barbieri and most notably, Arthur Custance.

Special thanks go out to Diana D'Itri, whose encouragement and unique editing capabilities were essential in accomplishing the completion of this book.

Any and all theological errors found within this work are the sole responsibility of the author, for which I do now duly apologize for.

In addition, one of the challenges of writing a study that is extremely broad in its scope is the occurrence of some redundancy of thought and examples. These were deemed to be necessary however, in order to make the arguments presented within each individual chapter sufficiently comprehensive.

www.paradigmstossed.com

Preface

While still a young Christian man, relatively new to the faith, I had the privilege of taking a Seminary level course taught by Dr. Louis Barbieri, who at the time was the Dean of Students at Dallas Theological Seminary. Dr. Barbieri would start each class session with the singing of a random hymn. Before the singing commenced, Dr. Barbieri would quickly scan through the text of the hymn, pick out a stanza from the hymn, and then read the stanza to the class. After reading the stanza aloud, he would then proceed to ask the class, "Now what is wrong with this verse from the hymn? Is what this statement saying, actually true?" Then he would quote Scriptures which exhibited to the class how the verse from the hymn was not 100% in agreement with God's Word.

During the first two or three sessions of the class, while Dr. Barbieri was going through this ritual, I can still remember myself getting upset with what I considered at the time to be "excessive nitpicking." But after the first few sessions, I began to realize the importance of what Dr. Barbieri was doing. For I could now see how some of my own perceptions of the Christian faith had been clouded to the truths revealed in the Word of God. The obvious point that Dr. Barbieri was trying to impress upon the class was that the writings of men, whether they are in the form of hymns, Christian literature, or even Church Doctrines, were to be considered suspect unless they were in complete agreement with the written Word of God. It was Dr. Barbieri's contention that when the writings of men are not held up to and examined by the light of God's Word, they can often lead to harmful misconceptions as to the truths that are revealed in Scripture.

The purpose of this study is to attempt to expose some of these common misconceptions or faulty paradigms that exist within the Church today, and to thereby provide fresh insight and understanding into the wonderful truths that are expressed in God's Word.

Foreword

At the time that I became a Christian at the tender age of 19, I became keenly aware of the newfound presence of God within my being. I also soon realized that the presence of the Holy Spirit within me now enabled me to better understand the Holy Scriptures. In addition to these things, I also recognized just how far "off base" my former theological views had been prior to my conversion. I became determined to never again adopt a stance on Biblical Doctrine or Topics unless I was as certain as I could be that the stance I was taking was absolutely true.

Over the course of the next 30 years, I slowly and methodically developed "my take" on what I thought the Lord was attempting to communicate to the "household of faith" through His Word. Scripture states that "natural" or unredeemed man is not capable of truly understanding spiritual things. Evidence of this blindness is often seen in Old World Architecture, where we find in the eaves of the buildings the spirit beings or "gargoyles" mockingly looking down at "the presumptuousness of man in his attempt to understand the ways of the unknowable God".

To the true spiritually enlightened "born again" believer however, the God of the Universe is not the "God of the Gargoyles," but is openly exhibited in His Word and in the Person of the Lord Jesus Christ. The God of the Universe does not hide from His family of faith. In the New Testament, Jesus told his disciples that He did not consider them to be mere servants, but rather as His friends, "For the servant knoweth not what his master doeth." The same holds true in the Old Testament, where we find Scripture stating that, "Abraham was the friend of God", in addition to the declaration, "Shall I hide from Abraham the thing that I do?"

This of course begs the question, "If God is so willing to be intimately known by His followers, why then is it that so few members of the household of faith seem to have a coherent understanding of His Word and of how He is accomplishing His Purposes in their lives"?

From my years of studying Scripture and observing my fellow believers, I have come to the conclusion that the failure of the majority of believers to adequately grasp Christian Theology is not because Christian Theology is all that difficult to understand. Christian Theology is in and of itself very simple. The main reason that the Word of God is so challenging for many believers is the fact that there exists within Christendom numerous faulty understandings of basic Biblical Doctrines. These theological errors have been initiated throughout the years of Church History when God's Word has become interpreted through the lens of secular culture, erroneous belief systems, and sadly, through many of the creeds of the formalized Church.

It is only after these theological errors, or "faulty paradigms" have been exposed and replaced by the truths of God's Word, that one can see and appreciate how the various topics and Doctrines of the Bible all interlock together in perfect harmony and create a beautiful mosaic that reveals the thoughts and mindset of the Almighty God.

The author fully realizes that there will be those who read this work who will be reluctant to accept the fact that many of their core beliefs are not in alignment with the Word of God, for it is human nature to want to cling to one's beliefs. I think that it was Mark Twain who stated, "It is far easier to fool someone than to convince them that they have been fooled." This strong reluctance to changing one's viewpoint is all part and parcel to what the Scriptures refers to as, "the pulling down of strongholds".

To those who approach this study with an open mind, I hope

it will not only offer a new appreciation for God's Word, but that it will also awaken a new awareness of God's intimate presence within the life of each and every believer.

Introduction

The Quest for Truth

"What is truth?" Although these words were spoken by Pontius Pilate 20 centuries ago, they are just as poignant today as they were when they were first uttered. Scripture tells us that God's Word is Truth (John 17:17). The further any society drifts away from the Word of God, the further that society drifts away from Truth. This is where our modern day culture finds itself today. It is a culture steeped in moral relativism. A culture that makes the same mistake that Pilate made in denying that there is such a thing as absolute truth. This cultural malaise is nothing new, for there truly is, "No new thing under the sun" (Ecclesiastes 1:9). The 21st Century moral relativism we are now experiencing is based upon the belief that, "What may be true for you, may not be true for me." This system of thought inevitably brings about a culture in which every man "does what is right in his own eyes" (Judges 17:6), and typically ends with a society filled with broken homes and failed relationships.

Truth is not only found in God's Word but also in other areas of life, such as in science. There are many truths in the physical laws that govern the Universe that God has created. For example, the Law of Gravity. Whenever the Law of Gravity is violated, the results are 100 percent predictable. The object doing the violating comes down to earth. Just as man needs to align himself with the Laws of Nature, or face the immediate consequences, so must he align himself with the written Word of God. Failure to do so brings about consequences not only in this life, but also in the life hereafter.

Although ultimate Truth is not relative, it can be multi-faceted. This is what is meant by the philosophical statement, "Truth is not reality, but a perception of reality." That absolute truth can have many facets is borne out by the fact that there are four Gospels, each taking a different approach to the Incarnation of Jesus Christ, a topic for later discussion.

Another aspect of Truth is that it brings about freedom. It has been said that "The Ten Commandments are really the Magna Carta of human freedom." For if the Ten Commandments were truly followed, then every man would be free to enjoy his life, property, and relationships without being violated by the misdeeds of others. When Jesus stated, "That you shall know the truth, and the truth shall make you free," He was confirming the fact that it is truth that is the great liberator of mankind. Without truth, there can be no real freedom. Without freedom, there can be no real human happiness. Although it is seldom overtly stated, "Human happiness is directly correlated to the amount of freedom, both real, potential, and/or imagined, that the individual believes they possess.

All people, believer and unbeliever alike, benefit from knowing the truth about the life situations that they find themselves in. For example, when a person who is experiencing psychological distress from an unknown source finally discovers the underlying causes of the distress, it is common for that person to experience a degree of exhilaration and relief when the truth as to the underlying cause of the distress comes to light. It can be like opening a window and taking in a deep breath on a clear spring day. Such is the nature of Truth. It is the Great Liberator.

The conundrum that the unbeliever finds himself in however, is that by nature, he seeks to avoid coming to the solution to his spiritual problems. Napoleon, an adept student of human nature, stated, "Mankind will believe almost anything, as long as it is not in the Bible." This of course is in direct agreement with the words of Jesus, who stated that man naturally hates spiritual light, and seeks to avoid it at all costs (John 3:20).

Although the believer in Christ can receive the truths found in God's Word, he still has a twofold problem in his quest for spiritual truth. The first being the old sin nature that remains hostile to God, that continues to live alongside of his new life in Christ. A struggle has begun between the new and the old man, with each nature striving for dominance. In order to grow in the grace and knowledge of His Lord and Savior, the believer has to actively resist the old man, and to feed the new man by seeking the Lord and His Word. When the old man rules in the life of the Christian, the capacity for growing in the grace and knowledge of the Truths found in Jesus Christ is greatly diminished.

The second problem that the believer has regarding truth is that there are quite a few misconceptions or false paradigms found within Christendom which the Church at large often erroneously accepts as truths. These faulty paradigms often serve to cloud the believer's vision from the truths contained in God's Word, even when he is actively seeking to learn more about his Lord and His ways.

Many spiritual treasures in God's Word are to be found just beneath the surface, and like buried treasure in the physical world, can only be found by doing a little bit of digging. When one's vision is blinded by layers upon layers of faulty paradigms, many of the wonders of God's Word can be difficult to see, and thus remain hidden to the eyes of the believer. Many of these faulty paradigms have their origins in the well-intentioned accepted Creeds of the established Church, from Christian Literature and Music, and from the Church relying solely upon "human reasoning" in its attempts to understand God and His ways.

The purpose of this study is to expose some of these faulty paradigms and to hopefully open the eyes of the Christian to fresh insights and a deeper understanding of the Truths that are to be found within the written Word of God. It is by no means meant to be contentious and should be read in the same spirit of understanding expressed by the poet John Keats, who wrote; "Opinion striking opinion ignites the spark that lights the lamp of truth".

Paradigms

Although the word "paradigm" can evoke thoughts of a word that has either esoteric or deep and mysterious connotations, loosely defined, paradigms simply refer to "patterns of understanding". It is through paradigms that we create our mental outlook or interpretation of the realities of the world in which we live. In essence, paradigms are "the lens through which we see our world". We typically develop our paradigms without any conscious effort on our part. They just materialize from a synthesis of the information that we gather in during the course of our daily existence. When the information upon which we develop our paradigms is accurate and complete, then our paradigms can be beneficial to us in our dealings with the issues and the problems that we face in life. However, when the information upon which we develop our paradigms is either false or incomplete, it is then that they can have very damaging effects upon our lives.

To illustrate, we will give three examples of the potential deleterious effects of faulty paradigms from the secular business world.

Decca Records

In the early 1960's, Decca Records was one of the leading record labels in popular music. When they received a musical demo from a new male guitar group, they declined to sign the group to a recording contract. The reason they cited, was that it was their belief that the future of pop music was in individual artists, and not in guitar groups. Decca Records was looking for the next Elvis Presley to come along and rule the airwaves. The history of the recording industry in the 1950's would surely seem to justify the paradigm that Decca was operating under, for in the 1950's solo acts such as Bobby Darin, Frankie Avalon, and Bobby Vee reigned supreme.

As any student of pop music would most assuredly know, Decca's paradigm of the future of pop music was totally erroneous, as the ensuing years were filled with numerous successful guitar driven groups. While Decca was out looking for the next Elvis, their faulty paradigm of the future caused them to miss out on what was really happening in the world of pop music, much to the financial harm of their record company.

Just in case you haven't guessed who the group was that Decca originally refused to sign, it was of course, "The Beatles".

Swiss Watch Industry

In 1968, the Swiss controlled fully 65% of the total luxury watch market in the world. For decades, the Swiss had been the world's premiere luxury watch maker. Then along came the quartz movement. The Swiss opted not to utilize the new movement due to their assumption that "the future of the luxury watch market was in the use of mechanical watch movements".

By 1978, by marketing the new quartz movement, Seiko and mainly other Japanese firms now controlled over 80% of the total watch market, with the Swiss possessing only about 20%. Due to their faulty paradigm of the future of the luxury watch market, the Swiss had quickly lost their dominance in the luxury watch industry, much to their financial harm.

The ironic part of the story is, that it was the Swiss who had originally invented the quartz movement! Not only had the Swiss missed out on the new manufacturing trend in luxury watches, but due to their unfounded love of mechanical movements and their indifference to the possibilities of the new quartz movement, they had failed to patent their new invention, losing out on even more financial gain in the process!

Again, this was all because the Swiss could not bring themselves to believe in, or envision a future for, anything other than the mechanical movement in the luxury watch business. They had lost out because they were living under a faulty paradigm.

IBM and Microsoft

Probably the greatest example of financial loss due to a faulty business paradigm occurred in the early 1980's. IBM had employed a contract worker named Bill Gates, who had developed the DOS Operating System for small computers. The paradigm that IBM operated under was a deep belief that the future of the computer industry was in large Main Frame Computers. They really did not have much if any interest at all in the new world of small computers, or PC's.

To make a long story short, IBM sold the DOS Operating System back to Bill Gates for a small amount of money, and soon Microsoft was born, and the rest of the story as they say, is history. IBM lost out on billions of dollars of financial gain due to the fact that the paradigm upon which they had based their business decisions was substantially false. Today the world is almost completely run on these small personal computers which are found in many forms.

Due to a faulty paradigm, IBM missed out on potentially becoming the largest corporation in the world.

Rightly Dividing the Word of Truth

To the Christian, faulty paradigms in the spiritual realm can often be just as detrimental as they are to financial businesses in the secular realm. Here, however, the potential for loss can be even greater, for the stakes are now no longer confined to the temporal but have eternal consequences. For to the Christian, faulty spiritual paradigms can not only inhibit one from experiencing God's best for their life while here on earth, but they can also leave one in an undesirable state in the Day of Judgment, as Paul's letter to Timothy specifically indicates:

"Study to show thyself approved unto God, a workman that needeth not to be ashamed, rightly dividing the word of truth." II Timothy 2:15

Here Paul is emphasizing the importance of having an accurate and correct theological framework as a standard upon which the Christian should live his or her life. In essence, what Paul was saying to Timothy was that if the Christian did not rightly divide or correctly interpret God's Word, they would be running the risk of standing before the Lord at The Judgment Seat of Christ, being ashamed of how they had conducted their life while on earth.

So how does one "rightly divide the word of truth?" One of the keys to rightly dividing or correctly interpreting God's Word is to follow the Biblical admonition of concordance, as expressed in the Book of Matthew:

"That in the mouth of two or three witnesses, may every word be established." Matthew 18:16

This is in complete agreement with the writings of Solomon, who wrote in the Book of Proverbs:

"Where no counsel is, the people fall: but in the multitude of counselors there is safety." Proverbs 11:14

In other words, if one is to make interpretive statements about Scripture, one should always invoke other Scriptures for the sake of corroboration. This is the Biblical way of avoiding the mistake of wrongful interpretation, or of taking Scripture out of context. The interpretation of Scripture should always be in agreement with other Scripture.

As an example, in analyzing Revelation 14:18, where the Apostle John is chronicling the events of the Great Tribulation, the Bible states:

"And another angel came out from the altar, which had power over fire; and cried with a loud cry to him who had the sickle, saying, Thrust in thy sharp sickle, and gather the clusters of the vine of the earth; for her grapes are fully ripe."

Here one might want to ascertain that, as a principle, that "God allows sin to come to a full fruition, before He judges it." In order to properly establish whether this conjecture is true, one must appeal not only to human reason, but more importantly to the rest of Scripture. In the Book of Genesis, we find a validating verse, where God informs Abraham that He will not judge and displace the Amorites until their iniquity is fully matured:

"But in the fourth generation they shall come hither again, for the iniquity of the Amorites is not yet full." Genesis 15:16

Hence, a Biblical principle can safely be established, that the reason that God may seem to be slow to judge sin in the world, is that He often allows sin to come to its full fruition before He judges it.

A second example of corroborating Scripture in order to categorize and establish Biblical Principles can be seen by examining Paul's statement in II Corinthians 4:15, which reads:

"For all things are for your sakes, that the abundant grace might through the thanksgiving of many redound to the glory of God."

This passage of Scripture seems to indicate the principle "that everything that exists in the Universe, the whole wonders of Creation, and everything that transpires throughout the history of man, is in reality being done for the eternal benefit of the believer in Christ." For while Paul is stating, "ALL THINGS" (emphasis mine) are for your sakes", there is clearly a wide range of possibilities included in such a broad statement. This is indeed an awesome, humbling, and tremendous thought.

The truth of this principle is also affirmed by David in the Book of Psalms, where he writes:

"I will cry unto God most high: unto God that "PERFORMETH ALL THINGS FOR ME." Psalms 57:2 (emphasis mine)

Therefore, it is safe to say that the whole grand display of the Universe, and all of the intricacies of life, are ordained by God for the express benefit of the believer in Jesus Christ.

So, we see how general conjectures that we make regarding the interpretation of Scripture needs to be in accordance with other Scripture. All too often grave theological errors and faulty paradigms get introduced into the Church through assertions of well-intentioned pastors and Christian writers when these assertions are not held up to corroborating verses and the full light of Scripture. When Scripture is interpreted without appealing to other Scripture, it is then that we run into the danger of "majoring in the minors" and developing faulty paradigms. As Paul had stated to Timothy, this can lead to us living our lives in theological error, and potentially being ashamed when Jesus assesses our lives upon His return.

This study will now attempt to expose some of the more common faulty paradigms that exist within the Church today. Hopefully, new light will be shed upon God's Word for the reader, so that they will experience a better understanding of some of the truths found within Scripture, and for the reader this would truly be a time of, "Paradigms Tossed".

10

The Tragedy of Faulty Paradigms in Christian Theology

One of the greatest tragedies that emerges from the many Faulty Paradigms that are found within Christendom, is the fact that these numerous Faulty Paradigms serve to blind the believer in Christ to the truths contained in God's Word. Not only do faulty paradigms promote spiritual blindness, but when they are considered all together, they are also instrumental in the creation of an additional Faulty Paradigm, a paradigm which essentially states that, "God's Word is very complicated, and extremely hard to understand." This pattern of understanding of course is totally contrary to the clear teaching of Scripture. Paul writes in his second letter to the Corinthians:

"But I fear, lest by any means, as the serpent beguiled Eve through his subtlety, so your minds should be corrupted from the simplicity that is in Christ." II Corinthians 11:3

Here we have Paul stating that the message of God's Word that is found in Jesus Christ (John 1:1), is one of simplicity, and by direct inference, "easy to understand."

Imagine if you will, a mechanical engineer operating under scientific assumptions and mathematical formulas that are contrary to the known Laws of Physics. The fruits of his efforts would most likely be nothing short of disastrous. He would then spend his working days in abject frustration, the inconsistent results of his labor never allowing him to be totally successful in his work.

Should we expect anything different for the Christian who lives his life under the guidance of the many Faulty Paradigms that are to be found within Christendom, paradigms that are contrary to God's Word? Not only do faulty paradigms cause the Christian to potentially miss out on what may be God's best for his or her life, but they also serve to frustrate individual

11

Christians in their quest for a better understanding of God and His ways.

The overriding goal of this study is to refute the faulty paradigm that suggests, "God's Word is complicated and extremely difficult to understand" and reveal to the reader the utter simplicity of Christian Theology. This shall be done by first exposing the more common basic faulty paradigms, and then by revealing what God's Word teaches on the particular subject at hand.

It is the contention of this study, that Scripture when viewed as a whole, is like a multi-dimensional tapestry, and that all the basic doctrines and topics of Scripture fit seamlessly together without contradiction into a beautiful literary mosaic, a mosaic that requires no more intellectual ability to understand than that possessed by a typical high school student.

Finally, and most importantly, it is with profound hope that this study will bring the reader to a greater awareness and understanding of the personal love and care that God has for the individual believer in Jesus Christ.

Mankind's Reality is not God's Reality

"Man's view of the Universe and God's, are one and the same"

Of all the faulty paradigms to be found within Christendom that are in critical need of debunking, the idea that God's perception of reality is the same as man's perception, is right at the top of the list. Therefore, I can think of no better place to start our study into the world of common theological faulty paradigms, than by dealing with this particular misconception first.

It's likely due to the fact that Scripture states, "God made man in His own image" (Genesis 1:27), that it is quite natural for man to assume that God's viewpoint, perspective, and concept of the physical universe is much the same as his own. That God has to somehow wait for the future to occur before He too can truly know what is going to happen. This mistaken belief is reinforced by much of Christian literature and often permeates the very fabric of our collective theological thinking.

Scripture is quick to point out however, that God's experience with the physical universe is quite different than our own. When man makes up his own designs as to how "God views the Universe" without appealing to Scripture, the end result is inevitably destined to result in error. This error can easily lead us into a false concept of who God is, one in which His Omnipotence can seem to be greatly diminished. We often assume that God is somehow subject "to His own Creation," when in fact as a spiritual being, He exists outside of it, as its Perfect Master.

To begin with, man is a finite physical being. God on the other hand, is an infinite Spiritual Being. When man superimposes his own view of reality and perceptions on to God, the results can predictably be seen to be way off base. The atheistic philosopher Friedrich Nietzsche was quick to pick up on this folly of mankind, remarking, "In the beginning, God created man in His own image..., and then man..., returned the favor."

For all of his foibles, this was a brilliant observation on Nietzsche's part ("Even a blind squirrel can find a nut every now and then").

The physical world unfolds unto man in three stages: past, present, and future, and that being only within his limited geographical surroundings. We are told by Scripture however, that God views everything in the total Universe, both past, present, and future as one, and all at the same time. With God, "That which hath been is now; and that which is to be hath already been" (Ecclesiastes 3:15). The fact that God views the total history (past, present, and future) of the physical Universe all at one and the same time, is corroborated in the New Testament where we read:

"All things (past, present, and future) are naked and open unto the eyes of Him with whom we have to do." Hebrews 4:13

God is an Omniscient, Omnipresent, and Omnipotent Spiritual Being. Due to His Spiritual Nature or Essence, God is able to see the totality of the physical history of the Universe as one event, this without having to exert any effort on His part whatsoever. God exists and also stands outside of time. Unlike us, God is Spirit (John 4:24), and is in no way subject to the constraints of time. This is how and why Scripture can proclaim that in God's eyes, Jesus Christ was, "The Lamb slain from the foundation of the world" (Revelation 13:8). In that God is Spirit, it is in His very Nature to see the total history of the physical world as one sequential event. It was only when Jesus emptied himself of His Godly privilege (Philippians 2:7), and in His humanity, that He became confined as it were, to time.

While from our perspective, life can at times seem to drag on and on, from God's perspective, we truly do "spend our years as a tale that is told" (Psalm 90:9). As finite human beings, the awareness of the past, present, and future all at one and the same time is hard for us to comprehend, but for God, it is no big thing. This is how He can answer our prayers even before we have prayed them (Isaiah 65:24, "Before they call, I will answer.").

Albert Einstein recognized the fact that the non-material world of pure spirit is not subject to time, and that time as we know it does not really exist outside of the physical world. After Einstein had developed his theory of relativity, he stated:

"If you don't take my words too seriously, before the theory of relativity and the creation of the Universe, time would have existed as an independent entity. But after the theory of relativity, and before the creation of the physical universe, there would be no such thing as time, for time would have no meaning."

Einstein recognized that the Universe was not created at some specific point in time, but rather, that time itself was created at the same moment that the physical Universe came into existence. The concept of time does not exist in the world of the purely spiritual. Without the physical Universe, time would cease to exist, not having any function in and of itself. God is a Spiritual Being and existed long before there was any physical Universe. He is not bound by the time space continuum that we as human beings experience, which may serve to explain how He is able to view the total history of the physical Universe all at once.

The ultimate or "real" reality, if you will, is the reality of the "spiritual world." What we as human beings experience in the reality of the "physical world", a reality which is strictly bound by space and time, is a mere anomaly when considered in the light of the reality of the purely spiritual world. Einstein addressed the shortcomings of the physical reality which we as humans experience when he stated, "Reality is an illusion, albeit a persistent one." Here Einstein is recognizing the fact that the reality of the physical world is in a sense subservient to the greater reality of the spiritual world.

The actuality that there are at least two separate realities of existence opens the door for much conjecture. For example, one might speculate that, "Perhaps time is only experienced by those who are subject to it, that is, physical beings." This may indeed be the reason why in Mark's Gospel the demonic beings exhibited a longing to be housed in physical bodies, even if the bodies in question were those of animals (Mark 5:12). Perhaps for the fallen angels to be without a physical body is to exist in a purely spiritual reality, one in which they are somehow subjected to a constant awareness of the horrors of their eternal damnation that await them. By acquiring a physical body, demons may in some way be able to mitigate the consciousness of these horrors. Conjectures such as this of course fall into the realm of "speculative theology", the answers to which we will probably never fully know this side of heaven.

What we do know is that God is Spirit, and that He is not bound by time in any way. This is how He is able to not only answer our prayers before we have even prayed them, but also of how He was aware of the total history of the Universe from the moment of its Creation:

"Known unto God are all His works from the foundation of the world." Acts 15:18

Nothing that happens in the Universe has ever been, or will ever be, a surprise unto God. The prophet Isaiah attests to this fact when he writes:

"Remember the former things of old: for I am God, and there is none else, I am God, and there is none like me,

Declaring the end from the beginning, and from ancient times the things that are not yet done, saying, My counsel shall stand, and I will do all my pleasure." Isaiah 46:9,10

Soul Sleep

This brings us to another common misconception in Christendom which deals with the physical world and time, the idea of "soul sleep". It is often taught and believed that in between the time of the believer's death and of his resurrection, that his soul is in a state of suspended animation or sleep. This suspended animation or "soul sleep" if you will, is merely from the perspective of those left behind. From the perspective of those who have died and left this earth however, they are transported immediately to their place in God's Resurrection program. For Scripture clearly declares, "To be absent from the body, is to be present with the Lord" (II Corinthians 5:8). This is how Jesus was able to say to the thief on the cross, "Today thou shalt be with me in Paradise" (Luke 23:43).

Scripture teaches us that when we step out of this physical world, we are immediately taken into the world of the spirit, with all of the intervening time being "eclipsed". Every individual at the moment of their passing arrives at their individual appointed place in God's Resurrection Program. Scripture refers to this as "every man in his own order" (I Corinthians 15:23). While it is common to view the Resurrection as being a singular event, it is the clear teaching of Scripture that the "Resurrection" occurs in a series of stages contained within the framework of world history.

As Paul taught in his first letter to the Corinthians, Jesus was the "first fruits" or opening phase of God's Resurrection Program. The second phase of the program will be the resurrection of all Church Age believers at the time of the Rapture of the Church (I Thessalonians 4:16,17).

This will be followed by the resurrection of the Old Testament saints at the physical 2nd Coming of Jesus back to the earth. This event occurs immediately before the initiation of Christ's Millennial Kingdom. At the conclusion of the Millennial Kingdom, the last phase of God's Resurrection Program will occur at the time of the Great White Throne Judgment. It is at this time that all those who have yet to be judged by God will be resurrected and have their lives assessed by the LORD (Revelation 20:11-15).

The issue of "soul sleep" and God's Resurrection Program shall be dealt with in greater detail in a later chapter of this book. For now, it is important for us to simply recognize that when any person dies, they immediately step out of the reality of the physical world and into the timeless reality of the eternal.

God's Power Over Time

Scripture teaches that God has not only power over the physical Universe, but also over time itself. A prime example of this is the "eclipsing of time" that occurs when one steps out of this physical world, and into eternity.

This is well illustrated in the case of Enoch. Although Enoch, an Old Testament Saint, was only the 7th generation from Adam (Jude 14), his vision for his future was that of the 2nd Coming of Christ coming back to the earth with His Bride, the Church, at the subsequent time of the Resurrection of the Old Testament Saints. For Enoch, the next event after his departure from the earth in the first millennia, was an immediate arrival to the 6th millennia, without the apparent passage of any time "Behold, the Lord cometh with ten thousands of his saints" (Jude 14).

While some might argue that this vision of Enoch's could well be the second time that he will have experienced the eclipsing of time, as he is often cited as potentially being one of the two witnesses mentioned in the Book of Revelation (Revelation 11:3), the principle remains the same. God has the ability to eclipse the passage of time.

In the New Testament, Jesus also spoke of this eclipsing of

time in the Book of John. In that Jesus was always a true gentleman, He addressed people from their particular perspective in life. To the believers who had lost a loved one, He comforted them by saying,

"I am the resurrection and the life: he that believeth in me, though he were dead, yet shall he live" (John 11:25).

To those who were still alive, He comforted and reassured them with these words, "Whosoever liveth and believeth in me shall never die" (John 11:26).

When we compare II Corinthians 5:8, which implies that as soon as we depart from this earth we are face to face with the Lord ("to be absent from the body is to be present with the Lord") with John 14:3, which seems to suggest that we won't be with the Lord until the actual time of the 2nd Coming ("I will come again and receive you unto myself"), we run into an apparent contradiction. But there is no contradiction here, only an affirmation that God has the ability to eclipse the passage of time when we depart from this life. For He is not only Lord of the physical Universe, but also the Lord over the realm of time. In John 5:25 we read:

"Verily, verily, I say unto you, The hour is coming, and now is, when the dead shall hear the voice of the Son of God: and they that hear shall live."

To those who are still alive, "the hour is coming". To all of those who have gone on before, having passed away, the hour "now is".

With God, there is no difference between "the hour is coming" and "the hour now is". All events that occur in our physical world whether they be past, present, or future from our perspective, are from God's perspective immediately known.

An Overlooked Miracle of Christ

Jesus performed many miracles while He was here on earth. The miracles were done in large part to prove that He was indeed the long awaited Messiah. Jesus showed that He had power over sickness and disease by His many healing miracles (Matthew 8:14; 9:22, Mark 7:35, Luke 18:43, John 9:7). He showed that He had power over nature by turning the water into wine (John 2:9), and by stilling the wind and seas (Matthew 14:32). Finally, He also exhibited His power over death by bringing at least three people back from the dead (Matthew 9:18-26, Luke 7:11-17, John 11:1-44).

One of the many miracles that Jesus performed however, is often overlooked. In this miracle, He showed that He had power over the time and space continuum. In John 6:16-21, we are told that after the disciples had rowed about 30 furlongs (approximately 3-4 miles) out into the Sea of Galilee, that Jesus had walked out from the shore over the troubled waters to meet them. Scripture then records an interesting phenomenon, for we are told that after the disciples had received Him into the boat, the boat was then "immediately" transported to the safety of the shore. Although the boat was 3-4 miles out to sea, the boat's return to dry land was accomplished without the passing of any time, for again, we are told that this event happened "immediately". This miracle was done in order to exhibit the fact that Jesus was God, and that He had the ability to not only physically control Nature, as shown by His "walking on water", but more importantly, was able to demonstrate His power over time itself by the "eclipsing of its passage" (John 6:21).

By analogy, when the Christian leaves the troubled waters of this world, he too is "immediately" taken into the safe and peaceful Presence of the Lord, without experiencing any passing of time ("To be absent from the body is to be present with the Lord." II Corinthians 5:8).

In summation, we as humans are made in the image of God and possess many of the same characteristics that He possesses. These characteristics include such things as the possession of a unique personality and a sense of justice, amongst other things. In terms of the realm of the experience of our existence however, this is where the similarities between God and man quickly begin to diverge. For while God exists outside of the time space continuum, we as humans are strictly bound by it. We do an incredible disservice to our understanding of God by imagining that He is observing the unfolding of history in the same manner that we are. That He is somehow acting like a one-man puppeteer, scurrying about in a frantic attempt to keep up with the answering of our prayers while at the same time endeavoring to work out His Plan for mankind. We must always remember however, that with God, when it comes to the future, that He is already there. That He did indeed answer all of our prayers, and provide for all of our needs and concerns, at the same moment that He created the Universe:

"Known unto God are all of His works from the beginning of the world." Acts 15:18

Again, we as believers must be cognizant of the fact that there exists more than one reality, and that the reality which we experience is far different than the one experienced by God. While we as humans are subjcct to time, God is not. God sees the past, present, and future as one event. For in God's reality, the reality of the eternal,

"Yesterday is as today, and tomorrow hath already been." Ecclesiastes 3:15

Free Will

"Man has a free will, and God won't violate man's free will in any way"

To most people, the idea that man possesses a total free will is foundational to their theological beliefs. However, as this chapter will now attempt to show, the concept of the total free will of man does not emerge when we carefully examine Scripture.

The idea that man's will is totally free in the choices he makes in life is often taught to us as children by our parents, and then reinforced culturally throughout the length of our lives. It is used as a mantra to encourage positive behavior, by assigning responsibility for negative actions.

Although it is seldom stated, we as humans recognize that our happiness is largely dependent upon the amount of free will that we possess. This can be readily seen by how we punish societal evil doers. We take away their "rights of choice", or "free will", either by lifestyle restrictions, imprisonment, or ultimately through capital punishment.

Because our happiness is dependent upon the amount of freedom, both actual and imagined, that we possess, it is easy to see why we constantly remind ourselves of the belief that "We are totally free in all of our actions." It is within our nature to be extremely resistant to even the notion that our wills may not be completely free.

We feel offended by the very idea that God might be restricting us or overriding our freedom of choice in any way, and so we tend to ignore any evidence to the contrary, whether this restriction is imposed upon us by God, or by man. Yet, Scripture clearly indicates that restrictions and limitations are placed by God upon mankind's ability to have total free will in the ordering of the events of our lives.

While we make elaborate plans for our lives, Scripture tells us that it is God who ultimately determines the places we shall go, and the resultant things that we shall do.

"A man's heart deviseth his way: but the Lord directed his steps." Proverbs 16:9

"Lord thou wilt ordain peace for us: for thou also hath wrought all of our works in us." Isaiah 26:12

In the Book of Job, we are informed that not only the events of our lives, but also the length of our days on earth are strictly regulated by God:

"Seeing his days are determined, the number of his months is with Thee, Thou hast appointed his bounds that he cannot pass;

Turn from him that he may rest, till he shall accomplish as an hireling, his day." Job 14:5,6

The primary reason that God places restrictions upon man's free will is that He has an overriding Plan for History, not only in the lives of believers, ("For I know the thoughts that I think toward you, saith the Lord, thoughts of peace, and not of evil, to give you an expected end." Jeremiah 29:11), but also for the world at large ("This is the purpose that is purposed upon the whole earth: and this is the hand that is stretched out upon all the nations" Isaiah 14:26).

If man's will were to be pre-eminent in the outworking of human history, then God would not have the ability to have His own unhindered Plan for the History of Mankind. Any plan that God might have for History, would be dependent upon the will of man, wills that Scripture is quick to point out, which are essentially sinful.

Thankfully, God does have a Plan for History, and where God's Plan is in conflict with the will of man, Scripture states that man's plans are overruled.

"For the Lord of hosts hath purposed, and who shall disannul it? And his hand is stretched out, and who shall turn it back?" Isaiah 14:27

"Who worketh all things according to the counsel of his will." Ephesians 1:11

Up until the 20th Century, it was common for educated and cultured people to recognize that many of the events of their lives seemed to be out of their own personal control. That there was the unseen Hand of God guiding the events of their lives. William Shakespeare wrote in Hamlet, "There is a divinity that shapes our ends, rough hew them as he will." In the play, "As You Like It", he reiterates the same sentiment, "All the world's a stage, the people its players."

The respected intellectual American patriarch Benjamin Franklin also acknowledged God's Providential Hand in his life, when he wrote:

"It is with great sincerity I join you in acknowledging and admiring the dispensations of Providence in our favor, America has only to be thankful and to persevere, God will finish His work and establish their freedom... If it had not been for the justice of our cause, and the consequent interposition of Providence, in which we had faith, we must have been ruined. If I had ever before been an atheist, I should now have been convinced of the being and the government of a Deity! It is He who abases the proud and favors the humble. May we never forget His goodness to us, and may our future conduct manifest our gratitude... I believe in one God, Creator of the universe. That He governs it by His Providence. That He ought to be worshipped."

The idea of a Sovereign God controlling both our personal and our nation's history permeated the thoughts of the pre-20th century American people. Interestingly, the first message that was transmitted by Samuel Morse on his telegraph in 1844 was an affirmation of the Providential Hand of God in our lives. When Morse typed his initial message, "What hath God wrought?", he was in fact acknowledging America's early 19th century cultural acceptance of Isaiah 26:12, "Thou also hast wrought all our works in us."

It was later on in the 19th century when things really began to change in Western philosophical thought. With Charles Darwin, the events of creation began to be explained by the process of "evolution". Suddenly, there no longer was a need for an Omnipotent God in Creation. With the advent of the scientific method, man began to have greater control over nature, furthering his tendency to push God out of the "ordering of the Universe".

By the end of the 19th century, the scientific community had in essence declared that "all things could be explained by physics and chemical reactions" (A. Custance). There was now no longer any apparent need to have a Providential God guiding the events of the Universe. When we come to the start of the 20th century, with Frederick Nietzsche, the process of removing God from our collective consciousness had become complete. For it was Nietzsche who had declared that God was no longer ordering the events of History, that God was in fact, "dead."

With our educational establishment now teaching the new religion of evolution and its companion "secular humanism", the concept of a Providential God has largely gone by the wayside in the thoughts of Western man. Although man now felt that he was totally free from the influence of a Sovereign God, he had instead become in a sense imprisoned intellectually. For according to Scripture, man was now "living a lie" (Romans 1:28). Thus the flood gates were opened for the secularization of the West, and the removal of God from Western society.

Putting aside how we arrived at our present cultural malaise, and letting "God to be true, and every man a liar" (Romans 3:4), we will now further examine what God's Word has to say on the matter of God's control over the events of human history. This will be done by examining instances in Scripture where God is seen to override the free will of man in order that He might accomplish His Purposes.

The Case of Pharaoh

A prime example of God overruling the free will of man in the Old Testament is the case of Pharaoh. God through Moses had demanded that Pharaoh let the Israelites be released from their bondage in Egypt. After a display of miracles carried out by Moses, Pharaoh would have let the people go, but Scripture tells us that God then hardened Pharaoh's heart so that he would not let them go (Exodus 7:13). Then after being subjected to further judgments of God, Pharaoh once again had a change of heart. He had decided that it was better to let the people go than to experience God's Judgments. Scripture tells us that God again hardened Pharaoh's heart to work against His expressed will (Exodus 9:12).

When Pharaoh decided to let the people go, time and again God would harden his heart to go against His stated demands. We are told that God overrode Pharaoh's free will in order that He might make a greater display of His Power and Might (Exodus 10:1, Romans 9:17).

Back and forth Pharaoh vacillated, all by the urging of God's Hand (Exodus 10:20). When Pharaoh would have let the people go, it was God who inspired him to do otherwise. Here we have an excellent example of how God works to control History, and an affirmation of Proverbs 21:1:

"The King's heart is in the hand of the Lord, as the rivers of water: he turneth it whithersoever He will."

If Pharaoh had been left to his own devices, he would have let the Israelites go early on in the process, but God had other plans, plans of making a full display of His awesome Power to mankind.

The Case of Jonah

God's control over history is not only accomplished by the rich and powerful, but also by the actions of ordinary men such as Jonah. Although God had ordered Jonah to go and preach to Nineveh, Jonah had instead opted to go in the opposite direction to Tarshish. It was Jonah's will that led him away from Nineveh, against the known desires of God upon his life. But Jonah's will soon became overridden by God's will, and he did indeed end up in Nineveh. God could have sent someone else to preach repentance to Nineveh, but that was not His Plan. God's Plan was to have Jonah be the one to preach to the city of Nineveh, which Jonah eventually did.

Again, this was totally against the dictates of Jonah's own free will! This is a clear example of Proverbs 16:9, that while Jonah's heart was devising his way, God was working to direct his steps! This truth is reiterated by Jeremiah:

"O Lord, I know that the way of man is not in himself: it is not in man that walketh to direct his steps." Jeremiah 10:23

The Case of the Apostle Paul

In the New Testament we have the case of Saul, later named Paul, whose free will was totally set upon destroying the Church. While on his way to Damascus to further accomplish his desire of persecuting and destroying the Church, God intervened in the life of Saul, and overrode Saul's free will.

"And as he journeyed, he came near Damascus: and suddenly

there shined round about him a light from heaven:

And he fell to the earth, and heard a voice saying, Saul, Saul, why persecutest thou me?" Acts 9:3,4

If Saul's will had been totally free, there never would have been the Apostle Paul, for Saul's will was totally bent upon destroying the Church, not building it. Saul was clearly a case of "a free will run amok." It was only by God overriding Saul's free will and turning him to Jesus, that the new-born Paul would start on the road to becoming one of the greatest heroes of the Christian faith.

After his conversion, we see that Paul had come to fully realize the limitations of his own free will. For when he was about to journey from Ephesus to Jerusalem, he told the Ephesians, that he would "return again unto them", but was careful to add, "if God willed" (Acts 18:21).

Limited Free Will

In truth, according to God's Word, man does not possess a total free will. What he possesses could best be termed as a "limited free will". As we have seen, when man's will is in direct conflict with God's Sovereign Plan for History, man's free will is overruled. When man's exercising of his will is outside of God's Plan for the Ages, presumably it could be said that his will would be free. Here however, we must be careful, for Scripture is quick to point out that God's Providence in our individual lives can be quite extensive ("For of Him, and through Him, and to Him, are all things." Romans 11:36).

In order to better understand how the limitations of our free will operate, it may be beneficial to compare our understanding of "Free Will" to our concept of "Democracy".

Most Americans would state that they believed they lived under a Democratic form of government, that they are indeed living in a "Democracy". However, in the reality of a true Democracy, every citizen is allowed to cast a vote on all political issues. The American form of Democratic governance typically only allows for voting on issues and laws by elected officials. As an ordinary American citizen, one really does not have a direct say about how the country is indeed actually governed. That work is done by the elected representatives. As citizens of the United States of America, we should therefore more aptly state that we live in a "Limited Democracy".

Such is the case with "free will." Under God's heaven, it is probably more accurate to say that we have a "limited free will." Where our plans do not affect God's Plan for the Universe, then presumably, our wills can be said to be free. However, if our plans are in conflict with God's Plan for History, then our plans, along with our free wills, are overruled.

Thankfully, we are not consciously aware of the many urgings and promptings of God in our lives. If we were, it would most likely have a profound negative effect on our sense of our own independence.

It will only be in the light of eternity that we will see the full extent of His Sovereign Guidance in the events of History, and of our personal lives. It is then that we shall most assuredly proclaim, as had Jesus' disciples:

"He hath done all things well." Mark 7:37

Good and Evil

"Everything that is Good comes from God, and everything that is Evil comes from the Devil"

From the time of our youth, we are taught that, "God is good", and that He is the source of all that is "good". Conversely, we are told that the Devil is the author of all that is "evil". It seems that everywhere we turn, whether it is in our literature, our television shows and movies, or through the daily news, we are constantly confronted with this dichotomy of "Good and Evil." It is not only deeply embedded within our common culture, but also in our general sense of justice, especially when we consider the many "injustices of life".

Throughout our lives this eternal conflict between "Good and Evil" is never far away from our thought processes. We often view our time here on earth in the context of this struggle, imagining that the "good" things we do as helping the cause of Good, and conversely, the bad things we have done as aiding the cause of Evil. "Good and Evil" often become synonymous with "God and the Devil" in our way of thinking.

There are at least two ways that the concept of Good and Evil are commonly misunderstood within Christendom. These pertain to Good and Evil in the matter of Salvation, and Good and Evil in the matter of God's Judgment of mankind.

Good and Evil in Salvation

Many people erroneously assume that their acceptability to God will be based upon whether their "good works" will somehow outnumber their bad or "evil works" in the Day of

Judgment. This they surmise, will be the criteria for their gaining acceptance into Heaven. They mistakenly believe that in order to be acceptable to God, one has to perform more good deeds than bad deeds. As if salvation were a matter of "the balancing of scales."

Thankfully, our salvation is not based upon our works, but rather upon our receiving Jesus Christ into our hearts as Lord and Savior. In John 1:12 we read:

"But as many as received Him, to them gave He power to become sons of God, even to them that believe on His name."

Salvation is not a matter of our actions, whether they are good or evil, but rather of faith.

"Knowing that a man is not justified by the works of the law, but by the faith of Jesus Christ, even we have believed in Jesus Christ, that we might be justified by the faith of Christ, and not by the works of the law, for by the works of the law shall no flesh be justified." Galatians 2:16

So, we see that Scripture plainly teaches that Good or Evil works will neither get one into, nor keep one out of heaven. When our time on earth has been completed, it is only through faith in Jesus Christ that we can be made acceptable unto God.

Good and Evil in Judgment

Again, it is common to believe that all that is to be equated with "good", is directly associated with God, and all that we consider to be "evil", as being in direct association with the Devil. However, when we carefully read Scripture, something strange to our way of thinking often occurs. For it is not uncommon to find the Word of God attributing Evil actions to God. The Prophet Isaiah writes:

"I form the light, and create darkness: I make peace, and create evil: I the Lord do all these things." Isaiah 45:7

In Amos 3:6, we read: Shall there be evil in a city, and the Lord hath not done it?"

These and many other Scriptures fly into the face of our understanding of God and His Ways. It is the tendency of most people to simply skip over these passages that associate God with Evil when we read them, as they are in conflict to the paradigm that all things "good" are synonymous with God, and all things "evil" with the Devil.

In order to understand how God can be connected with evil in any way, it is first necessary to take a fresh approach as to how we view the concepts of "Good and Evil".

Good and Evil Viewed from a Historical Perspective

In order to reconcile the conundrum that we find ourselves in when we read the many instances in Scripture that associate God with "Evil", we need to first change our approach as to how we view the terms "Good" and "Evil" as presented within Scripture. Instead of attaching a moral value to good and evil, we need to realize that "good and evil" when presented within Scripture, are often events to be considered from a historical or non-moral perspective. By historical perspective, we are referring to judging actions based solely on the effect that the action has upon the recipient of the action. The "moral aspect" of the action is removed from consideration. The primary reason for the confusion surrounding "good and evil" is that we tend to automatically attach a "moral value" to both, as if "good" and "evil" were synonymous with moral "right" and "wrong". We instead need to realize that in Scripture, "Good" and "Evil" are often morally neutral.

When Scripture refers to deeds in their moral context, they

are typically termed as being either "righteous" or "wicked". Good and Evil actions on the other hand, tend to be more commonly associated with actions viewed from a "non-moral" viewpoint as previously stated, being more concerned with the effect that the action has upon the recipient.

What makes an action either morally righteous or wicked is largely dependent upon the motivation that prompted the action. We shall see that from God's perspective, the morality of an act is not to be found necessarily in the deed itself, but rather is contingent upon what is going on within the heart both before and after the action has occurred.

Works: A Three Step Process

Every action that we perform in life is in reality a three-step process. First, we have the motive that inspires the action, which is then followed by the action itself, and finally, we have the response of the heart to the action.

1) Motivation

2) Action

3) Response of the heart

In the Judgments of God, the most important aspects of a person's works are steps 1 and 3, the aspects that concern the matters of the heart. While we as humans tend to judge actions based solely upon what we see regarding their affects upon others, God is more concerned with the before and after conditions of a person's heart in His assessment of our actions:

"For the Lord seeth not as man seeth; for man looketh on the outward appearance, but the Lord looketh on the heart." I Samuel 16:7

34

Good Actions

It is only when a "good deed" is done out of a proper motivation that the deed becomes an acceptable or "righteous deed" in God's eyes. For example, if a person gives a generous donation to the Church being motivated by his love for the Lord, his good action would be considered a righteous act. Conversely, if that same person had given the same donation but out of a selfish motive such as wanting to be held in high esteem by his fellow parishioners for his generosity, then that "good" act could never become a rewardable or "righteous" action in God's eyes. It is fit only for God's Judgment (I Corinthians 3:13).

Now if the person who had given the gift out of a proper motivation should later become proud of their act of giving, and brag about the gift to others, then that good and righteous act would then become morally neutralized in God's eyes. This is why Jesus warned his followers to, "... let not your left hand know what your right hand doeth" (Matthew 6:3).

So, we see that God's assessment of our actions is based initially upon our motivations, and then after the completion of our actions, upon the response of our heart to our actions. That everything we do in life from God's perspective is really a 3-part process consisting of motivation, action, and the response of the heart to the action. The action itself often being the least important part of the equation.

Evil Actions

When a parent spanks a child, it can be said that they have brought an "evil" action upon that child, for the child experiences hurt and pain. The action of disciplining a child is in and of itself neither morally righteous, nor is it morally wicked. What makes an "evil" action righteous or wicked is totally dependent upon the motivation behind the action. Now if the parent did the spanking out of the proper motive of attempting to correct bad behavior because of a deep concern and love for the child, then this evil action too becomes a "righteous" work. If the parent did the act of spanking the child solely out of the motivation that "the child was annoying them", having no ultimate concern for the child, then in this instance from God's perspective, the action could be deemed to be a "wicked" work.

So we can conclude that actions in and of themselves, whether they are either "good" or "evil", are often in God's eyes deemed to be morally neutral. When Scripture refers to actions strictly in their moral context, they are termed as being either "righteous" or "wicked", and not merely good or evil. This is what the Old Testament Prophet Samuel was alluding to when he wrote:

"For by God, actions are weighed." I Samuel 2:3

Now let us consider the Lord's statement concerning Judgment in Matthew 7: 22,23:

"Many will say to me in that day, Lord, Lord, have we not prophesied in thy name" and in thy name have cast out devils? And in thy name done many wonderful works?

And then will I profess unto them, I never knew you: depart from Me, ye that work iniquity."

Here we have people standing before the Lord in Judgment, attempting to proclaim their righteousness based upon the "good deeds" which they had performed during the course of their lives.

Notice that Jesus did not deny the fact that these people who were standing before him in Judgment had indeed accomplished many "good" things. What the Lord is saying here is that because they did not know Him on a personal level, that the good works which they had achieved could not have been done out of a proper God pleasing motive, and were therefore sinful, or "works of iniquity".

God and Evil

Due to a lack of understanding of these differences between the concepts of "Good and Evil", as opposed to "Righteousness and Wickedness" as found within the pages of Scripture, it is often very troubling for Christians to read of the many instances within God's Word where God is said to be associated with Evil.

The list of Scripture verses that attribute Evil unto God is quite long and extensive. Below are some of the more commonly cited examples:

"Therefore it shall come to pass, that as all good things are come upon you, Which the Lord your God promised you, so shall the Lord your God bring upon you all evil things, until he hath destroyed you from off this good land which the Lord your God hath given you." Joshua 23:15

"Then God sent an evil spirit between Abimelech and the men of Shechem; and the men of Shechem dealt treacherously with Abimelech." Judges 9:23

"But the spirit of the Lord departed from Saul, and an evil spirit from the Lord troubled him." I Samuel 16:14

"Now therefore, behold, the Lord hath put a lying spirit in the mouth of all these prophets, and the Lord hath spoken evil concerning thee." I Kings 22:23

"Did not your fathers thus, and did not our God bring all this evil upon us, and upon this city? Yet ye bring more wrath upon Israel by profaning the Sabbath." Nehemiah 13:18

"But he said unto her, Thou speakest as one of the foolish women speaketh. What? Shall we receive good at the hand of God, and shall we not receive evil? In all this, did not Job sin with his lips." Job 2:10

"Hear O earth: behold, I will bring evil upon this people, even the fruit of their thoughts, because they have not hearkened unto my words, nor to my law, but have rejected it." Jeremiah 6:19

"For the inhabitant of Maroth waited carefully for good: but evil came down from the Lord unto the gate of Jerusalem." Micah 1:12

We must always keep in mind that although Scripture records numerous instances where God is said to do evil, it is important to note that in no place does the Word of God ever state that God ever acts "wickedly" (Job 38:12). The works of God, whether they be good or evil, are always deemed to be righteous.

It is also essential to remember that when Scripture speaks of events strictly in their moral context, it typically describes these works as being either "righteous works" or "wicked works" as opposed to "good and evil". Within Scripture, Good and Evil are not always representative of true morality, and must often be viewed as simply being positive or negative events. Events that are morally neutral.

The true basis of morality in God's eyes, is dependent upon motives, and not necessarily upon actions in and of themselves. This again is a confirmation of His Holy Word:

"Then hear thou in heaven thy dwelling place, and forgive, and do, and give to every man according to his ways, whose heart thou knowest; for thou, even thou only, knowest the hearts of all the children of men;" I Kings 8:39

Solomon warned believers in the Old Testament about the necessity of being constantly aware of the condition of one's heart before God, when he wrote:

"Keep thy heart with all diligence, for out of it are the issues of life." Proverbs 4:23

Later, the Apostle Paul would deliver a similar admonition to believers in the New Testament, when he warned the Corinthian believers of the fact that God's assessment of their lives would be based primarily upon the hidden motivations of their hearts. It is only at this time that the Christian will fully realize the depths of his or her fallen condition:

"Therefore judge nothing before the time, until the Lord come, who both will bring to light the hidden things of darkness, and will make manifest the counsels of the hearts: and then shall every man have praise of God" I Corinthians 4:5

Thankfully, although we may not be totally aware of the depths of our sinful condition, God's Word does declare the fullness of His mercies:

"He hath not dealt with us after our sins; nor rewardeth us according to our iniquities,

For as the heaven is high above the earth, so great is his mercy toward them that fear him.

As far as the east is from the west, so far hath he removed our transgressions from us." Psalm 103:10-12

"...But where sin abounded, grace did much more abound;" Romans 5:20

God's forgiveness and grace knows no bounds. It is truly a Wonderful and Gracious Savior that we serve!

Faulty Paradigm #4

The Basis of God's Judgment of Mankind

"God's judgment of man is based primarily upon man's actions"

We as humans spend a good portion of our time considering the actions of not only ourselves, but also of others. If we believe that the rewards (and/or punishments) we receive in life are based solely upon our actions or deeds, we naturally assume that God will take the same approach when He makes His final assessment of our lives.

From the time that we are little children, we are told to be mindful of our actions or outward behavior. Our parents often warning us with the admonition that, "God was watching us." So logically, our perception of our moral accountability to God as being based primarily upon our actions, is just an extension of the lessons that we learned in childhood.

These lessons in turn later became reinforced by certain Scriptures which seem to indicate that God's Judgment will be based primarily upon our actions. Revelation 20:12,13 states:

"And I saw the dead, small and great, stand before God; and the books were opened: and another book was opened, which is the book of life: and the dead were judged out of those things which were written in the books, according to their works.

And the sea gave up the dead which were in it; and death and hell delivered up the dead which were in them: and they were judged every man according to their "works."

Here in Scripture, we are told that God will judge man

"according to his works". At face value this seems to indicate that God will judge man solely on the basis of the things that he has done. But, when we consider the totality of what the Bible has to say on the matter of God's judgment or assessment of our lives, we shall see that when Scripture is talking about "works", it is referring to something much broader than just our actions or deeds.

Scripture tells us that in addition to our physical actions, we will also be held accountable for the very words that we used in our conversations. In Matthew 12:36, Jesus states:

"But I say unto you, that every idle word that men shall speak, they shall give account thereof in the day of judgment."

The words we speak reveal not only what we are thinking, but also in turn, what is really motivating our actions. In the 12th chapter of the book of Matthew, Scripture confirms the fact that the words that come out of our mouth not only communicate our thoughts, but also serve to reveal what is going on in our heart:

"For out of the abundance of the heart, the mouth speaketh." Matthew 12:34

While we as humans are attaching a great significance to our actions or deeds, God is attaching an even greater significance to the motivations that are prompting these very same actions.

"For by Him, actions are weighed." I Samuel 2:3

"I the LORD search the heart, I try the reins, even to give every man according to his ways, and according to the fruit of his doings." Jeremiah 17:10

So, we see that what Scripture really means by "works" is not an exclusive reference to our actions, but it also entails our actions when viewed in the light of the motivations that have prompted them.

The Motivations of Our Hearts

In God's eyes, hating someone without a cause is the same as committing the act of murder (Matthew 5:22). To look upon a woman to lust after her, is the same as engaging in the act of adultery itself (Matthew 5:28). In the Old Testament we find David exhorting and instructing his son Solomon to be diligent in keeping his heart perfect before the Lord:

"And thou, Solomon my son, know thou the God of thy father, and service him with a perfect heart and with a willing mind; for the LORD searcheth all hearts, and understandeth all the imaginations of the thoughts:..." 1st Chronicles 28:9

Nothing escapes the eyes of God, and man will not only have to give an account for every idle word that he has spoken (Matthew 12:36), but also for every false and selfish motive that has emanated from his deceitful heart. In Jeremiah 17:9 we read:

"The heart is deceitful above all things, and desperately wicked: who can know it?"

Not only does God hold mankind accountable for the motivations that inspire our actions, but as we shall see, also for the general condition of our heart in response to our actions.

The Case of the King of Assyria

In order to better understand how God judges or assesses man in terms of the motivations and conditions of his heart, let us now examine His dealings with the king of Assyria in the tenth chapter of the Book of Isaiah. Here we read that Israel had been walking in disobedience to God, and that God desired to judge the nation of Israel for her disobedience to Him. God's chosen vessel to discipline or "judge" Israel, was the king of Assyria. Isaiah 10:5,6, states:

"O Assyrian, the rod of mine anger, and the staff in their hand is mine indignation.

I will send him against a hypocritical nation, and against the people of my wrath will I give him a charge, to take the spoil, and to take the prey, and to tread them down like the mire of the streets."

Isaiah then goes on to tell us that the king of Assyria was unaware that he was being prompted by God to discipline Israel:

"Howbeit he meaneth not so, neither doth his heart think so." Isaiah 10:7

Here in Scripture we see that the king of Assyria was an unwitting tool in the Hand of God. Now, after the king of Assyria had completed the work that God had prompted him to do in the matter of disciplining Israel (Isaiah 10:12), we find an interesting thing occurring. The response of the king's heart to his military victory over Israel had caused his heart to become filled with pride over what he considered to be his own accomplishment. In Isaiah 10:13 we read:

"For he saith, By the strength of my hand I have done it, and by my wisdom; for I am prudent: and I have removed the bounds of the people, and have robbed their treasures, and I have put down the inhabitants like a valiant man."

The response of God towards the arrogance of the Assyrian king is one of retributive judgment:

"Wherefore it shall come to pass, that when the Lord hath performed his whole work upon mount Zion and on Jerusalem, I will punish the fruit of the stout heart of the king of Assyria, and the glory of his high looks" (Isaiah 10:12). The Word of God then goes on to state:

"Shall the axe boast itself against him that heweth therewith? Or shall the saw magnify itself against him that shaketh it? As if the rod should shake itself against them that lifteth it up, or as if the staff should lift up itself, as if it were no wood." Isaiah 10:15

Here we have an unbelieving king unknowingly being used by God to accomplish the task of disciplining Israel. Then after having accomplished the task, of being punished himself by God. This punishment was not for his actions themselves, for his actions were in reality the work of God, and therefore must be deemed to be morally neutral. The Assyrian king was punished solely for the proud response of his heart to these actions.

This is a prime example of how all of mankind, both believing and unbelieving, are held accountable to God for not only their actions, but also for the motivations and the conditions of their hearts. Again, we are reminded in God's Word, that "By the Lord, actions are weighed" (I Samuel 2:3).

Man's Works: A Three-Part Process

So, we see that our "works" in the eyes of God, consist of not only our actions, but also of our motivations, and the responses of our heart to our actions.

As we have mentioned in our study of "Good and Evil", our "works" are actually a 3-step process. The first step of the process is the motivation for our actions, which then in turn is followed by the second step, the actions themselves. Finally, after the action or deed has been completed, we have the third step in the process, the response of our hearts to the action.

From God's view, man is responsible for each part of the process, but chiefly for steps 1 and 3. For as we have seen in the case of the Assyrian king, his actual actions were in fact the works of God and were not of his own doing. God did not punish the king of Assyria for judging Israel, but rather for the proud response of his heart after he had performed the Lord's work.

We must always remember that God is typically more interested in the state of the heart of man, than He is in our actual actions themselves. For oftentimes, man's actions are the work of God. For it is God who has ordained and inspired man to do specific actions in order to accomplish His Plans, and therefore on the basis of his actions themselves, man can hardly be held accountable while being used as a tool in the Hand of God (Isaiah 10:15).

From this side of eternity, we will never know the full extent of God's influence in ordaining the things that we will do in our lives, but we do know that God's influence over our actions is far more extensive than we typically imagine.

"Lord, thou wilt ordain peace for us: for thou also hast wrought all our works in us." Isaiah 26:12

If at any time man's actions should somehow be irrelevant to the Plan of God, it is then that man's will would hypothetically be in a state of total freedom. It is at this time that he would become not only totally responsible for his motivations and the responses of his heart, but also for his actions as well.

The Judgment of King Nebuchadnezzar

The King of Assyria was not the only king judged by God for having a prideful heart. In like manner, King Nebuchadnezzar of Babylon was also on the receiving end of God's Judgment. In the 4th Chapter of the Book of Daniel, Nebuchadnezzar had a troubling dream, after which he called in Daniel to interpret the meaning of the dream for him. In Daniel 4:24-26 we read:

46

"This is the interpretation, O King, and this is the decree of the most High, which is come upon my lord, the king:

That they shall drive thee from men, and thy dwelling shall be with the beasts of the field, and they shall make thee to eat grass as oxen, and they shall wet thee with the dew of heaven, and seven times shall pass over thee, till thou know that the most High ruleth in the kingdom of men, and giveth it to whomsoever he will.

And whereas they commanded to leave the stump of the tree roots; thy kingdom shall be sure unto thee, after that thou shalt have known that the heavens do rule."

King Nebuchadnezzar failed to heed Daniel's warning of God's impending judgment upon him. After a year had passed from the time of his dream, as he was walking through his palace, Nebuchadnezzar's heart became filled with pride as he considered his empire:

"The king spake, and said, Is not this great Babylon, that I have built for the house of the kingdom by the might of my power, and for the honor of my majesty?

While the word was in the king's mouth, there fell a voice from heaven saying, "O king Nebuchadnezzar, to thee it is spoken; the kingdom is departed from thee.

And they shall drive thee from men, and thy dwelling shall be with the beasts of the field: they shall make you to eat grass as oxen, and seven times shall pass over thee, until thou know that the most High ruleth in the kingdom of men, and giveth it to whomsoever He will." Daniel 4:30-32

In that same hour, Nebuchadnezzar was driven out from among men. For the next seven years, he ate grass as the oxen, and slept outside in the damp. His hair became like eagle's feathers, and his nails grew like bird claws. At the end of the appointed time for his judgment, God restored Nebuchadnezzar, who then later stated in Daniel 4:34,35:

"I Nebuchadnezzar lifted up mine eyes unto heaven, and mine understanding returned unto me, and I blessed the most High, and I praised and honored Him that liveth forever, whose dominion is an everlasting dominion, and His kingdom is from generation to generation.

And all the inhabitants of the earth are reputed as nothing: and He doeth according to His will in the army of heaven, and among the inhabitants of the earth: and none can stay His hand, or say unto Him, What doest thou?"

Here again, we see God judging a man, not for his action(s), but rather for the sinful condition of his heart.

The Crucifixion and Human Accountability

A prime example of the role that motivations play in the judgments of God is the Crucifixion. Revelation 13:8 tells us that the Crucifixion was ordained by God to occur from the "foundation of the world." It was a part of the express Will and Plan of God. In Acts 2:23, we read:

"Him being delivered by the determinate counsel and fore-knowledge of God, ye have taken, and by wicked hands have crucified and slain."

We are told here that the Crucifixion was an event that was not only foreknown by God, but was actually a result of His "determinate counsel." There was no power on earth that was going to stop the Crucifixion. It was an event that was fore-ordained by God to occur, being entirely needful in order to bring about man's salvation from his sins. Even though the Crucifixion was a totally necessary action in the Plan of God, the Jewish authorities were still held accountable to God for the atrocity. We shall see this accountability as based not upon the actual Crucifixion itself, but rather for the motive that had prompted the Crucifixion. For the Jewish rulers had hated Jesus without a cause, which in turn made them accountable for their actions. Note the wording at the end of Acts 2:23:

"And by "wicked" hands have crucified and slain."

In God's analyses, the fact that the Jewish authorities had hated Jesus without a cause had made their actions "wicked". When we consider the Roman soldier, whose job it was to administer the Crucifixion, we find no such animosity and apparent accountability, only a reverent acknowledgment of the fact that Jesus was indeed who He claimed to be, "the Son of God" (Matthew 27:54). This soldier was only doing what his job had called him to do, and in all likelihood, may not have been morally culpable for his actions.

From God's perspective however, the Jewish authorities were to be strictly held accountable for this, the most heinous act in human history. For in God's eyes, they had already murdered Jesus long before they had Crucified Him. Note the order of the words that Peter used in Acts 5:30:

"The God of our fathers raised up Jesus, whom ye slew and hanged on a tree."

Here we read that the Jewish authorities had first "slew Jesus", after which they had "hung him on a tree." Long before they had done the actual act of crucifying Him, the Jewish authorities had been guilty of "murdering Him." For they had hated Jesus without a cause. Although the Crucifixion was a part of the Plan of God, the Jewish authorities were still held morally responsible for their participation, even though the Crucifixion was part of the express will of God. The Jews were held accountable on the basis of the motivation of their hearts, and not necessarily for their actions.

To make sure that there is no confusion in the matter, God's

Word again repeats this same account of the Jewish authority's accountability in the Crucifixion in Acts 10:38-39, which reads:

"How God anointed Jesus of Nazareth with the Holy Ghost and with power: who went about doing good, and healing all that were oppressed of the devil; for God was with him.

And we are witnesses of all things which he did both in the land of the Jews, and in Jerusalem; whom they "slew and (then) hanged on a tree." (Emphasis mine)

In summation, it is necessary for all Christians to be constantly vigilant when it comes to matters of the heart. For with God, the motivations of our heart are often seen to be of more importance than our actions themselves. The Apostle Paul tells us that we all have an appointed day in the future, when God will make an assessment of our lives:

"In the day when God shall judge the secrets of men by Jesus Christ according to my gospel." Romans 2:16

At this time the full extent of our motivations and condition of our hearts will be made known. The Apostle Paul wrote to the Church at Corinth:

"Every man's work shall be made manifest: for the day shall declare it, because it shall be revealed by fire; and the fire shall try every man's work of what sort it is." I Corinthians 3:13

It is only in God's Judgment that we will become fully aware of the full extent of the depravity of our sinful nature. As the Scripture states, it is then that we shall all have praise of God for what He has done for us in securing our salvation.

"For now we see through a glass, darkly; but then face to face: now I know in part; but then shall I know even as also I am known." I Corinthians 13:12

Even so, come quickly Lord Jesus.

God's Ultimate Purpose for Man Is His Own Glorification

"Man's ultimate purpose in life is to "Glorify God"

"Man was created to glorify God and to enjoy Him forever," so states the famous declaration from the Westminster Confession. Seldom have more noble sounding words been spoken by man. To borrow a phrase from the noted Christian apologist Norman Geisler, "The words sound so good that they are enough to give you a quiver in your liver."

Although most of Christendom regards this lofty sounding statement as being a part of acceptable Christian Dogma, there is a big problem with this edict from the Westminster Confession. This problem being the fact that when held up to the light of the Word of God, the statement, "IS SIMPLY NOT TRUE!"

God's ultimate purpose in the creation of man was not, and is not, "To Glorify Himself," as this chapter will now attempt to demonstrate.

Now some might say, "What is the harm done, if indeed what you are saying is correct, that God's ultimate purpose in creating man was not to "Glorify Himself". What's the big deal? Well, the big deal is that when we are talking about the ultimate purpose for which man was created, we are in essence stating the basis upon which man will ultimately be judged by God.

In the light of cold analyses, this is much the same for example, as when a manufacturing company creates a new product. The company's final assessment of that product will ultimately be judged (by both the company and the marketplace) by how well the product performed the function

51

for which it was created. In like manner, God's ultimate assessment of mankind will most certainly be based largely on how the individual performed the function for which he or she was created. We are not talking about an individual's personal vocational calling here. We are referring rather to the general calling of all mankind.

What we believe to be the ultimate purpose of our lives is very important. For if we are serious about our Christian faith, what we believe to be the ultimate purpose for our lives will eventually become the "ultimate focus" of our lives. Focusing on God's ultimate purpose for our lives will have a profound impact on not only our behavior, but also on how we approach our relationship with God as we live out our journey of faith. It will be the measuring rod to which we must constantly refer, to make sure that we are staying "on the proper track." If our understanding of what the ultimate purpose for which God created us is erroneous, then we run the danger of living our lives with our spiritual ladders being "placed on the wrong wall" so to speak. Scripture exhorts us to be wary of this and of all theological error. Paul wrote to Timothy:

"Study to show thyself approved unto God, a workman that needeth not to be ashamed, rightly dividing the word of truth." II Timothy 2:15

God's Purpose for Man in Creation

To my knowledge, there are only two Scriptural references that deal with the question of, "What is man's ultimate purpose in God's Creation?" These two Scripture references are Isaiah 43:7, and Revelation 4:11.

Isaiah 43:7 states: "Even every one that is called by my name: for I have created him for my glory, I have formed him; yea I have made him."

Revelation 4:11 reads: "Thou art worthy, O Lord, to receive glory and honor and power: for Thou hast created all things, and for Thy pleasure they are and were created."

The writers of the Westminster Confession chose Isaiah 43:7 to explain the ultimate purpose that God had in mind for mankind within His creation. It is this writer's contention that much of the confusion that exists within Modern Christendom regarding the outworking of the Christian's life is a direct result of this choice. For again, when we talk about "Why man was created", we are also talking about, "On what basis that man will ultimately be judged", which in turn leads us to, "What should be the proper focus of man while living out the days of his life." There are at least three problems with choosing Isaiah 43:7 to explain man's created purpose.

The first problem is that a careful analyses of the passage in Isaiah 43:7 reveals that the writers of the Westminster Confession really attempted to show that the statement "For I have created him for my glory" is to be interpreted as, "That I have created man to Glorify Me". This rendering obviously conveys an entirely different meaning to the verse. For this interpretation implies that the verse is a direct call for man to exhibit obedience to God by "Glorifying Him".

This is an incredible leap indeed, for if the verse is interpreted as it is written, "I have created him for my glory", we do not find any plea for obedience or call to action to be exhibited by man towards God. The verse simply states that God has glorified Himself by creating man.

If we think about it, God is glorified by man regardless of whether man is being obedient to Him or not. In reality, God is glorified by man even when man is in a state of disobedience. For when man is being stiff necked and antagonistic towards God, God's long suffering and tender mercies are put on display for all the Universe to see and observe. God is glorified by man whether man behaves himself or not! Hence, the specific ordering of the words, "I have created him for my glory."

If God had wanted to convey the fact that man was created for the express purpose of "Glorifying Him", then He would have likely stated in Isaiah 43:7, "I have created man to Glorify me", instead of, "I have created him for my Glory."

The second problem with the Westminster Confession's interpretation of Isaiah 43:7 is contextual. Throughout the context of the Book of Isaiah, we find God himself performing acts, whereby He is said to be "glorified".

"For thou hast made of a city a heap; of a defenced city a ruin: a palace of strangers to be no city: it shall never be built.

Therefore shall the strong people glorify thee, the city of the terrible nations shall fear thee." Isaiah 25:2,3

"Thou hast increased the nation: thou art glorified: thou hadst removed it far unto all the ends of the earth." Isaiah 26:15

"Sing, O ye heavens; for the LORD hath done it: shout, ye lower parts of the earth: break forth into singing, ye mountains, O forest, and every tree therein: for the LORD hath redeemed Jacob, and glorified himself in Israel." Isaiah 44:23

It can be easily seen that within the context of the Book of Isaiah, that Isaiah 43:7 is just another instance whereby God is performing acts by which He is bringing glory unto Himself.

The third problem with choosing Isaiah 43:7 to support the idea that God's ultimate purpose for the creation of man is to "glorify God" is that to this writer's knowledge, there are no other apparent verses within Scripture that work together to corroborate such an interpretation. We are warned numerous times in Scripture that we should verify all things in the mouths of two or three witnesses (Deuteronomy 17:6, Matthew 18:16, II Corinthians 13:1). If we fail to do this, we are in danger of misinterpreting God's Word. We must always base our assertions of what the Word of God is saying by backing these assertions up with other corroborating Scriptures.

So again, to interpret Isaiah 43:7 as meaning, "God's ultimate purpose for mankind is to Glorify God", can be considered as standing on shaky ground, for the following reasons:

1) The structure of the wording of the verse simply does not imply any such responsibility on the part of man to "glorify God". God is seen within the wording of this verse to be "glorifying Himself" by His own actions.

2) To state that Isaiah 43:7 should be seen as a call for man to Glorify God does not fit within the context of other verses in the Book of Isaiah, where once again, God is seen to be bringing glory to Himself by "His own actions."

3) There are no apparent verses within Scripture that when combined together would serve to justify interpreting Isaiah 43:7 to mean, "That man's ultimate purpose in life, is to Glorify God."

This is not to say that man should not be glorifying God, for we are instructed on numerous occasions in Scripture to "Glorify God":

"Let your light so shine before men, that they may see your good works, and glorify your Father which is in heaven." Matthew 5:16

"For ye are bought with a price: therefore glorify God in your body, and in your spirit, which are God's." I Corinthians 6:20

"Having your conversation honest among the Gentiles: that, whereas they speak against you as evildoers, they may by your good works, which they shall behold, glorify God in the day of visitation." I Peter 2:12

We are to give God all glory not because that is our ultimate purpose in life, but rather, simply in the interest of truth. In Scripture, God is said to be Wonderful (Isaiah 9:6), and we as fallen sinners, are anything but. Paul in his letter to the Romans describes our condition not as being Wonderful, but rather as being "wretched" (Romans 7:24).

The notion that God created man to "glorify Himself" also suggests that God somehow "needs" to be glorified by man. Nothing could be farther from the truth. For God's Word tells us that He is totally self-sufficient ("blessed forever" Romans 1:25) and in no way needs anything from man ("If I were hungry, I would not tell thee" Psalms 50:12).

In defense of the writers of the Westminster Confession, they did not set out to mislead Christendom through their writings, they simply chose the wrong verse to explain the purpose that God had in mind when He created man and the Universe.

Man's Ultimate Purpose in Creation, to Please God

In Revelation 4:11, it is written, "And for Thy Pleasure, Thou hast created all things." Or, to rephrase, "God created man in order that man might please Him." Nothing more. Nothing less.

According to this rendering of the verse, the believer's main purpose, and ultimately the primary focus of his life, should be that of "pleasing God." So very simple, yet so very profound. Unlike the misinterpreted verse of Isaiah 43:7, Revelation 4:11 clearly states that God created all things for the purpose of being pleasing to Himself.

In addition to the fact that Scripture states that man was created in order that he might please God, we also have numerous other Scriptural references that corroborate this position. For we find the theme of "pleasing God", repeated time and time again throughout the pages of Scripture, from Genesis to Revelation.

In the Old Testament, we must first consider the life of Enoch. In Genesis 5:24, we are told that Enoch did not have to taste death, for God simply translated him from time into eternity without Enoch having to physically die. In Hebrews 11:5, we are told that the reason that Enoch did not have to go through the pains of death, was that "before his translation into eternity, he had this testimony, that he had "Pleased God."

In the New Testament, we have God the Father, introducing His Son to Israel with the qualifying statement, "This is My Beloved Son, In Whom I Am Well Pleased" (Matthew 3:17).

Jesus, in explaining His close relationship with God the Father to His disciples, which in reality should be viewed as a summation of His life, stated, "For I do always those things that Please Him" (John 8:29).

This brings us to the obvious question, "If man was ultimately created in order that he might "please God", then how does one accomplish this task of "Pleasing God."

The Pleasing of God

Scripture tells us that the believer can please God in many ways. The first way that man can please God is through his actions. By being obedient to the things that God has commanded. In John's first letter we read:

"And whatsoever we ask, we receive of him, because we keep his commandments, and do those things that are pleasing in his sight." I John 3:22

In the Book of Hebrews we are told that we please God by doing good works and openly communicating to the world the things of God:

"But to do good and to communicate forget not: for with such sacrifices God is well pleased." Hebrews 13:16

"Make you perfect in every good work to do his will, working in you that which is well pleasing in his sight, through Jesus Christ: to whom be glory for ever and ever. Amen." Hebrews 13:21

Conversely, Scripture tells us that God is not pleased with believers when they commit actions that are contrary to His Laws. In reference to the Hebrew people who had engaged in idolatry, revelry, and fornication in the Wilderness Wanderings, the Word of God states:

"But with many of them God was not well pleased: for they were overthrown in the wilderness." I Corinthians 10:5

Scripture is quick to point out that while our good actions are pleasing to God, the attitudes of our hearts towards Him are of even greater importance:

"I will praise the name of God with a song, and will magnify him with thanksgiving.

This shall please the LORD better than an ox or bullock that hath horns and hoofs." Psalm 69:30,31

Here we find the Psalmist informing us that although God is well pleased with our sacrificial actions towards Him, He is even more pleased when our hearts are in fellowship and agreement with His. When we are totally preoccupied and trusting in both Him and His mercy towards us:

"The LORD taketh pleasure in them that fear him, in those that hope in his mercy." Psalm 147:11

Likewise, when our hearts drift away from God, and we become worldly and indifferent to Him, it is then that we run the risk of living lives that are not pleasing to Him. The Apostle Paul warned Timothy, and all believers, of the dangers of becoming too preoccupied with the things of this world:

"No man that warreth entangleth himself with the affairs of this life; that he may please Him who hath chosen him to be a soldier." II Timothy 2:4

Perhaps the ultimate way that we please God is when we no longer are motivated to live to please ourselves, but when our sole motivation in life is to "please Him". This was exhibited to us in the life of Jesus, as was pointed out by the Apostle Paul in his letter to the Romans:

"We then that are strong ought to bear the infirmities of the weak, and not to please ourselves.

Let every one of us please his neighbor for his good to edification.

For even Christ pleased not himself; but as it is written, The reproaches of them that reproached thee fell on me." Romans 15:1-3

As we shall now see in this study, the primary way in which a believer pleases God is spelled out by the Apostle Paul in his letter to the believers at Philippi:

"For it is God that worketh in you, both to will and to do of His good pleasure." Philippians 2:13

In other words, the Pleasing of God is primarily accomplished in the life of the believer by not only doing God's will, but more importantly, "by willing God's will in one's life." This requires some further explanation.

The Plan of God

First of all, from the beginning of Creation, God has had a

plan for the world. No tinkering or meddling on the part of man can disannul this plan. This is spelled out in the Book of Isaiah, where we read:

"This is the purpose that is purposed upon the whole earth: and this is the hand that is stretched out upon all the nations.

For the Lord of hosts hath purposed, and who shall disannul it? And His hand is stretched out, and who shall turn it back?" Isaiah 14:26,27

As we have seen, God's view of the Universe and man's view are not the same. Man is finite, and can only have immediate awareness of the present, while God is infinite, and is capable of seeing the past, present, and future all as one (Ecclesiastes 3:15). Because God is spirit, He knew the totality of human history right from the moment of Creation (Hebrews 4:13). If there were anything that was going to affect His Plan for man and the Universe, then God would have made the necessary allowances for any deviations from His Plan from the very beginning. Although this ability to see the total past, present, and future of the physical world as one event is beyond our comprehension, it is nonetheless something that God is more than capable of doing.

In that God incorporates both Good and Evil in the outworking of this Plan, we as humans have a difficult time understanding and grasping the justness and rationale of what God is doing. This may indeed be what inspired the prophet Isaiah to write in Isaiah 28:21:

"That He may do his work, His strange work, and bring to pass His act, His strange act."

While we by nature tend to attribute only good things as being a part of God's will in this world, Scripture is quick to point out that God incorporates not only good, but also evil to accomplish His ends.

"I form the light and create darkness: I make peace, and create evil: I the Lord do all these things." Isaiah 45:7

When it comes to the Plan of God, there are certain acts or works that each of us are predestined to fulfill. Scripture states that "He hath wrought all of our works in us" (Isaiah 26:12). In order that He might accomplish His Plan, God uses not only godly people, but also the ungodly, the lowly, and the mighty. Regarding the outworking of His Plan, all of mankind are seen to be "servants" of God.

"They continue this day according to thine ordinances: for all are Thy servants." Psalm 119:91

It seems that in the accomplishing of God's Sovereign Plan, events which require evil actions are typically appointed to those "outside of the faith", or the non-believing segment of mankind. Good examples of this are the priorly mentioned actions of Pharaoh in the Book of Exodus, and of the King of Assyria in the Book of Isaiah. For both of these rulers were inspired by God to bring evil actions upon the children of Israel.

The believer in Christ can never claim that their evil and/or sinful works were committed due to any promptings or inspiration from God, for Scripture explicitly states that believers are appointed to do good works and not evil ones.

Paul addressed this issue in his letter to the Church at Ephesus when he wrote:

"For we are His workmanship, created in Christ Jesus to do "good works", which God hath before ordained that we should walk in them." Ephesians 2:10

So we see how all that occurs in the Universe is sovereignly controlled by God.

When a man's plans do not coincide with God's Plan, then man's plans are over-ruled.

"A man's heart deviseth his way, but the Lord directs his steps." Proverbs 16:9

When a man's actions are outside of God's Plan for the Universe, then presumably, his actions are free. We as humans never really know however if what we are doing is by God's Design, or our own. As Arthur Custance stated, "In eternity I think that we will find that what we considered to be insignificant actions, such as the choice of the color of tie to wear on a particular day, will prove to be "the hinges upon which the gates of destiny have swung."

We must keep in mind that the Hand of God is so prevalent in the outworking of human history that Paul wrote, "For of Him and through Him, and to Him, are all things: to whom be glory forever. Amen" (Romans 11:36).

The Will of God

Much to our dismay, all of the Good and all of the Evil that is happening in our world, is either prompted by, or allowed to occur, by the express Will of God. It can be stated that, "There is no prayer in Scripture that asks for God's Will to be done." To this, many would say, "Wait a minute, the Lord's Prayer does ask for God's Will to be done." But this is really only looking at one-half of the prayer request, the full prayer reads:

"Thy Will be done in earth, as it is in heaven." Matthew 6:10

You see, God's Will (both perfect and permissive) "IS" done on earth. If there were an event in man's history that did not fit into His Master Plan, then He would have made the necessary corrections for it at the time of creation. God's Word tells us that from God's perspective:

"The works were finished from the foundation of the world." Hebrews 4:3

The request being made in the Lord's Prayer is not that God's Will be done, but rather that God's Will be done on earth "as it is in heaven". And how is God's Will done in heaven? It is done, "WILLINGLY"!

Which leads us back to Paul's letter to the Philippians where he states:

"For it is God that worketh in you, both to will and to do of His good pleasure." Philippians 2:13

What Paul is saying here, is that while God is working in the lives of non-believers to "do" His good pleasure or will, within the lives of believers, God is going one step further and is working to have the believer to not only "do His will", but also to "will His will" in their lives. This is how believers ultimately accomplish the purpose for which they were created, that of being "Pleasing to God."

Paul addresses this issue in the Book of 1st Corinthians while explaining his own accountability to God:

"For though I preach the gospel, I have nothing to glory of: for necessity is laid upon me; yea, woe is unto me, if I preach not the gospel!

For if I do this thing willingly, I have a reward: but if against my will, a dispensation of the gospel is committed unto me." I Corinthians 9:16,17

What Paul is saying is that his work in this world of preaching the gospel is something that he will do, he cannot escape it, it is foreordained. The real merit or basis of any rewards for doing this work is to be found not in his doing of the work itself, but rather in Paul's "willingness" to do the work. The works themselves are what Scripture deems to be Paul's "reasonable service."

Jesus addressed this issue in the Gospel of Luke, where we read:

"Doth he thank that servant because he did the things that were commanded him? I trow not. So likewise ye, when ye shall have done all those things which are commanded you, say, We are unprofitable servants: we have done that which is our reasonable service." Luke 17:9-10

From God's point of view, He has made a plan for the course of history, created the Universe, and then died on a cross to redeem fallen humanity from the effects of their sins. He thus considers the doing of His Commandments by the believer, as being "our reasonable service."

The basis for the rewardability of doing His works does not rest in the works themselves, for Scripture tells us that it is God Himself who has "wrought all of our works within us" (Isaiah 26:12). The rewardability of our actions is dictated by the motive that prompts them.

As Paul stated in Corinthians, if he was not willingly preaching the gospel, then his efforts in preaching were of no value (I Corinthians 9:17). At some point in time, Paul in his human frailties had probably grown tired of all of the arguing, deprivations, and hardships that he had to endure in his efforts to spread the Gospel. In this, Paul's struggles were much the same as any believer's struggles. For it is difficult to maintain a proper attitude when life is hard. All believers are called to recognize God's sovereign control over their individual lives, and then be willing to "will God's will" in their lives. No matter how dull or distasteful our daily routine may appear to be at the time, the believer is called to live in joyful and thankful obedience to God. By so doing, he or she exhibits the fact that they are indeed "willing God's will" and thereby accomplishing God's ultimate purpose for their life, that of being found to be, "pleasing unto Him".

It should also be noted that nowhere in Scripture is man ever commanded to "Please God." If he were, then according to the parable in Luke chapter 17, the pleasing of God would hold no merit for rewards, for it would be a part of his or her "reasonable service". Mankind however is commanded to "glorify God", on numerous occasions:

"Ye that fear the LORD, praise him; all ye the seed of Jacob, glorify Him; and fear Him, all ye the seed of Israel." Psalm 22:23

"Wherefore glorify ye the LORD in the fires, even the name of the LORD God of Israel in the isles of the sea." Isaiah 24:15

"For ye are bought with a price: therefore glorify God in your body, and in your spirit, which are God's." 1st Corinthians 6:20

This of course makes the "Glorification of God" a part of man's "reasonable service", and is not necessarily a basis for rewards.

Again, while mankind is more concerned with the outward physical appearance of things, God is more concerned with the inner man, the conditions of a man's heart.

"For the Lord seeth not as man seeth; for man looketh on the outward appearance, but the Lord looketh on the heart." I Samuel 16:7

This is why the Scripture admonishes the believer to: "Keep your heart with all diligence, for out of it are the issues of life." Proverbs 4:23

In the Old Testament, a good case in point on this matter is the story of Jonah. God ordered Jonah to go to Nineveh and preach to the Assyrians. Jonah however went in the opposite direction and headed towards Tarshish. We all know what happened then. God brought a great fish to swallow up Jonah and bring him to Nineveh. You see, it was ordained that Jonah would go and preach repentance to Nineveh, and this he did (with a little change of direction directed by God). The works that we are foreordained to do, these we will do. Job writes:

"Seeing his days are determined, the number of his months are with Thee, thou hast appointed his bounds that he cannot pass;

Turn from him, that he may rest, till he shall accomplish, as a hireling, his day." Job 14:5,6

Next, we see that Jonah held what was probably the most successful evangelistic campaign in the Old Testament, whereby the many people living in Nineveh repented and were spared by God. Yet Jonah still refused to "will God's will" in his life. He actually became angry that God had spared Nineveh. Although Jonah did eventually do the works that he was commanded and ordained to do, judging from God's stinging rebuke of him as recorded in the Book of Jonah, we can only deem that in the end Jonah remained "an unprofitable servant."

"And God said to Jonah, Doest thou well to be angry for the gourd? And he said, I do well to be angry, even unto death.

Then said the LORD, Thou hast had pity on the gourd, for the which thou hast not laboured, neither madest it grow; which came up in a night, and perished in a night:

And should not I spare Nineveh, that great city, wherein are more than six-score thousand persons that cannot discern between their right hand and their left hand; and also much cattle?" Jonah 4:9-11

In that Jonah had performed his "reasonable service" unto God reluctantly, Jonah's work in God's eyes had no rewardable merit. Hence God had harshly rebuked him. The story of Jonah should serve as a constant reminder to believers of all ages of the importance of maintaining a proper attitude in their walk with the Lord. That the duties that we are called to do, no matter how distasteful or mundane they may appear to be at the time, should be done in a loving, joyful, and willing manner.

There were aspects of Jesus' life and ministry that were far from pleasant, especially when we consider the pains of the Crucifixion. Jesus did not want to go through the horrors of the cross, as is evidenced by His prayer in the Garden of Gethsemane:

"Father if thou be willing, remove this cup from me: nevertheless not my will, but Thine, be done." Luke 22:42

Here we see Jesus accomplishing what man was originally created to do, that being, "He Pleased God". He did this not by willing His own will, but rather, by "Willing God's Will in his life."

The Will of God and Human Responsibility

(Why doth He yet find Fault)

When we consider that God has a Plan that takes precedence over the plans of man, and the fact that many of the things that men do are a direct result of the inspiration of God, then the question arises as to where human responsibility comes into play. This is the direct question that Paul was confronted with in the 9th chapter of the Book of Romans. For here we are reminded that it was Pharaoh's will to let the Israelites go, but it was God who had hardened Pharaoh's heart so that he would not let them leave. So, the argument is presented, "If God overrules many of our actions, how can He be just in judging man for doing what He Himself hast ordained to be done?" Or, in other words as is stated by the argument in Romans 9:19:

"Why doth He yet find fault?"

If you will notice, Paul never directly answers this question. To some this might seem to be suspect, but there is a reason why Paul does not directly answer the question. The reason Paul does not answer the question is because the question is based upon the false assumption that the judgment of God is determined primarily by man's actions. Therefore the question in and of itself is not a valid question, and requires no response on the part of Paul.

As we have stated in previous chapters, God's judgments are based more on motives than upon actions themselves.

In God's economy, the basis for his judgment, "Pleasing God", is primarily accomplished by mankind presenting the Lord with a "willing heart".

In the Old Testament, we find David desiring to build a house for God. But God would not allow it because David had been a man of war, and God did not want to have His Name associated with war. Although God did not allow David to build a house, He rewarded David as if he had, "For it was in David's heart to build it" (II Chronicles 6:8).

Time and time again in Scripture we find the necessity of doing the works of God with a "willing heart". In the Old Testament we read:

"And they came, everyone whose heart stirred him up, and everyone whom his spirit made willing, and they brought the LORD's offering to the work of the tabernacle of the congregation, and for all his service, and for the holy garments. And they came, both men and women, as many as were willing hearted..." Exodus 35:21,22

Moses then went on to write: "The children of Israel brought a willing offering unto the LORD, every man and woman, whose heart made them willing to bring for all manner of work, which the LORD had commanded to be made by the hand of Moses." Exodus 35:29

Paul in the New Testament also stressed the importance of believers having a willing heart:

"Now therefore perform the doing of it; as there was a readiness to will, so there may be a performance also out of that which ye have.

For if there be first a willing mind, it is accepted according to that a man hath, and not according to that he hath not." II Corinthians 8:11,12

68

The pleasing of God is the only proper eternally rewardable motivation in life. In reality, it is also the basis for what constitutes sin in the eyes of God. The unbeliever does not know God, and hence cannot will to please God (will God's will), as Paul points out in the Book of Romans:

"They who are in the flesh cannot please God." Romans 8:8

I believe that it was Augustine who pointed out that because the unbeliever does not know God, they cannot perform any action with the proper motivation, and hence, every action that they do in this life amounts to sin in the eyes of God.

Although God does reward unbelievers for doing His bidding here on earth, as He is no man's debtor (Ezekiel 29:17-20), these rewards are only in this life, and are only dispensed in eternity in terms of receiving a less severe judgment (Luke 12:45-48).

The unbeliever has no basis for receiving rewards in the eternal, for nothing that they have done could ever have been done with the proper rewardable motivation. In that they have never known God, he or she can never truly "will to choose to please God" by their actions. Ultimately, their actions can never be deemed as being righteous actions.

From a strict moral perspective, unbelievers in various ways can only choose to please themselves, which is the essence of sin. As Augustine and many others have stated, "The unbeliever's freedom of choice lies only in choosing what manner of sin they will commit."

When a person comes to faith in Christ, it is then and only then that they have a restoration of "their moral free will." They are now capable of making their actions righteous and with eternal merit, when offered out of love for his or her Savior. The believer in Christ has a choice of seeking to either please themself, or of seeking to please God as the motivating factor in life.

This is the struggle of our day to day lives. This is the end to which God is now constantly working out in the believer's life while still on earth. To not only do God's will, but to also "will God's will" (Philippians 2:13).

In the eternal state, God's Will, will be accomplished in the same manner that it is now being performed by the Unfallen Angels in Heaven, and that being, "His Will is being done Willingly."

In summation, the overriding goal of the Christian should be that at the end of his or her life, that God would say, "Well done thou good and faithful servant." This can be accomplished by doing what he or she was created to do from the beginning, that is, to live a life that is found to be, "Pleasing unto God" (Revelation 4:11).

The Christian "pleases God" by not only doing the godly works that we are commanded to do, but also more importantly, by choosing to do these works (Philippians 2:13). Christians are to will that "God's Will be done" in their lives," never reluctantly, but gladly. That is why Paul constantly reminds the Christian to live with a spirit of joyful thankfulness. For when we live in a constant state of thankfulness, it is a good indication that we are indeed willing God's Will in our lives.

"Giving thanks always for all things unto God and the Father in the name of our Lord Jesus Christ." Ephesians 5:20

"Do all things without murmurings and disputings." Philippians 2:14

"Rejoice in the Lord always, again I say rejoice." Philippians 4:4

"And let the peace of God rule in your hearts, to the which also ye are called in one body; and be ye thankful." Colossians 3:15

"Rejoice evermore." I Thessalonians 5:16

"In everything give thanks: for this is the will of God in Christ Jesus concerning you." I Thessalonians 5:18

"By him therefore let us offer the sacrifice of praise to God continually, that is, the fruit of our lips giving thanks to His name." Hebrews 13:15

For when we are joyful and thankful, we are not only glorifying God to the Universe at large, but more importantly, it is evidence that we are "willing His Will", and thereby fulfilling the ultimate calling of our lives, that of being "Pleasing unto God."

Heaven Helps Those Who Help Themselves

"God helps those who help themselves"

The idea that "God helps those who help themselves", is a paradigm whose origination can be traced back to the Protestant work ethic that was so influential in the formation of America. This Biblically based ethic stressed the importance of being industrious in our day to day lives:

"He that is slothful in his work is brother to him that is a great waster." Proverbs 18:9

Hard work gave man not only the means to support himself and family, but also the ability to be charitable to those in need:

"But rather let him labor, working with his hands the thing that is good, that he may have to give to him that needeth." Ephesians 4:28

The problem with the Protestant work ethic was that it took on a life of its own. Work in and of itself too often became the focal point for many as they lived out their lives. It became a "false god". Eventually this gave rise to the erroneous belief that, "God helps those who help themselves". Many believe that this phrase is an actual quote from Scripture. We can rest assured however that this statement is nowhere to be found within the Word of God, and neither is its sentiment. In fact, the exact opposite is true. Scripture tells us that God is in the business of "helping the helpless", not the so called self-sufficient. In the Book of Isaiah we read:

"He giveth power to the faint; and to them that have no might, he increaseth strength." Isaiah 40:29

The Christian walk is a walk of faith that centers upon a reliance on God, and not on oneself. The believer in Christ is admonished to "rest in the Lord", and to not trust solely upon their own abilities. This is not a call to laziness on the part of the believer, but rather a call to the realization that God had provided for all the needs of believers for their journey here on earth from the moment that He had created the universe. Believers are admonished to rest in this fact:

"For we which have believed do enter into rest, as he said, As I have sworn in my wrath, if they shall enter into my rest: although the works were finished from the foundation of the world." Hebrews 4:3

Again, God knew the total history of the world from the time that He had created the heavens and earth ("Known unto God are all his works from the beginning of the world." Acts 15:18). At the moment of Creation, God supplied all of the needs that believers would encounter during their pilgrimage here on earth, in addition to providing the answers to all of their prayers:

"That before they call, I will answer; and while they are yet speaking, I will hear." Isaiah 65:24

To accomplish the maturation of faith in the lives of His followers, it is God who leads the believer into situations where there are no human solutions. This He does in order that the believer might learn to trust in Him. It is an intricate part of Christian growth. The Christian is to acknowledge the fact that God knows their every need and concern and has made provision for them to be granted in His perfect timing. This of course often involves waiting on and trusting in the Lord on the part of the Christian. As most Christians realize, this is a task that oftentimes is not all that easy to accomplish.

74

This is why the writer of Hebrews implores the believer to "labor" to enter into God's rest:

"For he that is entered into his rest, he also hath ceased from his own works, as God did from his.

Let us labor therefore to enter into that rest, lest any man fall after the same example of unbelief." Hebrews 4:10,11

It takes a lot of effort to learn to trust God. Yet this is what the Christian is both called and admonished to do. This process of growing in faith by entering into God's rest is just a continuation of the process that God had used to mature Israel in the Old Testament. This in turn dispels another common faulty paradigm, that "God's way of facilitating the growth of believers in the New Testament is somehow different than the methods that He employed in the Old Testament."

God's method of maturing believers in both the Old and the New Testaments is essentially the same. He brings about spiritual growth by teaching believers to trust in Him to daily supply all their needs, especially when there are no human solutions available. The believer's faith calling is therefore often seen to be one of waiting on and resting in God, as opposed to that of constantly "doing".

The Wilderness Wanderings

This resting in the Lord is the same walk of faith that the nation of Israel had been implored to do after they had been released by God from their bondage in Egypt. In the Book of Exodus, we are told that God led them to a place in the wilderness, where there was no water. He did this to test them, that they might learn to walk by faith. God had already supplied the big thing, their release from the bondage of Egypt. Now He was asking them to trust in Him for the "little things".

When the Israelites reached Marah, they found there only bitter waters to drink (Exodus 15:23). God knew this, for it was God who had led them there. God had brought the people to Marah in order to test them. They had just seen the many miracles that God had performed for them in Egypt. They had also been delivered from a lifetime of living as slaves to the Egyptians. What God was now asking them to do, was to simply trust in Him to supply the daily needs of their lives. What did the people do? Scripture tells us that, "they murmured against Moses", God's chosen representative (Exodus 15:24). God in His grace however, sweetened the waters, and the children of Israel drank.

Later when they had journeyed farther on into Meribah, they again found no water. Here too they once again murmured against the Lord (Exodus 17:2,3). Time and time again the Lord would bring Israel to a place of testing, and continually the people failed to learn to "rest in Him." Instead, they murmured against Him, and refused to believe in His goodness and in His ability to provide for them. For this the Lord was grieved and consigned this generation to 40 years of wandering in the wilderness (Numbers 14:33).

In like manner, the Christian has been released not from the bondage of Egypt, but rather from the bondage of sin. God has provided the big thing, salvation, and now, as in the case of the Israelites, He asks the Christian to trust in Him for the little things; the day to day needs of their lives.

Like the Israelites, God leads the Christian into places of need. For some it is a case of having no job. For others, it is living without a car or a house or spouse. From God's point of view, He is waiting for the believer to trust in Him. He knew from the "foundation of the world" all the predicaments of necessity that Christians would find themselves in throughout the course of their lives. And, from the foundation of the world, He had already made provision for these needs. Not in our timing, but in His perfect timing. What God is now asking of those who believe in Christ, is to not fall apart and murmur and complain like the Hebrew people had done in the Wilderness, but rather to simply "rest and trust" in Him to supply their daily needs. This is not easy, for it goes against our fallen nature.

76

It is however the method that God has chosen to mature believers in their faith. According to Scripture, it is almost as if God is "tapping His foot" waiting for the Christian to trust Him in all things:

"And therefore will the Lord wait, that He may be gracious unto you, and therefore will He be exalted, that He may have mercy upon you: for the Lord is a God of Judgment: blessed are all they that wait for Him." Isaiah 30:18

The Christian is to accept this period of waiting on the Lord to provide for his or her needs as their "labor in the Lord" (Hebrews 4:11). During this time, the believer in Christ is commanded to "rejoice in the Lord" (Philippians 4:4), and refrain from "murmuring or complaining".

Again, for the Christian to murmur and complain to God about the problems in their life is tantamount to the children of Israel's complaining to God in the wilderness. When Christians come to the junctures in life where they are lacking something, and there are no human solutions, it is at these times that "They are supposed to be looking up." Just as God led Israel into situations where they were lacking necessities, so too does He lead the Christian into situations where they are forced to turn to Him for help. It is at these times that the Christian is called upon to resist the urge to murmur and complain, and thereby repeat the mistakes of the Children of Israel. Rather, the Christian is called to simply enter into God's rest. To trust in His goodness and faithfulness to provide. This life of resting in God, which some have called "The Faith-Rest Life", is really an acknowledgment that it is God who is in control of the events of the Christian's life. By leading the believer into situations of need, God teaches the believer to learn to fully trust in His Sovereign Plan for their lives.

In some respects, the faith-rest life is the modus-operandi by which God matures the faith of the believer so that the believer develops a complete and total trust in Him. For it is only through these trials of trusting in the Lord in times of need that the believer can become mature and fully capable of praying the prayer that Jesus prayed in the Garden of Gethsemane, ("Nevertheless, not my will but thine will be done" Matthew 26:39), in all situations of life.

It is easy to see that this life of resting and trusting in God is another way for the Christian to be found to be, "pleasing unto God". For it is an acceptance of God's Will over the believer's own will. It is also an acknowledgment of the fact that God has a perfect timing for the events of our lives, and that He, not ourselves, has everything under control. The Book of Hebrews states:

"Wherefore as the Holy Ghost saith, today if ye will hear his voice, Harden not your hearts, as in the day of provocation, in the day of temptation in the wilderness:

When your father tempted me, proved me, and saw my works forty years.

Wherefore I was grieved with that generation, and said, they do always err in their heart; and they have not known my ways.

So I swear in my wrath, they shall not enter into my rest.

Take heed, brethren, lest there be in any of you an evil heart of unbelief, in departing from the living God." Hebrews 3:7-12

Again, it is important to realize that God is maturing the Christian in the same manner that He matured the Children of Israel. Paul cites these failures of the children of Israel to warn the Christian so as not to repeat these same mistakes in their walk:

"Neither let us tempt Christ, as some of them also tempted, and were destroyed of serpents.

Neither murmur ye, as some of them also murmured, and were destroyed of the destroyer.

78

Now all of these things happened unto them for examples: and they are written for our admonition, upon whom the ends of the world are come." I Corinthians 10:9-11

In summation, the principles found in Paradigms 5 and 6 of this study, show that the focus of the Christian life should be:

1) To seek to "Please God" by consistently "willing God's Will" in one's life during the time of our pilgrimage here on earth.

2) To fight the natural inclination to murmur and complain about the things that may be lacking in one's current life situation. To rest in the faith that God both knew about and provided for all of our needs from the moment He created the Universe. That God will provide for these needs in His perfect timing, and that there is no need for the Christian to continuously wander out of fellowship with the Lord for the majority of their earthly lives (as did the children of Israel for 40 years in the wilderness).

Christian Growth

When Jesus was asked what the greatest commandment of the law was, he replied:

"Thou shalt love the Lord thy God with all thy heart, and with all thy soul, and with all thy mind.

This is the first and great commandment.

And the second is like unto it, Thou shalt love thy neighbor as thyself.

On these two commandments hang all the law and prophets." Matthew 22:37-40

In essence, what Jesus was saying here is that the purpose or totality of the Old Testament record could be summed up in these two complementary principles: "That man is to love God with all of his heart, and his neighbor as himself."

In like manner, if one were to point to the two aspects of the Christian life which are the essence of how God matures the believer in Christ, it could be argued that God primarily accomplishes His work of maturing the New Testament believer by employing the two aforementioned complementary principles, reiterated here:

1) Working on the heart of the Christian to learn to not only do His will, but to also "will His will", and in so doing, to thereby become "Pleasing unto Him" (Philippians 2:13).

2) By teaching the Christian to recognize that it is God who is leading them into various places of "need" in his or her life, by which they are to learn to refrain from murmuring and complaining, but rather by faith, to learn to rest in and trust the Lord to supply all of their needs. That God's methodology for spiritual growth is still the same as it was in the Old Testament.

Sadly, these two Christian Life Principles are rarely if ever recognized nor given much attention from our nation's pulpits. Too often, the themes of sermons are more concerned with topics that might be more appropriately addressed in "self-help" books.

The faith-rest life is all a part of the "simplicity that is in Christ" that Paul not only talks about, but also warns against straying away from (II Corinthians 11:3).

If our lives are constantly exhibiting less than a thankful and joyous attitude, it is a clear indication that we are in our own way murmuring against God, much like the Hebrew people of the Exodus (I Corinthians 10:10,11). A large part of how a Christian's life becomes "pleasing unto God", is accomplished by the Christian entering into the mechanics of the faith-rest life, a life of resting in the Promises of God. A daily self-examination of our attitudes is a good measuring rod of whether we are faithfully living with a proper Godly focus, and are joyously resting in His Promises to supply all our needs, "according to his riches in glory by Christ Jesus" (Philippians 4:19).

God's View of the Races

"It is the desire of God that racial divisions should cease to exist"

In the modern secular world, the subject of racial harmony is a constant and ongoing concern. In both the print media and in our nightly news broadcasts, we are continually reminded of the friction that often exists between the races in our society, with the implication that somehow the world will not become a better place in which to live until the day that racial distinctions cease to exist. In recent times, it has even become common for man to misguidedly proclaim, "There is only one race, the human race." While this statement is long on Utopian sentimentality, it is short on historical facts, as there are obvious racial variances amongst the peoples of our world.

On a theological basis, we assume that because God is love, He too is all in favor of removing racial distinctions. This sentiment is seemingly backed up by certain passages of Scripture that appear to ask for peace and harmony amongst the peoples of the world. In the Book of John, Jesus states:

"Neither pray I for these alone, but for them also which shall believe on me through their word.

That they all may be one; as Thou Father art in me, and I in thee, that they also may be one in us: that the world may believe that thou hast sent us." John 17:20, 21

In writing to the Galatians, Paul states:

"For you are all the children of God by faith in Christ Jesus.

For as many of you as have been baptized into Christ have put on Christ,

There is neither Jew nor Greek, there is neither bond nor free, there is neither male or female: for ye are all one in Christ Jesus." Galatians 3:26-28

When we carefully consider these verses and the context in which they were delivered we realize that they are both directed at the Church, and not to the world at large. This begs for an answer to the question, "How does God view the separation of the peoples of the world along distinctive racial lines?"

God's Program for the Races

As we shall soon see in this study, that since the time of Noah, God has had a purpose in the division of mankind into three distinct and separate races. This purpose becomes more evident as we study the historical record and note the particular contributions that each race has made to their fellow man in the betterment of Civilization.

Although these contributions are not specifically spelled out in Scripture, nonetheless they do exist. We must always remember that the focus of Scripture is not upon history, science, or anthropology. The focus of Scripture is always concerned with the Salvation of Man. On this subject, God's Word is totally accurate and complete. When Scripture refers to these other subjects such as history, science, and anthropology, it is always 100% accurate, but seldom complete. Here we have to refer to the written historical record.

A special acknowledgment must be given to Arthur Custance for his exhaustive research and insights contained in his monumental book "Noah's Three Sons", which has provided much of the historical information contained within this study.

The Division of Mankind into Three Racial Groups

According to Scripture, at the time of the Flood, all of mankind was destroyed excepting the family of Noah and the families of his three sons: Shem, Ham, and Japheth. From these three sons have emerged three separate and distinct racial lines that have remained intact to this day.

It is an interesting fact that many of the aspects of God's Creation exist in three divisions or parts. First and foremost, we see that God Himself is a three-part Being consisting of Father, Son, and Holy Spirit. Next, we see that the physical world is separated into three divisions: animal, vegetable, and mineral. Then we note that the world of matter also exists in three different states: solid, liquid, and gaseous. When we refer to time, we again find a three-part division of past, present, and future.

Of special interest to this study is the fact that Scripture states that man too is made up of three parts: body, soul, and spirit (I Thessalonians 5:23). This we shall see is of great significance when we examine the history of the three races.

Genesis Chapter 10: The Table of Nations

In the 10th chapter of the Book of Genesis, we find a listing of the family trees of Noah's three sons. This chapter in the Bible is often referred to as "The Table of Nations", as it lists both the family trees or lineages of each of the three sons of Noah, and the original geographical areas in which they settled. Although throughout the history of mankind there has been some mixing of the three races, these three lines have remained remarkably intact and distinct from one another.

The 10th chapter of Genesis shows that the different peoples of the world have all come from the same family, that of Noah. It has been said that "Just as the Magna Carta is the original document of human equality, the 10th Chapter of the Book of

Genesis is the original document of the unity of man." All of mankind can trace their origins back to one of Noah's three sons: Shem, Ham, or Japheth.

The children of Shem have become known as the Semitic race, which includes the Jewish and Arabic peoples of the world, who for the most part have remained concentrated in the Middle East.

The children of Ham have become known as the Hamitic or Black Race, consisting of the darker skinned peoples of the world who are now mainly concentrated in Africa and Asia. In addition, the children of Ham were also the original settlers of the far reaches of the world, including the continents of Australia, and North and South America.

The offspring of Japheth have become known as the Japhetic or Indo-European peoples, commonly referred to as the White Race. This branch of mankind originally settled in what is known as Europe and India but have subsequently branched out into the rest of the world, especially into the Americas and Australia.

The Blessings and Curse upon the Three Sons of Noah

After the Flood, Scripture records that Noah had planted a vineyard, and subsequently after partaking of the fruits of the vineyard, had become drunk. Noah became so drunk in fact, that he had fallen off to sleep naked. Scripture records that upon finding his father in this inebriated state, Ham had done nothing to cover his father's nakedness (Genesis 9:22). Shem and Japheth however, had respectfully proceeded to place a covering over their father. When Noah awoke and had realized what had transpired, he pronounced blessings upon Shem and Japheth, and a curse upon Ham through his son Canaan:

"And he (Noah) said, Cursed be Canaan; a servant of servants shall he be unto his brethren.

And he said, Blessed be the Lord God of Shem; and Canaan shall be his servant.

God shall enlarge Japheth, and he shall dwell in the tents of Shem; and Canaan shall be his servant." Genesis 9:25-27

This seemingly obscure pronouncement that Noah had placed upon his three sons would eventually play a rather significant role during the course of the history of mankind. For we shall see that it has been the framework of God's plan for the setting up of Civilization.

We know from world history, that the blessings given to Shem were ultimately of spiritual prominence and would eventually come down to the Semitic race through Abraham. We also know that Japheth's descendants later shared in these spiritual blessings at the advent of the Church Age, when the Japhetic Gentiles arose to worldwide spiritual prominence over the next two millenniums. This occurred after the children of Israel had been set aside by God for a season due to their rejection of their Messiah, thus fulfilling the blessing given to Japheth of "dwelling in the tents of Shem."

History also shows that since the time of the overthrow of Semitic Babylon in 538 B.C. by Cyrus the Persian, that God had indeed "enlarged Japheth" on the world's secular stage, bringing the Japhetic race into the political dominance which it has maintained to the present day.

This leads us into the third aspect of Noah's pronouncement, the curse placed upon the children of Ham, that of being "a servant" to both Shem and to Japheth.

The Curse Placed Upon Canaan

When we read of the curse that was placed upon Canaan for Ham's act of negligent disrespect, we immediately ask the question, "If it was Ham who had sinned, then why did Noah curse his son Canaan?" There are at least two reasons why Noah cursed Canaan instead of Ham himself:

1) In the Oriental Culture, the actions of the children were typically tied directly to the father. A good example of this is when the mighty feats of David had been brought to the attention of King Saul, Saul's reaction was to ask the question, "Whose son is this" (I Samuel 17:55)? Saul asked this question because he wanted to know who the person was who deserved credit for the great acts of valor that had been performed by David. Not only were the good deeds performed by one's children attributed to the father, but likewise so were the bad deeds. In a very real sense, for Noah to have cursed Ham would have been akin to pronouncing a curse upon himself.

2) By having Noah curse Canaan as opposed to Ham, it also becomes apparent that the blessings placed upon Shem and Japheth, and the curse that was placed upon Ham, were meant to extend beyond their own lifetimes. That these pronouncements were indeed intended to be multi-generational. It also thereby implied that the distinctions between the three families or racial branches of mankind would also remain to some degree intact throughout mankind's history.

An Analyses of Genesis 9:25

When we consider the meaning of the curse that was pronounced upon Canaan by Noah in the Book of Genesis, we read in Genesis 9:25:

"Cursed be Canaan; a servant of servants shall he be unto his brethren."

At face value, it sounds as if the children of Ham were destined to be literal servants to the other two races. History has shown that this misinterpretation of the text in Genesis has only served to exacerbate the problems faced by the Hamitic peoples of the world. Throughout the ages, many people have felt that this verse of Scripture suggests that the calling of the children of Ham was one of subjugation to the other races, and tragically in the extreme, to a justification for the enslavement of the children of Ham. But as we shall see, this is not an accurate depiction of what the Hebrew idiom "servant of servants" really means.

In the Hebrew language, when a condition is repeated, such as when Jesus Christ is referred to as "King of Kings", it is an indication that merely denotes excellence. When Jesus is said to be the "King of Kings", what is meant is that Jesus is to be a king par excellent, or restated, "a great King, having no equals". In like manner, so it was with Canaan. Canaan was to be a "Servant of Servants", or in other words, a Servant par excellent, having no equal in his contributions to the physical welfare of his fellow man.

Contrary to what many believe in our culture, there is nothing undignified about being a servant. Time and time again Jesus Christ Himself is depicted as being a servant in Scripture. When considered in its proper context, in God's eyes being called to be a servant can be just as noble as being called to be a king. When we look at the subsequent outworking of world history regarding the three races, we shall see that the Hamitic peoples have indeed been of great service or "servanthood" to the descendants of Shem and Japheth. For anthropological history shows that it was the children of Ham who were the original trailblazers in the repopulating of the earth after the Flood. It was Ham's descendants who had left the Middle East's "Cradle of Civilization" and had roamed to the four corners of the world, preparing the land for its future habitation by all of mankind.

Ham's descendants include the peoples who had populated the continent of Africa (including Egypt), Asia (China, Japan, Indonesia, etc.), North and South America (Eskimos, Native Americans, Incas, Mayans, et al), and Australia (Aborigines). The early history of anthropology is a story of the children of Ham time and time again creating ever far reaching settlements, until they were eventually overrun by the children of Japheth. It can be said that it was Ham who had tamed the lands of the world, by both clearing them and removing obstacles to civilization such as the dangerous wild animals from them. Scripture confirms this fact in I Chronicles 4:40 where we read:

"And they found fat pasture and good, and the land was wide, and quiet, and peaceable; for they of Ham had dwelt there of old."

When considering Ham's contributions to Civilization, of even more importance than his taming of the world's lands is the fact that the Hamitic peoples have in conjunction developed almost all of the basic technologies that were necessary for mankind's survival in the world. An inventory of Ham's inventive prowess reveals that it was the descendants of Ham who have led the way in the technological development of Architecture, Agriculture, the Domestication of Animals, Mathematics, Metallurgy, Pharmacology, and Textiles, thus paving the way for a more orderly and advanced Civilization.

History has shown that part of the curse that was pronounced upon the children of Ham by Noah seems to be that the benefits of their labors have been enjoyed far more by the children of Japheth and Shem than by the Hamitic peoples themselves. In addition, another important aspect of the Hamitic curse may lie in the fact that the Hamitic peoples have very seldom been given proper credit for their technological contributions to Civilization. Very often the other races have falsely taken credit for what was the inventive genius of Ham, when in fact most of their contributions have been only slight modifications to original Hamitic creativity.

Sadly, this ignorance of Ham's creative genius has often led to the other races disparaging the Hamitic race. The truth be known, without the technological accomplishments of the Hamitic peoples, civilizations throughout the history of the world would have most certainly been far less advanced and physically comfortable for their inhabitants.

In order to better understand the scope of the contributions of Ham to his two brothers, it is necessary to list some of these technological advancements that have been made by the various Hamitic peoples throughout the history of mankind.

The Descendants of Ham

The Sumerians

The Sumerians were one of the original groups of Hamitic peoples. They lived in the area of Mesopotamia, until they were displaced by the Semitic Babylonians and Assyrians. Some of the early contributions to civilization made by the Sumerians include the development of pottery, the origination of written records, banks, postal systems, and the concept of the division of labor. In Metallurgy, it was the Sumerians who had first fabricated bronze. (their ratio of 10% tin to 90% copper still being used to this day).

In the area of Mathematics, the Sumerians had discovered the correct value of Pi in the third millennium B.C. In conjunction with the Egyptians (who were also of Hamitic descent), the Sumerians developed Mathematics to the point that they could not only calculate the areas of irregular rectangles, circles, cones, and triangles, but also solve algebraic equations with up to four unknown variables.

The Sumerians were also employing the so called "Pythagorean Theory" as early as 2000 B.C., long before Pythagoras had even been born in the 6th Century B.C.

In addition to developing algebra, the Sumerians were also the world's first chemists and cartographers.

The Sumerians were working with glass as early as 2700 B.C., and early on had created a plywood that is similar to the plywood still used today.

The Egyptians

Like the Sumerians, the Egyptians made vast inroads in the area of Mathematics, especially in geometry. These developments were created out of necessity due to the fact that the Nile River flooded annually, changing the landscape and thus making the determination of property lines rather difficult.

In addition to making great advances in Mathematics, the Egyptians were also accomplished architects and stone masons. Like the Sumerians, the Egyptians were also adept at working with glass. Almost all of the tools of carpentry were invented by the Egyptians, including the level. From the Egyptians came many mechanical devices, including the original dead bolt door lock mechanisms.

The Egyptians also developed paper from papyrus, and black ink for writing. Other items that have come down to us from Egypt include the calendar, the pipe organ, moving picture sequencing (cartoons), and a form of the game of bowling.

On the personal hygiene front, it was in Egypt that the world's first soap, toothbrushes, toothpaste, breath mints, eye make-up, and hair shears were developed.

In Agriculture, it was the Egyptians who invented the plow, and then later domesticated oxen in order to pull it. Around 2000 B.C. the Egyptians developed the art of making cheese.

In order to successfully navigate the Nile River, the Egyptians had become the world's first sailors by inventing and employing the use of the sail to propel their boats.

The Chinese

The civilized world owes an incredible debt to the ancient Chinese and their fellow Hamitic Asiatic peoples. Their contributions to mankind have truly been remarkable. It was the Chinese who first cultivated rice and soybeans, two of the largest staples of our world's diet. Agriculturally, the Chinese also developed millet and tea, and went on to produce the world's first noodles.

Between 2000-3000 B.C., the Chinese also domesticated oxen and buffalo for agricultural use. In Textiles, they domesticated the silk moth for use in the production of silk.

From China have also come many advances to Metallurgy. It was the Chinese who developed the first blast furnaces, hydraulic powered bellows, and cast iron. In the 3rd Century B.C., they produced the world's first stainless steel by introducing chromium with iron in the steel making process. Chinese arrow tips which were produced 2,000 years ago to this day still show no indication of oxidation. In 150 B.C. the Chinese developed the first cast iron stoves, and then built the world's first suspension bridge ten centuries before Europe had accomplished the same feat.

What is now famously known as the "Bessemer Process" for making various types of steel, was not originally developed by either William Kelly or Henry Bessemer (the two Americans who have both made claims for its creation in the 19th Century). For the process had already been in use in both China and Japan many centuries before. We now know that Kelly had in fact hired four Chinese iron workers in 1854 to "assist him" in the development of his process.

The watertight compartment method of boat construction came from China, as did the sternpost rudder, and canal locks for inland water transport. China's neighbor to the south, Korea, had made the first iron clad battleship in the 16th Century, long before America tried to make the same claim with the construction of "The USS Constitution" at the close of the 18th Century.

Around 2000 B.C., the Chinese had developed glass mirrors, and later created the world's first glass windows, the term "window" itself, being an embellishment of the inventor's name, Wing Dow.

The Chinese also created porcelain and fine pottery, and in 450 B.C. were the first people to both harness and use natural gas.

Long before our F.B.I. began using fingerprints for identification purposes in solving crimes, the Chinese had known about their uniqueness to each individual, and had been employing them for purposes of identification as early as the 7th Century A.D.

China also developed their own version of paper in addition to moveable type and printing ink. Paper money was also first employed in China, which allowed for a vast expansion of commercial exchange. By employing paper money, a person no longer had to carry his wealth with him wherever he went, and economic exchange was greatly expanded and facilitated. Like our nation's original currency, this paper money was also redeemable in precious metals or gems.

In Aviation, it was the Chinese who had produced the world's first gliders, rockets, kites, balloons, and parachutes. In addition, the inspirational idea for the modern helicopter can be found in an ancient Chinese toy.

Numerous weapons of war have also come from China, including gunpowder, cannons, hand grenades, iron clad bombs, and flame throwers. For psychological warfare, the Chinese invented large arrows that whistled in flight. The Chinese were also the first people to incorporate lethal gas in warfare, having created a form of the world's first mustard gas.

Two of the major innovations from China, the invention

of the stirrup and of gunpowder, played a major hand in the history of Europe. With the introduction of the stirrup, armored warriors took control of the battlefields, causing the introduction of feudalism to the continent. When gunpowder was perfected, it brought about the end to the feudal state, as the walls of the castles of the feudal Lords came crashing down.

The Native Populations of North and South America

The Native North and South American populations were big contributors to the world's agricultural progress. It was they who had first developed corn (maize), beans (kidney and lima), and potatoes, items which have also become some of the major dietary staples of the world. They were also the first to cultivate and use other common foods such as peanuts, squash, peppers, and tomatoes.

In Pharmacology, it was the Peruvians who employed cocoa leaves (cocaine) for use as an anesthetic, and in medicine developed the practice of suturing cuts and of cauterizing wounds. In South America, quinine was first used in the treatment of malaria. In Dentistry, it was the Incans who had developed the use of Portland Cement for the filling of tooth cavities.

On the technological front, long before Mr. Goodyear had started manufacturing tires, the Brazilian Incans had learned how to vulcanize latex into rubber, and were making watertight shoes, ponchos, flasks, and dolls out of this natural material.

Other Hamitic inventions that have come out of the Americas include the hammock, the chain, and new methods of bridge and paved road construction. The water pumps which the Native Central American Indians had developed were so effective that the Spaniards upon their arrival into the New World immediately began to employ them as bilge pumps on their boats.

From the Eskimos in North America have come new methodologies for tailored leather clothing, and the invention of the thimble. In Peru, numerous advancements in Textiles in the fields of tapestry, embroidery, and weaving were accomplished. In addition to this, the Peruvians were also big contributors to the creation of many dyes.

Out of Africa

From out of Africa not only did the world receive the many contributions of the early Egyptians, but also much of our knowledge of metal working. Almost every village throughout the African continent had its own furnace for smelting. The African peoples became adept at making sheet metal, wire, and various items that they cast out of iron for common usages.

From Ethiopia, the world was blessed with its first coffee.

Through Africa have come the original necessary basic technologies that were employed in the creation of the first civilized European societies. It was only later that the technological contributions of the Chinese and the Native populations of the New World were to come into play in the further shaping of modern Western Society.

Some of the other technological innovations of the Hamitic peoples of the world not previously mentioned include:

Mechanical Devices: Gears, pulleys, block and tackle, lathes, clock mechanisms, chain drives.

Mechanical Principles: Cantilever construction, dome and arch construction.

Materials: Copper, cement, glues, shellacs, and varnishes.

Building Tools and Materials: Nails, saws, hammers,

sandpaper, drills, and hinges.

Building Techniques: Running water pipe systems, wide scale sewage disposal systems, street drainage systems, central heating systems, cement road construction, and all manner of building types, including skyscrapers.

Textiles: Cotton, wool, felt, lace, all types of thread, needles, feathered and fur garments, dyes, silk screening methodology, and mechanical looms.

Writing: Textbooks, encyclopedias, libraries, and mailing envelopes.

Animals domesticated: Horses, camels, alpacas, llamas, cows, sheep, pigs, dogs, and cats.

Medical: Pills, lotions, ointments, adhesive tape, gauze, bandages, vaccine for smallpox, tranquilizing drugs, enemas, splints, and pain medications.

Musical instruments: Wind instruments such as the organ, pipes, horns, and flute. Tuning fork, early percussion instruments, and many modifications of the harp.

Miscellaneous: Umbrellas, safety pins, spectacles, snow goggles, compass, drinking straws, and safety pins.

Semitic and Japhetic Contributions to Basic Technology

History has shown that neither the Semitic nor the Japhetic races have made much if any contributions to the basic technology that was necessary to create civilized societies. The only technological advancements that have been attributed to either of these peoples are the screw from ancient Greece (although some dispute that it was developed in Egypt), and the windmill from ancient Persia. Almost everything else that the children of Shem and Japheth have employed to build their own societies, have been borrowed from the children of Ham.

Today we know that the building blocks of the Japhetic Greek Civilization were derived mainly from Egypt via the Minoans. Rome too was developed largely from technology taken from Egypt and the rest of the African continent. The contributions to Roman society made from these outside African sources was so prevalent in fact that the ancient Romans had a saying, "Ex Africa semper aliquid", which loosely translated means, "There is always something new coming out of Africa."

In addition to these contributions from Africa, the creation of Roman society was also greatly influenced by the Etruscans. The Etruscans were displaced Hamitic peoples who had settled in Italy after their arrival from the Near East.

So, we see that the many things that Roman Civilization is famous for such as its architecture, systems of weights and measures, surveying prowess, organizational skills, and calendar, had all come down to them from these outside Hamitic sources. Even the so-called Roman method of child delivery, "Caesarean births", was practiced in Africa many centuries before Rome had taken credit for its development.

Although most people in the Western world have been brought up to believe that the White or Japhetic race has exhibited the greatest capacity for invention, nothing could be further from the truth. The basic building blocks for all Civilizations have all come down to us from the children of Ham. In this it can truly be said that "Ham has indeed been a "servant of servants" unto his two brothers."

The Descendants of Shem

Next, we come to Noah's son Shem. From Shem have come

the peoples who are today known as the Semitic Race. This race consists of what we now refer to as the Jewish and the Arabic peoples. The distinguishing characteristic of the Semitic Race is that their identities are by and large connected to religion. It is not that all Jews or Arabs are religious people, for many are not. What is meant is that their racial and cultural identities are deeply tied to their respective nation's religious histories. Their cultural mindset itself being more pastoral and spiritually contemplative, thus making the Semitic people more prone to adaptation than to invention.

The Semitic peoples have essentially stayed within the Middle Eastern Cradle of Civilization. It has only been since the Jewish dispersion brought about by the Roman destruction of Jerusalem in 70 A.D., that the Jewish people have begun to "wander" across the face of the globe. The many persecutions that they have had to endure in foreign nations has finally led to the return of the Jews back to the land of Israel in the 20th Century.

World history has shown that the contributions to mankind made by the children of Shem, the Semitic peoples, have been largely in the realm of the spiritual. For from out of Shem have come the three leading monotheistic religions of the world: Judaism, Christianity, and Islam. All religious revelation, both true and false, has come down to mankind through the Semitic race.

To this statement, one might ask, "But what about the other major religions of the world such as Hinduism and Buddhism?" In Buddhism we find no recognized God at all. The Gods of the Hindu faith, Brahman and the various other Hindu gods who are merely different expressions of Brahman, really don't place a strict moral code upon the devotees of Hinduism. So technically, these other belief systems are not religions at all, but rather at best systems of Philosophy or Ethics. This demands a little explanation.

Apart from the relatively insignificant number of nature-worshipping Pagan cults that are scattered throughout the world, belief systems in general tend to be either Religious or Philosophical in nature. While the main goal of Religion is to find God through Revelation, the primary goal of Philosophy is to find truth through human reason. Religion rejects human reason as the final arbitrator of truth, while in turn Philosophy rejects Revelation.

While Religion's primary focus is upon man's relationship to God, Philosophy is more concerned with man's relationships with his fellow man. If we define morals as referring to man's relationship to God, and ethics as being concerned with man's relationship to his fellow man, then we see that it can be said that "Religion's main focus is upon "morality", while Philosophy is more concerned with "ethics".

While religious morals tend to be absolute, ethics tend to be relative in nature. These are some of the basic differences between Religion and Philosophy.

So, we see that both Hinduism and Buddhism should more properly be termed as being Philosophical systems rather than Religious ones. For they are both based upon human reasoning as opposed to direct Revelation and have little or no concern for any exacting demands made by a monotheistic God. The same holds true for many of the other so-called religions of the world such as Confucianism and Taoism. For in the final analyses, they too are not concerned with Revelation, but rather with human reasoning, with ethics as opposed to morality.

It is only in Judaism, Christianity, and Islam that we find belief systems that are based upon Revelation, and a Creator God imposing a strict and specific moral accountability upon mankind.

The Descendants of Japheth

Lastly, we come to Noah's son Japheth. The descendants of Japheth are essentially what we know today as the Indo-European or White Race. They initially settled in Europe, Russia, Persia, and India. They have since spread out to the rest of the world, primarily in the American and Australian Continents. The contributions of the Japhetic Race to Civilization have been largely in the area of the intellect. History has shown that the mindset of the White race has been more prone to delve into the theoretical as opposed to the practical. From the Japhetic race have come almost all of the leading Philosophers of the world.

By definition, a philosopher is "a lover of wisdom," and philosophy itself might best be defined as:

"Wisdom solely for the sake of wisdom, without any concern for religious or practical value." (Arthur Custance).

Although mankind has always engaged in philosophical speculation as to the truths concerning his existence, it was not until the 7th Century B.C. that Philosophy emerged onto the world scene. This happened at the same time in both India and Greece.

From out of India emerged the Hindu philosophy, which later on morphed into Buddhism in China. These are two of the largest philosophical belief systems of the world, claiming many millions of adherents.

Out of Greece came many schools of philosophical thought, including the early great philosophers: Socrates, Plato, and Aristotle. The effects of these three men have continued on throughout history, and to this day still have a large influence on how Western Man views the world. The many European and New World Philosophers such as Aquinas, Descartes, Kant, Locke, Spinoza, Rosseau, Hobbes, Kierkegaard, and others, are in many ways, continuations of the contributions to Philosophy of these early Grecian thinkers.

By and through these various Philosophical systems, the Japhetic peoples have attempted to discover the ultimate nature and meaning of reality through rational speculation.

Divergence

So, we see that each race of mankind has developed its own unique mindset and characteristics. The Semitic peoples have typically been reflective or pastoral peoples and have exhibited a tendency to be adaptive to their environments. The children of Ham on the other hand have been intensely practical in their approach to life and have sought to change and adapt their environments in order to satisfy their immediate physical needs. The children of Japheth have exhibited a more theoretical approach to life than have his two brothers, placing more emphasis on the importance of intellect above the physical or spiritual.

An example of this difference in mindset has been pointed out by Arthur Custance, who observed that if one were to ask a typical Indo-European the hypothetical question,

"If you had 2 oranges, and I gave you 2 oranges, how many oranges would you have? He would by nature immediately answer, "4 oranges."

If the same question were presented to a Hamitic Native American or Eskimo, he would be just as likely to answer, "But I don't have 2 oranges" as he would be to state, "4", the mindset of the Hamite being typically more prone to practicality and reality as opposed to the theoretical."

While the theoretical mindset of the Japhetite in many instances can cause him to not be able to "see the forest because of the trees", the practical mindset of the Hamitic people has in some way given them the ability to visualize the solution to a problem long before the solution exists.

We can also note these differences of mindset between the races even in the false gods and mythologies that they created for themselves since ancient times. While the pagan gods of the Hamitic peoples have tended to be physical "gods of power", the gods of the Japhetic race have been more prone to be "gods of illumination".

Nature or Nurture

Whether the differences between the races and the unique way in which they approach life has been brought about by nature or nurture is hard to determine. But it is obvious that each race has their own unique way of viewing and approaching reality. God may have programmed man to think in certain ways simply by virtue of his DNA or physiological make-up. Another solution to the question of racial divergence may be found by looking into the respective language systems that are employed by the three racial groups as opposed to their DNA. For all three of the races of mankind employ three different and distinct families of languages.

While we typically look at language as only being "the vehicle by which we express out thoughts", it is also the vehicle by which we "shape our thoughts". As B.L. Whorf insightfully observed, "We see things not as they are, but as we are." Whorf went on to state, "Language is not merely a reproducing instrument for voicing ideas, but rather is itself the shaper of ideas." Due to the fact that the three language groups that are utilized by the three races of man each contain their own unique peculiarities, it may well be true that the differences in mindset that are exhibited by each of the three races is the result of different nuances found within their respective language systems.

In the final analyses, there is no way of knowing exactly how these differences in mindset that have been historically exhibited by each of the races have come about. Whether it has been by nature or nurture is not the important aspect of the issue. What is important is to realize that each of the three races by their particular individual mindset has served to uniquely develop one of the three parts of which man is constituted: body, soul, and spirit. For from the time of the Flood in the Book of Genesis, the three families of mankind have to a large degree maintained their own unique path and mindset throughout history. That this social ordering was ordained by God should be evident to all who recognize His Sovereignty in the affairs of mankind. The blessings and curse that were pronounced by Noah upon his three sons in the Book of Genesis have in the end been very significant in establishing the framework for subsequent world history. The children of Ham have served to address the physical needs of man's body, the children of Shem have addressed the needs of man's spirit, and the children of Japheth have contributed to mankind in the nurturing of man's soul or intellect.

The Historical Role of Philosophy

Both in Greece and in India in the 6th Century A.D., the respective philosophical communities conterminously began a quest for ultimate truth which lasted for many centuries. In that their attempts were made apart from any religious revelation their search was destined for abject failure. By the time of Christ, much of the world had become cloaked in both intellectual and spiritual despair.

This failure of Philosophy to find ultimate truth through human reasoning had brought about deep spiritual malaise in the world. In India, the prevailing philosophical approach to life had become what is known as Nihilism, or the destruction of self and of all desires. In ancient Greece, there also existed this same sense of hopelessness. So much so that in ancient Greece and Rome, suicide came to be thought of as being a noble, rational act. This was the world into which Jesus was born.

Philosophy had failed to provide mankind with any sense of ultimate truth, hope, or meaning. When Jesus had presented claims of ultimate truth to Pontius Pilate, the only response that Pilate could give to Him was a cynical, "What is truth" (John 18:38)? Pilate's response was a mere reflection of the mindset of 1st Century culture, for by then the futility of finding ultimate truth through human reasoning had been firmly established.

The Apostle Paul addressed this same issue of the failure of Philosophy to come to ultimate truth apart from revelation in I Corinthians 1:21: "For after that in the wisdom of God the world by wisdom knew not God, it pleased God by the foolishness of preaching to save them that believe."

So, it is evident that up until the time of Christ, the benefits of Philosophy would have been limited to producing a greater understanding of life strictly on a natural level, along with providing some degree of intellectual stimulation. This reality however was soon to change.

The Advent of Theology

When the Japhetic peoples rose to spiritual prominence after the Jewish Dispersion in 70 A.D., it brought about an interesting phenomenon. For when the theoretical philosophical mindset of Japheth began to be applied to the spiritual revelations of Shem, it was at this time that Theology emerged onto the world stage.

105

From the time of the early Church Fathers through to Augustine, Thomas Aquinas, John Calvin, and many others, man has become much more capable of coming into a better understanding of God and His ways through the merging of Japhetic Philosophy with Semitic Revelation. When Scripture began to be studied and analyzed from a philosophical approach, it was then that the wonderful truths found within the Word of God began to be more fully recognized and discovered. It also allowed for the categorization of Scripture into specific Doctrines, and thus greater enabling and enriching man in his understanding of God and His Ways.

The Advent of Science

Later, in the 2nd millennium A.D., this same Japhetic philosophical mindset was applied more fully to both the natural world and to the many basic technologies that had been developed by the children of Ham. It was at this time that true Science emerged onto the world stage. This in turn brought about much greater mastery by man over nature, and advances to Civilization that were far beyond the dreams of earlier generations. With the dawning of the Scientific Age and the development of the scientific method, man came into a much greater understanding of the truths of the natural order. This in turn led to far greater advancements in the technologies that were necessary for the creation of far more advanced societies. Simple gears and mechanical devices now became printing presses, internal combustion engines, and many other forms of advanced machinery. Man's ability to disseminate knowledge and to travel would also grow by leaps and bounds, eventually giving him the ability to not only explore and communicate with the whole planet, but also the capability of going to the moon and back.

Great gains in productivity were also made in Manufacturing and Agriculture, thus freeing man up for more leisure time. Electricity would also come to be understood, produced, and harnessed, thus blessing mankind with not only night-time illumination but also with street cars, televisions, and microwave ovens.

With the advent of the Scientific Age, the practice of Medicine and Pharmacology would also come into full bloom, eliminating many of the illnesses that had plagued mankind for centuries.

With the introduction of the computer in the 20th century, there was now seemingly no limits as to how far man's scientific technical advancements might go.

God's Synergy

So, we see that with the teaming up of Japhetic Philosophy with Semitic Revelation to create Theology, and the marriage of Philosophy to Hamitic technology to create Science, that great advancements have been made for the betterment of mankind in the shaping of our modern Civilization. When we remember that all things in history are under God's Sovereign control, we recognize that this marriage of the efforts of Shem and Ham to the philosophical mindset of Japheth is really a synergy that only God could have both planned and provided for.

When we view the history of man from this Biblical perspective, we find that God's plan for man's proper development and happiness was not accomplished by maintaining a unity of man, but rather by separating man into three distinct races. Each race has maintained a degree of uniqueness of mindset which has served to aid them in the development of a particular aspect of life that was necessary in order to fulfill the needs of man's body, soul, and spirit.

While secular history teaches that all societies have a natural organic process by which they are born, develop, and die, a more accurate interpretation of the historical rise and fall of nations may indeed be that societies tend to stagnate and/or die when one or more of the three basic needs of the people's body, soul, and spirit have not been met within that particular society. Such societies tend to not only be ineffective in providing for the general well-being and happiness of its inhabitants, but also in their ability to spread the Gospel.

For when a society lacks in Revelation, it will soon suffer moral and ethical problems. When the physical needs of a society are not met, ill health and a sense of despair sets in. When a people's intellectual needs are not nurtured within a society, its inhabitants will soon develop a certain poverty of the soul, and their happiness and vibrancy can be greatly diminished.

Noah's Three Sons and the History of Salvation

Although Scripture does not fully elaborate on the individual contributions that have been made by Noah's three sons in the betterment of Civilization, it does have much to say when it comes to the involvement of the three races of mankind in the history of man's salvation.

One of the wonders of Scripture is that there are many golden nuggets that can be found when one simply does a little digging into God's Word. For in the history of salvation, we shall see that God is not only careful to include the mentioning of all three races at the various stages of the story of man's salvation, He is also careful to mention the three sons of Noah in a specific order at each phase of salvation's history. In so doing, God verifies the fact that while Scripture was written by many different human agents, it was all inspired by one Omniscient Person.

The first instance of Scripture's noting of the three races in the History of Salvation begins with the Father of Salvation, Abraham. Although God's Word declares that "Salvation is of the Jews" (John 4:22), God has Providentially made a point of including all three races at the initial phase of salvation's story by having Abraham marry three wives, one from each respective race. Abraham's first wife Sarah was a Semite. Next, we find Abraham with the Hamitic Egyptian Hagar, and lastly, Abraham married the Japhetic Gentile, Keturah. In so doing, God established the fact that all three races were to be included in, and were to be a part of, the salvation of man. The chronological order of these unions is also by no means an accident. For regarding the outworking of Salvation's story, the same ordering is always employed by Scripture. First, we have the mentioning of Shem, followed by Ham, and then finally Japheth. It is as if God has left His Fingerprint behind in order to personally bless the careful students of His Word.

At the time of the first Advent of Jesus, we find all three races come looking for Jesus. Again, we first find the Semitic shepherds who were watching their flocks by night (Luke 2:8). These were followed by the three Wise Men, who we now know to be children of Ham ("for we have seen his star in the east" Matthew 2:2). Lastly, we find the children of Japheth looking for Jesus, the "certain Greeks", who proclaimed, "We would see Jesus" (John12:20-21).

Next in the History of Salvation, we observe each of the three races participating in the Crucifixion. First, we have the Semitic Jews, who bore the moral responsibility for the Crucifixion, "His blood be upon us, and our children" (Matthew 27:25). They were followed by the Hamitic black man, Simon the Cyrenian, fittingly bearing the physical burden of the Cross (Mark 15:21). Lastly, the Crucifixion itself was administered by the Japhetic Romans.

Next, we find all three races included in the receiving of the gift of Salvation through Jesus Christ. First, we have the Semitic Jews receiving salvation at Pentecost (Acts 2:41), followed by the Hamitic Ethiopian to whom Philip had preached while on his journey back home to Ethiopia (Acts 8: 26-40), and lastly, we have the Japhetic Roman soldier Cornelius, in the 10th Chapter of the Book of Acts, coming to salvation in Jesus Christ.

109

Not only do we see the Guiding Hand of God at work in Scripture during the course of the outworking of Salvation's story, but we also see the indication of His ongoing Providence after the accounts of Scripture had been written. For when it came time to determine the ordering of the four Gospel accounts found in the Bible, we again find the same chronological sequencing of the mentioning of the races.

The first Gospel record is that of Matthew. To theologians of all persuasions, the Book of Matthew is considered the Gospel that is directed towards the Semitic Jewish people. Its focus is on the credentials of Jesus as being qualified to be both their Messiah and King, with its genealogy leading back to the Father of the Jewish nation, Abraham.

Following the Book of Matthew, we have the Book of Mark. In Mark we find Jesus depicted as a man of action, portrayed as a Suffering Servant, an overt appeal to people of Hamitic descent.

Next when we come to the Gospel of Luke, we find that Luke's genealogy traces Jesus back to Adam. This was to show that Jesus was related to all of mankind, an obvious appeal to the Universal man, and the philosophical mindset of the children of Japheth.

Lastly, we have the Book of John, which is unlike the other three Gospel accounts. This is because John does not stress any of the human characteristics of Jesus, but rather His Divinity.

So, we see that God has always been careful to include all three races of mankind in the historical narrative of the outworking of His Plan for man's salvation. No race has ever been excluded in any phase of Salvation's History.

The Case of the Missing Genealogy

Although it is commonly believed that there are only two genealogies to be found in the New Testament, those in the

Gospel accounts of Matthew and Luke, when we pay closer attention, we can see that the Book of John also contains a genealogy. It is the personal genealogy of God Himself:

"In the beginning was the Word, and the Word was with God, and the Word was God." John 1:1

In that we know that Jesus is the Word (John 1:14), it is here in the Book of John that we find Jesus' genealogical lineage being traced not to any person or moment in historical time, but rather back to eternity and His own personal identity as the 2nd Person of the Trinity, the Creator God Jehovah!

This begs the question, "If there are four Gospel accounts, why then are there only three genealogies given? Why is there no genealogy given in the Book of Mark?

The answer to the question lies in the fact that the Gospel genealogies are given in order to establish credentials. These credentials were needed in order to show that Jesus Christ was qualified to be the prophesied Messiah who would save the world from their sins.

While Matthew's genealogy establishes the fact that Jesus was eligible to be the prophesied Jewish Messiah because He was both Jewish and from the line of David (Isaiah 11:1), in Luke we find Jesus lineage being traced back to Adam, thereby making Him qualified to undo the works that had been wrought by the first Adam (Romans 5:12, I Corinthians 15:45), and therefore being not only the Savior of the Jewish people, but also the Savior of all mankind.

In John's genealogy, we see that Jesus Christ was truly God in the Flesh, and thus eligible to fulfill God's promise to mankind that He would Personally undo the disaster of Adam's Fall. For in the Book of Genesis, it was the same Jesus, as the 2nd Person of the Trinity, who had made the promise in the Garden of Eden:

"I will put enmity between thee and the woman, and between thy seed and her seed; it shall bruise thy head, and thou shalt bruise his heel." Genesis 3:15

When we remember the fact that "No man hath seen God at any time, the only begotten son hath declared Him" (John 1:18), it is then that we realize that the member of the Trinity who had walked with Adam in the Garden, was also the same Person who had later died on the Cross for our sins, thus Personally fulfilling the Promise that He had made in Genesis 3:15.

So, the genealogy given in the Book of John fully establishes Jesus' credentials in being the only Person capable of fulfilling the prophecy given in the Garden of Eden.

Now when we come to the Book of Mark and ask the question, "If there are genealogies given in each of the other three Gospels, why is there no genealogy given in the Book of Mark?", we can surmise that a fourth genealogy is unnecessary. For in the Book of Mark, Jesus Christ is presented to the world as being a Servant, and a servant needs no credentials! For in the grand scheme of things, "Who cares where your servant has come from!"

In Summation

It is evident that contrary to human logic and reasoning, God has ordained that there should be racial distinctions or divisions within mankind. In His Wisdom, God has used these divisions to allow for each individual race to uniquely contribute to the development of one of the three parts of which all of mankind is constituted: body, soul, and spirit.

History has borne out the fact that to Shem was given the task of the nurturing of man's spirit. The work of Ham being that of attending to man's physical needs, while Japheth was Providentially ordained to address the intellectual needs of mankind.

Although there has been a lot of mixing of the races down

112

through the millenniums, the racial lines themselves have remained remarkably intact. Each race has kept its own "bent" or mindset if you will. Whether this bent is caused by the peculiar format of the language system that each race incorporates, or whether DNA may play a part in racial differences is hard to determine. It is important to recognize that the differences of mindsets that do exist between the races does not imply that there are superiorities of one race over another. The differences that exist between the races are simply that, only differences.

It is also important to state that God's Word never speaks out against the mingling of the races through interracial marriages. The only marriages that Scripture condemns are interfaith marriages.

While many secular historians tend to believe that societies or cultures tend to arise and die out as part of a natural or organic cycle, the truth of why cultures tend to stagnate and die may lie in the fact that one or more of man's three basic needs may have been neglected within that particular culture or group, leading to its demise.

We know that at the future time of God's rule on earth known as The Millennium, that the nations will still exist as nations (Daniel 7:27, Matthew25:32). Accordingly, the races will still exist as races, maintaining their own peculiar abilities to contribute to the betterment of mankind. Under the governance of Christ, when the curse will be taken off of the earth, and the nurture of the whole man (body, soul, and spirit) will be kept in perfect balance, there will be few if any limits to the potential heights that Civilization will at this time attain.

Sin and Sins

"The words "sin" and "sins", when found in Scripture, are synonymous terms, with the word "sins" simply being the plural form of the word "sin"

At face value, it is perfectly logical to view the word "sins" as simply being the plural form of the word "sin" in our study of God's Word. However, when we examine how Scripture utilizes the words "sin" and "sins", it soon becomes apparent that the differences between the two words goes well beyond the scope of "sins" merely being the plural form of the word "sin". To some, it may appear to be nitpicking that one would want to delve into a serious study as to the difference that a single letter can bring to a word, but we must always remember that the Lord was quick to point out that even the dotting of an "i" and the crossing of a "t" can be of great significance when it comes to the proper interpretation of God's Word:

"For verily I say unto you, Till heaven and earth pass, one jot or one tittle shall in no wise pass from the law, till all be fulfilled." Matthew 5:18

Not only are the subtle nuances of language such as the Hebrew jot and tittle important in the study of God's Word, but so too can the inclusion or exclusion of a single letter be of great significance in our understanding of Scripture. We see a clear example of this in Paul's letter to the Galatians:

"Now to Abraham and his seed were the promises made. He saith not, And to seeds, as of many, but as one, and to thy seed, which is Christ." Galatians 3:16

In this passage, we have Paul informing the Galatians that the blessings of the Abrahamic Covenant, which were beforehand thought to be solely directed at Abraham and his immediate progeny, were also meant to not only point to, but to also be directed at the Lord Jesus Christ. So, we see that the land and seed blessings of the Abrahamic Covenant as found in the Book of Genesis go far beyond the scope of just Abraham and his earthly progeny.

"In the same day the Lord made a covenant with Abram, saying, Unto thy seed have I given this land, from the river of Egypt to the great river, the river Euphrates." Genesis 15:17

What Paul was stating in his letter to the Galatians is that the blessings given to Abraham and his seed were also ultimately meant to include Jesus Christ. This is a prime example of the theological truism, "In the Old Testament, what was once concealed, in the New Testament, is now revealed."

Sin and Sins

As in the case of the differences between "seed" and "seeds" as enumerated in Scripture, there are also profound differences between the words, "sin" and "sins", as presented in the Word of God. While in the Old Testament, the word sin is typically used to denote wrongful acts, both singularly and in plurality, in the New Testament, its meaning is more commonly broadened to include the fact that "sin" is also a deleterious physical condition that mankind immediately inherits through Adam when born into this world:

"Wherefore, as by one man sin entered into the world, and death by sin; and so death passed upon all men, for that all have sinned." Romans 5:12

Here in Paul's letter to the Romans we see that "sin" is a disease or contagion which all of mankind inherits due to Adam's disobedience. It is this disease of "sin" which ultimately causes our physical death.

"For as in Adam all die, even so in Christ shall all be made alive." I Corinthians 15:22

It is by Adam's disobedience that "sin" was brought into the world, and with "sin" not only was a death sentence pronounced upon all men, but also a curse was placed upon the earth:

"And unto Adam he said, because you listened unto your wife, and have eaten of the tree of which I commanded you, saying, you shall not eat of it: Cursed is the ground for your sake; in sorrow shall you eat of it all the days of your life.

Thorns and thistles shall it bring forth to you; and you shall eat the plants of the field;

In the sweat of your face shall you eat bread, till you return unto the ground; for out of it were you taken; for dust you are, and unto dust shall you return." Genesis 3:17-19

Scripture also points to the fact that it is this disease or contagion called "sin", that also has infected our bodies and creates the constant war between right and wrong within us:

"But I see another law in my members, warring against the law of my mind, and bringing me into captivity to the law of "sin" which is in my members." Romans 7:23

When Scripture mentions the word "sins" however, it is always in reference to our individual wrongful acts. The word "sin" is much broader in scope, and can either denote wrongful acts, or the disease or contagion that ultimately brings about our physical deaths. We are told in Scripture that "sin" also negatively affects our whole "nature" or being. It is the fact that we possess a "sin" nature, that brings about our impulses to commit personal "sins":

117

"But "sin"... wrought in me all kinds of evil desires." Romans 7:8

While it is "sin" that causes our physical death, Scripture indicates that it is our individual "sins" which bring about our spiritual death in our relationship with God. It is through our unconfessed sins that we lose our communion with God.

"But your iniquities have separated between you and your God, and your "sins" have hid his face from you, that he will not hear." Isaiah 59:2

God's prescription for the treatment of "sin" is different than His methodology for the treatment of "sins". We are told in Scripture that "sin" is "covered" (Psalm32:1), "taken away" (John 1:29), and "cleansed" (1 John 1:7). "Sins" on the other hand, are said to be forgiven. Nowhere in Scripture are we told that the disease of "sin" is ever "forgiven". It is only our "sins" that are in need of forgiveness:

"If we confess our "sins", he is faithful and just to forgive us our sins, and to cleanse us from all unrighteousness." 1 John 1:9

"To him give all the prophets witness, that through his name whosoever believeth in him shall receive remission of "sins". Acts 10:43

"I write unto you, little children, because your "sins" are forgiven you for his name's sake." I John 2:12

In that we are born into this world with a sinful nature through no choice of our own, we are not held responsible by God for the condition of "sin" that we find ourselves in. It would neither be appropriate, or just, for mankind to be condemned for possessing the disease and curse of "sin". Again, this is because we are all unwittingly born into this world with this condition. It is only for our personal "sins" that we find ourselves in need of forgiveness.

It is easy to see how a degree of confusion could arise in this matter because Scripture often uses the word "sin" to denote wrongful acts (both in the singular and in the plural sense), while at other times "sin", is used to denote the physical disease or contagion that we have been referring to here. It is up to the student of the Word of God to make the differentiation within the given context of Scripture as to which aspect of "sin" is being discussed.

There can also be problem passages in the Old Testament concerning this difference between "sin" and "sins" in regard to the "forgiveness of sin", as is expressed in 2nd Chronicles 7:14:

"If my people, which are called by my name, shall humble themselves, and pray, and seek my face, and turn from their wicked ways; then I will hear from heaven, and will "forgive their sin", and will heal their land."

In this Old Testament passage, we find the idea of the forgiveness of "sin", a concept which is foreign to the New Testament, where "sin" is never said to be "forgiven". It is easy to see however that within the context of this passage of Scripture, that the word "sin" is in fact referring to the wrongful acts or "sins" of Israel ("their wicked ways"). Theologians address this apparent inconsistency of Scripture by explaining that "in the Old Testament religious principles are being established, while in the New Testament a more exacting theology is presented, the Greek language being more precise in its scope than the Hebrew of the Old Testament"(A. Custance).

Age of Accountability

While mankind is not held responsible for possessing the disease of "sin", a disease which we have all unwittingly acquired through no fault of our own, we do pay for the effects of "sin" from the time of our conception ("Behold, I was shapen in iniquity; and in "sin" did my mother conceive me." Psalm 51:5). Regarding our personal "sins", we are also not held responsible unto God while we are still in the early formative years of life. Only in our later years do we become accountable to God for our individual "sins". This is attested to in Scripture through an examination of the death of the newborn son of David and Bathsheeba.

When David's son died seven days after his birth, David was comforted in his grief because he knew that one day he would again be united with his son in heaven ("I shall go to him, but he shall not return to me" II Samuel 12:23). It is also important to note that the child had not yet been circumcised, as circumcision was performed on the 8th day of a child's life, and that David's son had died on his 7th day. In this we see that the rite of circumcision, and by default the rite of infant baptism, are not necessary for one's salvation.

Here it is the clear indication of Scripture that infants are not held morally responsible for either their "sin" nature, or for their personal "sins". It is only further on in our development, at a time known only to God, that we become morally responsible to Him. Scripture clearly indicates that it is not from the time of our conception or our birth that we become morally responsible for our "sins", but only from the time of our "youth up".

"For the imagination of a man's heart is evil from his youth." Genesis 8:21

Here we have seen how the knowledge of the difference between "sin" and "sins" is beneficial to our understanding of certain aspects of God's Plan for the Salvation of man. The same is especially true when it comes to our understanding of the pivotal event in human history, the Crucifixion of Christ.

"Sin" and "Sins" and the Crucifixion

It is common for mankind to view the Crucifixion of Christ as largely being a symbolic act in which God's esoteric demands for justice were somehow satisfied by His Son Jesus Christ when He shed His Blood and died on the Cross at Calvary. When we consider what transpired on the Cross from the aspect of both "sin" and "sins" however, many different avenues of inquiry and understanding begin to emerge. For when God's Word points out that there is a difference between "sin" and "sins", this difference demands that in some way, the issue of both "sin" and "sins" had to have been dealt with separately by Jesus while on the Cross.

In analyzing how the issues of "sin" and "sins" were addressed on the Cross, we must first recognize that there must have been more than just a "Symbolic" aspect to the Crucifixion. That there was indeed an additional and significant "Literal" element associated with the sufferings that Jesus experienced that went far beyond the mere shedding of His blood.

"Sin" and the Crucifixion

In the matter of "sin" and the Crucifixion, we see that Jesus Christ symbolically took upon himself the curse of "sin", as was exhibited by His wearing of the "crown of thorns" while on the Cross.

Again, it was due to Adam's disobedience that the curse and disease known as "sin" had come into the world. When "sin" became a part of mankind's members, it was now impossible for man to be totally obedient to God and His Law, thus making the Law also a curse unto man. For with the giving of the Law, mankind became more fully aware of the high standards of God, and was now judiciously obligated to fulfill the Law in order to be accepted by God:

"For until the Law, "sin" was in the world; but "sin" is not imputed when there is no law." Romans 5:13

Jesus literally took upon Himself this aspect of the curse of "sin" that Adam had brought into the world by His hanging on the Cross.

"Christ redeemed us from the curse of the Law by becoming a curse for us, for it is written, Cursed is everyone who hangeth upon a tree." Galatians 3:13

In the literal sense, Jesus also took on the curse of "sin" because Scripture informs us that on the Cross, "He literally became "sin" for us.

"For he hath made him to be sin for us, who knew no sin." II Corinthians 5:21

Jesus was able to do this because he had totally fulfilled the obligations of the Law by living a sinless life. He was literally qualified to undo the works of Adam through His perfect obedience to God's Law.

"For by one man's disobedience many were made sinners, so by the obedience of one shall many be made righteous." Romans 5:19

While on the Cross, Jesus also literally physically died and was later resurrected, thus judiciously overcoming the curse of death that was the result of Adam's transgression:

"Wherefore, as by one man "sin" entered into the world, and death by "sin": And so death passed upon all men, for all have sinned." Romans 5:12

And by living a perfect life and becoming a sin offering on the cross, Jesus paved the way for all of mankind to be resurrected.

"For since by man came death, by man came also the resurrection of the dead.

122

For as in Adam all die, even so in Christ shall all be made alive." I Corinthians 15:21,22

With Jesus' removal of the "sin" curse of physical death initiated in the Garden (Genesis 2:17), "all" of mankind will now one day be resurrected. This is just a small part of what Jesus accomplished in his life and on the cross. We must remember however, that although Scripture tells us that "all of mankind will be resurrected (I Corinthians.15:22), not "all" of mankind will be made righteous, only "many" (Romans 5:19).

By living a perfect life and removing the death curse of "sin" on the cross, Jesus also made mankind accountable for the effects of their possessing a sinful nature, their personal "sins". Jesus stated in the Book of John:

"If I had not done among them the works which none other man did, they had not had sin: but now have they both seen and hated both me and my Father." John 15:24

As an interesting sidelight, it is important to recognize that while Jesus died "on" the Cross, He did not die "because" of the Cross. When Jesus died on the Cross, he did so because He voluntarily gave up His own life, not because anyone had taken it from him.

"Therefore doth my Father love me, because I lay down my life, that I might take it again.

No man taketh it from me, but I lay it down, I have power to lay it down, and I have power to take it again. This command-ment have I received of my Father." John 10:17,18

123

"Sins" and the Crucifixion

In the matter of "sins" and the Crucifixion, we see that Jesus symbolically shed His blood to exhibit to the world that the work of the Cross was to supply redemption from the effects of our "sins". In the Book of Matthew we read:

"For this is my blood of the new testament, which is shed for many for the remission of sins." Matthew 26:28

This symbolic necessity of the shedding of blood for the remission of sins is also taught in Leviticus 17:11 and in Hebrews 9:22.

When we examine the literal aspect of Jesus shedding His blood for the remission of sins, we come to a very interesting occurrence in the Book of John. Immediately after Jesus' resurrection from the dead, he was seen by Mary Magdalene at the Garden Tomb. He told Mary, "Touch me not, for I am not yet ascended to my Father" (John 20:17). The explanation for this statement from the Lord lies in the fact that Jesus fulfilled many roles in the short time that He was here on earth. One of these roles was that of being our High Priest:

"Seeing then that we have a great High Priest, that is passed into the heavens, Jesus the Son of God, let us hold fast our profession." Hebrews 4:14

If we remember the duties of the High Priest on the Day of Atonement, we know that he was to wear a simple but clean garment in order to enter the Holy of Holies. No one was to touch him, for this would defile him and render his offering of the blood of the spotless sacrificial ram to be of no value. This in turn would result in the death of the High Priest should he then enter the Holy of Holies, much in the same way as the occurrence of the death of Aaron's two sons, who had gone into the Holy of Holies and offered strange incense unto God (Leviticus 10:1). When Jesus told Mary not to touch him, he was acting in the role of High Priest, and had not yet brought His precious Blood up to the Holy of Holies in Heaven, to be accepted by God the Father, as the offering for the "sins" of believers.

After Jesus had returned from the Heavenly Holy of Holies, He now encouraged His disciples to freely touch Him ("handle me and see." Luke 24:39), as this aspect of His work as our High Priest was now complete. This was also clear evidence that His Blood offering had been formally accepted by God the Father.

It is also of great interest to note that when Jesus later came upon his disciples, he referred to his resurrection body not as having flesh and blood, but rather "flesh and bones" (Luke 24:39). Evidently, the resurrection body may no longer need to have blood, and the Precious Blood of Jesus was to forever remain in Heaven's Holy of Holies.

When we consider the judicial aspect of the Crucifixion in terms of "sins", we run into a rather interesting legal conundrum. For if Jesus' sacrifice on the Cross was infinite, that would mean that under the legal principle of "double jeopardy", God would have no basis for judging or condemning non-believers. For if Jesus had paid the price for all "sins", then the penalty for all wrongful acts has been fully paid, and there could be no further recourse or punishment that could be judiciously meted out for the "sins" of unbelievers. For, as in our legal system, the judge has no further say in a matter where all harm and damages have already been taken care of or paid for. Peter in writing to believers, tells us that Jesus, "bore our sins", and not the world's sins, "in His own body on the tree" (I Peter 2:24).

This brings us to the place where we realize that for there to be an accountability for non-believers, and for justice to truly be served, then the penalty for "sins" that was paid on the Cross by Jesus had to be finite and accomplished only for the specific "sins" of believers. The punishment for sins that Jesus experienced on the cross therefore also had to be literal, and not merely symbolic.

125

This in turn begs the question, "How could Jesus personally acknowledge and pay for all of the individual "sins" of all of those who would ever believe in Him, in the matter of only 3 hours of time?" This question leads us to a re-examination our concept of space and time.

The Relativity of Experienced Time

It is a common experience for almost all of mankind during times of great stress or danger, of having the sensation of time standing still. Einstein's Theory of Relativity confirms this phenomenon by revealing that the passage of time is in no way absolute. Research conducted in the mid-20th Century has shown that under the influence of certain drugs and/or hypnosis, human beings are capable of accomplishing incredible mental feats in a very short period of time. That time, in some way, can be "stretched out".

In a study done by Linn F. Cooper and Milton H. Erickson entitled "Time Distortions in Hypnosis", a metronome was set to one beat per second. The human subjects used in the study were hypnotized, and then told that the metronome had slowed down from 1 beat per second, to 1 beat for every 2 seconds, then for every 5 seconds, once per minute, and then to ever slower and slower rates. The subjects in the study were then given certain tasks to do. One person was assigned the task of picking and counting bolls of cotton. This person was able to mentally pick and count 862 bolls of cotton in only 3 seconds of elapsed time, even though he imagined that 80 minutes had passed. Another subject was able to count 9200 bb pellets in a matter of only 5 seconds. The fact that the human mind could accomplish such things is truly incredible, but even more incredible is the wide variance that is possible in the experience of the passage of time. These scientific experiments do exhibit how Jesus Christ during those 3 hours of darkness on the Cross, could have felt the shame, guilt and suffering for the billions upon billions of individual "sins" that His followers would have committed during the course of their lifetimes.

While our human clocks meaninglessly clicked off 3 hours of "time", Jesus had to endure what was most likely a seemingly endless expanse of time, an "eternity of time" if you will. To give a degree of perspective, we know that 1,000 years for man is like a day unto the Lord (Psalm 90:4, II Peter 3:8). Therefore by extrapolation, those 3 hours on the Cross for God would have amounted to 125 years of straight 24/7 non-stop suffering for us as human beings. Quite unscientific, but you get the point.

The sufferings that Jesus had to experience while on the Cross go far beyond the limits of our imaginations. In addition to experiencing the shame, guilt, and punishment for each of our individual sins as believers while on the Cross, Jesus also had to experience a break in His eternal fellowship with God the Father and God the Holy Spirit, for God cannot be a part of sin in any way (Habakkuk 1:13). During the time of the 3 hours of darkness on the Cross, when God laid the penalty for our "sins" upon Jesus, from Jesus' perspective, may have seemingly taken an eternity to pass. For God the Father, God the Son, and God the Holy Spirit had eternally enjoyed perfect fellowship with one another. At the cross, this fellowship was broken, as is evidenced by Jesus' crying out, "My God (God the Father), My God (God the Holy Spirit), why hast Thou forsaken me" (Matthew 27:46)? Knowing of these great horrors that awaited Him, is it any wonder that He would have sweated great drops of blood in the Garden (Luke 22:44)?

This of course also brings a whole new perspective to the meaning of the hymn, "Were You There When They Crucified the Lord". For if you are a believer in Jesus Christ, then all of your personal "sins", were literally there at Calvary during the Crucifixion. Jesus Christ was personally aware of you, and internally felt the pain and shame for each and every transgression that you would ever commit, in order to secure your salvation. As 21st Century believers, it is hard for us to imagine how God could have been aware of every sinful thought and action that we would ever commit two millenniums before we were even born, but we must always remember that God exists outside of time, and the realities of the future are just as real to Him as the reality of the present is to us from our finite perspective. Not only were the events associated with the Crucifixion known unto God from the moment of Creation ("The Lamb slain from the foundation of the world" Revelation 13:8), but so too was the total physical history of the Universe. In the Book of John, Jesus reminds His disciples that God exists in a different reality than the reality that is experienced by mankind:

"But the hour cometh, and now is, when the true worshippers shall worship the Father in spirit and in truth: for the Father seeketh such to worship him." John 4:23

From man's perspective, the future is coming, "The hour is coming...", but from God's perspective, the future has already occurred, "...and now is" (John 4:23).

The fact that Jesus literally experienced the guilt and shame for each of our individual personal "sins" long before many believers had even been born is truly an astounding thought. The recognition of this fact may indeed be what Paul had in mind when in addressing the severely backslidden, he stated that by their actions they, "Crucify to themselves the Son of God afresh" (Hebrews 6:6). In other words, if one sins willfully after they have received Jesus as their Savior, they should be aware of the fact that each time they sin they are literally heaping more anguish upon Jesus while He was on the Cross, even though from man's perspective, the Cross is a past historical event. This is truly a sobering thought and a poignant call for holy living.

The two most amazing events in the history of the world are the birth and death of Jesus Christ. At Jesus' birth into this world, we have the Creator of the vast Universe appearing as a baby in a manger ("He was in the world, and the world was made by him, and the world knew him not" John 1:10). That the Creator could condescend into becoming a helpless child in an insignificant town in a tiny country is simply an astounding thought.

It is also of interest to consider that as a child, Jesus was wrapped in swaddling clothes, in much the same way that He was wrapped while He lay in the Garden Tomb. By this we can surmise that Scripture is indicating that Jesus Christ was truly, "Born to Die".

Still even more incredible is the fact that at Jesus' death, He not only overcame the power and effects of the disease of "sin", but He literally took upon Himself the punishment and shame for each of the individual "sins" of those who would come to believe in Him, even though many of these believers had yet to be born! While our finite minds may find this impossible to comprehend, we must remember that with God, "all things are possible" (Luke 1:37)!

Just as the events concerning the Crucifixion were known to God from the moment of the creation of the world (Revelation 13:8), so too were each and every one of our individual sins! The Psalmist David reminds us of God's amazing ability to know the total history of the physical creation from the moment of its inception:

"Thine eyes did see my substance, yet being unperfect; and in thy book all my members were written, which in continuance were fashioned, when as yet there were none of them." Psalm 139:16

While on the Cross, Jesus was painfully aware of every sinful thing that you and I as believers would have ever thought or done. This is how intimately connected He is to every person who comes to Him for salvation from their sins! It truly is an Incredible, Loving, and Wonderful God that we serve!!!

"Thanks be unto God for his unspeakable gift." II Corinthians 9:15

God the Father, the Creator of the Universe

"God the Father is the Creator of the Universe"

One of the worst theological errors to be found within the Christian Church is the belief that it was God the Father who had been the Creator of the Universe. One of the greatest causes of this Biblical misunderstanding is to be found within the words of the Apostle's Creed. This man inspired Statement of Faith has been recited liturgically throughout the history of the New Testament Church. It has found use in not only the Roman Catholic Church, but also in many of the Protestant Churches, including the Anglican, Presbyterian, Methodist, Congregationalist, and Lutheran denominations. Its influence upon the Church has obviously been quite vast and extensive.

The origin of the use of the Apostle's Creed goes back to at least 390 A.D., where it is mentioned in the writings of Ambrose. It is often associated with the 4th Century belief that the 12 Apostles themselves were the authors of the Creed. The Roman Catholic Church incorporated the Creed into their Catechism and divided the Creed into 12 separate statements in order to denote the contributions of the 12 separate Apostles.

The Creed in its entirety, reads as follows:

"I believe in God the Father Almighty, creator of Heaven and Earth. I believe in Jesus Christ, God's only Son our Lord, who was conceived by the Holy Spirit, born of the Virgin Mary, suffered under Pontius Pilate, was crucified, died, and was buried: He descended to the dead. On the 3rd day he rose again; he ascended into Heaven, and is seated on the right hand of God the Father Almighty. He will come again to judge the living and the dead. I believe in the Holy Spirit, the holy catholic Church, the communion of saints, the forgiveness of sins, the resurrection of the body, and the life everlasting." Amen

Jesus Christ the Creator of the Universe

The main problematic issue of the Apostle's Creed can be found within the words of its opening statement: "I believe in God the Father Almighty, Creator of Heaven and Earth."

The reason that this statement poses such a theological problem, is that it is in direct conflict with the written Word of God. For the idea that the 1st Person of the Trinity, God the Father, created the Universe, is nowhere to be found within the pages of Scripture. The Member of the Godhead to whom the act of Creation is attributed to, is none other than the 2nd Person of the Trinity, Jesus Christ. The following are some of the numerous Scriptural references that attest to this fact:

"All things were made by Him (Jesus Christ); and without Him was not any thing made that was made." John 1:3

"He was in the world, and the world was made by Him, and the world knew Him not." John 1:10

"For by Him were all things created, that are in heaven, and that are in earth, visible and invisible, whether they be thrones or dominions, or principalities, or powers: all things were created by Him, and for Him." Colossians 1:16

"God, Who at sundry times and in diverse manners spake in times unto the fathers by the prophets,

Hath in these last days spoken unto us by His Son, whom he hath appointed Heir of all things, by Whom also he made the worlds." Hebrews 1:1,2

The Plan of God

Scripture is implicit in its declaration that all of the historical events that have both already occurred, and that will yet occur, are a part of the Plan of God. This of course includes the act of Creation. David the Psalmist tells us that it is God who rules over both heaven and earth:

"The LORD hath prepared his throne in the heavens: and his kingdom ruleth over all." Psalm 103:19

The Prophet Isaiah later informs us of God's sovereign power in the control of history:

"Declaring the end from the beginning, and from ancient times the things that are not yet done, saying, My counsel shall stand, and I will do all my pleasure." Isaiah 46:10

The Apostle Paul wrote to the Ephesians regarding God's sovereign plan:

"In whom also we have obtained an inheritance, being predestinated according to the purpose of him who worketh all things after the counsel of his own will." Ephesians 1:11

When it comes to the outworking of world history, God's Word teaches us that God the Father functions primarily as that of the "planner", for all things that do occur are said to be, "of him". God the Son on the other hand, functions chiefly as the implementer of the Father's Plan, for all things are said to occur "by him". The Apostle Paul wrote of these facts in his first letter to the Corinthians:

"But to us there is but one God, the Father, of whom are all things, and we in him: And one Lord Jesus Christ, by whom are

133

all things, and we by him." I Corinthians 8:6

So, we see that it was Jesus Christ, as the 2nd Person of the Trinity, whose duty it was in the Plan of God the Father to be the actual Creator of the Universe. At the moment of Creation, which our 21st Century scientists often refer to as "The Big Bang", Scripture informs us that it was accomplished by Jesus, simply by the waving of His hand. Such is the power and might of the Lord Jesus Christ!

"Who hath measured the waters in the hollow of His Hand, and meted out heaven with the span, and comprehended the dust of the earth in a measure, and weighed the mountain in scales, and the hills in a balance?" Isaiah 40:12

The Enormity of the Creation

No study of Jesus Christ as the Creator of the Universe would be complete without some discussion as to the size and scope of the Universe itself. When viewed from a comparative format, the total amount of the structures that mankind has built throughout the time of his existence upon planet earth pales when compared to the size and depth of the Universe that Jesus created at the very beginning of time. Theologian Eric Sauer in "The Dawn of World Redemption", stated that as of the early 20th Century, "All that man has built on the whole world, ships, cities, and villages, taken together, would not occupy 300 cubic miles; Professor Betex, indeed, reckons only 98 cubic miles. But the physical Earth itself contains 260,000 millions of cubic miles!"

It is extremely difficult for mankind to grasp the enormity of what Jesus Christ did in the Creation of the Universe. For not only does the size of the earth in and of itself make the accomplishments of mankind's creative building efforts seem trivial at best, when we compare the Earth and all of its glory to the size of our Sun, we see that our Planet Earth is also quite insignificant in its magnitude. Our sun measures out to be 2,713,406 miles in circumference. It would take over 1 million earths (1,297,000 to be exact), to fill up the interior dimensions of our Sun, which of course, is also a part of the creative handiwork of Jesus Christ.

When we consider the size of our Sun in relation to the size of some of the other stars in the Universe, it too can be seen to be rather insignificant in its magnitude. The star Betelgeuse for example, is approximately 700 times larger than our Sun, and shines with an intensity that is 14,000 times brighter! The star known as UY Scuti is 1,700 times larger than our Sun and shines with an intensity that is 400,000 times brighter!

While there are many stars that are only 1/10 the size of our Sun, cosmologically speaking, our sun is merely an average sized star. When viewed within the context of the galaxy in which it resides, the Milky Way, our Sun can be seen to be a rather insignificant star amongst a group of well over 100 billion other such stars.

Our galaxy, the Milky Way, is also insignificant in terms of the countless other galaxies that are spread out over the vast expanses of space. For many years of the 20th Century, it was believed that there were approximately 100 billion galaxies in the observable Universe. In recent years however, with the improvements made to the Hubble Telescope, the latest astronomical observations made by NASA and others now show that there could be over 2,000 billion galaxies in the observable Universe. When we consider that each of these galaxies in turn contain on the average approximately 100 billion stars, we can further begin to realize the enormity of Jesus' handiwork in Creation.

While at one time in the 20th Century, it was believed that the entire visible Universe consisted of over 10,000 million, million, million stars (100,000,000,000,000,000,000,000), we are now aware that the actual number of stars within the visible Universe greatly exceeds that earlier estimate. This has prompted many scientists to state that there could be more stars in the Universe than there are grains of sand on the earth! That such a correlation should be mentioned within the scientific community is truly a tremendous fact. For this same direct correlation between the number of stars in the heavens and the "sands of the sea" is also made within the pages of Scripture.

In the Book of Hebrews, we are reminded that God had told Abraham that the number of his descendants would be so numerous, that they could be likened to the innumerable number of "stars in the sky, and the sands of the sea" (Hebrews 11:12).

This brings us to another facet of the immensity of the Universe that was created by Jesus. For the Universe is not only large regarding the magnitude of the celestial bodies of which it constituted, but it is also large in the scope of the distances between these bodies. Science tells us that light travels at a speed of 186,000 miles per second. At this speed, it takes the light reflected by our Moon a full 1 1/2 seconds to reach the Earth. The light emitted by our Sun takes a full 8 1/2 minutes to reach us here on the Earth! Within the expanse of our solar system, the light reflected from the Planet Neptune takes approximately 4 hours to reach our planet. The closest star to our solar system, Alpha Centauri, is yet another story within itself. For the distance to our closest star is measured not in terms of speed of light-minutes or in speed of light-hours, but rather in terms of light-years. One light-year, the total distance that light will travel in a full year of time, is a distance of approximately 6 trillion miles. It takes the light emitted from Alpha Centauri over 4 years to reach the Earth, a distance of over 24 trillion miles! The light from the closest galaxy to our Milky Way, the Andromeda Galaxy, takes a full 2 1/2 million of said light years to reach the Earth, a distance of over 15 million trillion miles!

Yet this distance is small in comparison to the other far outreaches of the visible Universe. Scientists tell us that this light comes to us from a distance of over 13.7 billion light years away, 13.7 billion years being modern science's estimated age of the Universe. That is a total of 78,000 billion trillion miles.

In that we can only see as far out into the Universe as there has been time for light to get to us, scientists recognize the fact that not only is there a visible Universe, but there is also an invisible Universe that we are not physically able to observe. In recent years, astronomers have speculated that the total Universe could actually be 250 times larger than what we can observe in our actual known visible Universe!

The immensity and vastness of Jesus' Creation stands as a testament to the veracity of Scripture as proclaimed by Paul in his letter to the Romans:

"O the depths of the riches both of the wisdom and knowledge of God! How unsearchable are his judgments, and his ways past finding out!" Romans 11:33

The enormous size and magnitude of the Universe begs the question, "Why did God find it necessary to make the Universe so large? An obvious answer would be, "To reveal to man the awesome power of God."

Another explanation for the incomprehensible vastness of the Universe might be found in the fact that God ultimately does all things for the sake of the believer (II Corinthians 4:15). God in His omniscience may have known that, "If man could find the boundaries of the Universe, he might in some way have felt a sense of emotional or intellectual confinement."

In the same light, yet another possible explanation for God's purpose in creating such an enormous Universe would be that "God made the Universe on such a massive scale so as to quell any thoughts that man might have, that would lead him to believe that Eternal life in heaven might somehow get to be confined and boring."

On a purely physical basis, man's natural existence is dependent on the Universe being both enormous and vast. For all of life depends upon carbon, and the formation of carbon itself can only occur in a large expansive Universe.

Regarding the physical make up of the Universe, our Universe consists mainly of hydrogen (92%) and helium (8%). All of the other elements, including carbon, are considered to be "trace elements", and constitute a mere 0.001% of the total mass of the Universe. Biochemists recognize the fact that the basis of life is found within DNA, and DNA itself requires carbon. John A Wheeler writes:

"DNA demands carbon for its construction. Carbon in turn comes into being by thermonuclear combustion in the stars. Thermonuclear combustion requires billions of years of time."

But according to general relativity, a Universe cannot provide billions of years of time unless it also has billions of light-years of extent. From this point of view it is not the Universe that has dominion over man, but man who governs the size of the Universe.

The Importance of Natural Law in Christ's Creation

With the act of Creation, not only did Jesus create a massive and expansive Universe, but He also created an environment on Planet Earth that would be uniquely capable of supporting all manner of life, especially that of the life of man. Isaiah tells us that the Earth was created expressly for the purpose of it being inhabited (Isaiah 45:18). Along with the Earth's Creation, Jesus also created the natural laws by which it is governed. The relationship between the physical properties of the Earth and the Laws of Nature that govern it are critical for mankind's survival. The following are some of these relationships:

1) The size of the Earth itself is of the utmost importance for establishing the right atmospheric gases which are necessary for man's survival.

2) The distance of the Earth from the Sun allows for a suitable

temperature range for the formation and survival of carbon chains.

3) The rate of revolution of the Earth provides for the alternating light that is required by plants for oxygen formation.

4) The tilt of the Earth's axis allows for the changing of seasons, which in turn keeps the proliferation of disease causing bacteria in check.

5) The land to water ratio of the Earth is appropriately suited for the proper irrigation of the land.

It is also of great interest to realize that when Jesus established the Laws of Nature, He also made man's survival dependent upon the occasional violation of these established Laws. Arthur Custance points out in "Man in Adam, and Man in Christ", the following three Laws of Nature that of necessity, have to be "violated" in order for mankind to survive:

1) Natural Law dictates that as liquids cool, their density increases. This Law remains in effect until water reaches a certain temperature level, 32 degrees Fahrenheit, at which time its density decreases, and forms ice. Ice acts as a natural insulator to the possible future deleterious effects of continuous cold temperatures. If it were not for this abrogation of this Natural Law, that cooler liquids become more dense, then most of the waters on the Earth's surface would annually freeze out, and any life that was within these waters would cease to exist.

2) The second Natural Law that is broken in the interest of mankind's survival is the Law of Gravity. In regard to the Earth's atmosphere, if the Law of Gravity was not overruled by the Law of Diffusion of Gases, then all of the harmful heavier gases would settle to the lower parts of the atmosphere, and thereby eliminate all life.

3) The third Natural Law that is superseded is the Law of Heat. The Law of Heat dictates that when temperatures are exceedingly low, chemical reactions slow down and then eventually cease to exist, should the temperature become too low. The combustion that occurs in our Sun is of such a volatile nature however, that as the temperatures rise, the Sun would literally burn itself out if it were not for the fact that the Law of Heat is also abrogated during extremely high temperatures. At a certain high temperature, combustion in the Sun also ceases, thereby stopping it from experiencing a "heat death".

By designing the Laws that govern our Universe as such, it is almost as if the Father Designer and the Son Creator were taunting those future members of mankind who would make a God out of "Mother Nature." For it is one thing to believe that the Laws of Nature could have evolved naturally, but it is entirely preposterous to believe that somehow these laws had to be abrogated in order for life to exist, and that this abrogation in turn also came about by natural forces! God truly does indeed, "take the wise in their own craftiness" (Job 5:13).

It is simply awe-inspiring to consider that the little baby lying in the manger in Bethlehem, was also its all-powerful Creator. Although this defies both human comprehension and reason, it is nonetheless the Truth as revealed in the Word of God.

How different would be the depth of our Christian experience if we would simply be more cognizant of the reality of who Jesus Christ really is!!! In that we do not recognize Him as being the Creator, we tend to over emphasize His role as the Son of God, when in fact, He is much, much, more than that. Although Jesus' role as the Son of God is easy for children and new believers to understand, there does come a time in every Christian's life in which he is to "grow up", so to speak. The Apostle Paul addressed this issue in his first letter to the Church at Corinth:

"When I was a child, I spake as a child, I understood as a child, I thought as a child: but when I became a man, I put away childish things." I Corinthians 13:11

A significant part of Christian growth is to have an intellectual grasp of who Jesus Christ really is. Not only are we to recognize Him in his role as our Redeemer, but we are also to be aware of His magnificent Power, as was demonstrated in His role as the Creator of all things, both visible and invisible (Colossians 1:16)! This is all part and parcel to why Jesus commanded His disciples to, "learn of me" (Matthew 11:29).

The idea that the Creator of the Universe would also be mankind's Redeemer is taught throughout the pages of Scripture. In Genesis 3:15, Jesus, whom Adam knew as his Creator, proclaimed that it would be He himself who would redeem the wrong that Adam and Eve had committed in the Fall.

The Prophet Isaiah echoed this same sentiment in recognizing that the Creator of the Universe was also going to perform the role of Redeemer:

"Thus saith the LORD, thy redeemer, and he that formed thee from the womb, I am the LORD that maketh all things; that stretched forth the heavens alone; that spreadeth abroad the earth by myself;" Isaiah 44:24

Not only does the Old Testament teach us that the Creator would also be the Redeemer, but the very disciples of Jesus taught this same message within the pages of the New Testament. We must remember that Jesus' disciple John, who was fully aware of the redemptive work of Jesus (John 1:29), also wrote that Jesus Christ was indeed the world's Creator: "He was in the world, and the world was made by him, and the world knew him not" (John 1:10).

To this, Paul had also added that not only had Jesus been responsible for saving us from our sins, but that He had in fact also been the Creator of "all things" (Ephesians 3:9), both in heaven and on the earth (Colossians 1:16).

141

Now if both the Old and the New Testaments teach us that the Redeemer of mankind was also the Creator of all things, should we not as modern-day believers also be careful to be fully aware of this fact in our theological understanding? Regrettably, the role of Jesus as Creator is not only obscured by the Creeds of the Church, but also by omission from many of our pulpits today.

A good method to remind us of Jesus' true power and majesty is, that when reading the pages of the New Testament, and coming across references to our Lord, replace the name of "Jesus" with that of "God". By incorporating this simple little exercise, we could go a long way in bringing ourselves back to a more accurate understanding of who our Savior really is.

While it is one thing for us to comprehend that the Son of God died for us on the Cross, the reality that this same Jesus, our Redeemer, was also the Creator of our vast Universe, is a stupendous truth that much of Christendom is sadly unaware of.

When we view Jesus Christ in the light of the tremendous Power that He exhibited in the Creation of the Universe, how utterly vain do the actions of the Jewish religious leaders appear to be during the days of His Incarnation. For they defied and questioned both his being and authority at every turn. They then later foolishly conspired to kill this same Person who had created both them and the vast Universe in which they resided.

In like manner, how vain too can we as believers be, when in the course of living our lives, we flippantly choose to live to please ourselves, rather than seeking to live a life that would be found to be "pleasing in His sight" (I John 3:22).

Jesus Christ in the Old Testament

"Jesus Christ came into existence, at the time of his birth in Bethlehem"

As we have seen in a prior study, Jesus Christ is not simply the only begotten Son of God, but He is also the 2nd Person of the Trinity, and as such, co-equal with God the Father, and God the Holy Spirit. Scripture informs us that as the 2nd Person of the Trinity, Jesus Christ is the very Creator of all things in the Universe (John 1:10). But the full story of Jesus in the Old Testament does not stop at the time of the Creation of the Universe (Genesis 1:1). We are told by both the Psalmist in the Old Testament and the writer of The Book of Hebrews in the New Testament, that the Pre-Incarnate Christ was very active indeed throughout the pages of the Old Testament.

"Then said I, Lo I come: in the volume of the book it is written of me,

I delight to do thy will, O my God: yea Thy law is within my heart." Psalm 40:7,8

"Then said I, Lo, I come (in the volume of the book it is written of me,) to do Thy will, O God." Hebrews 10:7

These statements concerning Jesus in the Old Testament are not referring solely to the prophecies concerning His coming into the world at Bethlehem. For if they were, Scripture would surely have stated, "Then said I, Lo, I come: as was foretold by the Prophets."

In that the Word of God clearly states, "In the volume of the book it is written of me", the reader should then recognize the fact that from Genesis to Malachi, one is going to find constant references to Jesus throughout the Old Testament record. These references to the Pre-Incarnate Christ are indicated mainly through four different vehicles:

1) The apparent visible manifestations of God in the Old Testament.

2) The various alternate names assigned to Jesus in the Old Testament.

3) Grammatical nuances in the typeface incorporated by the translators of the King James text.

4) Cross referenced Scriptures from the New Testament that indicate which Person of the Trinity the particular Old Testament Book was referring to.

The Visible Manifestations of God in the Old Testament

When we consider the visible manifestations of God in the Old Testament, we know that it was God the Son, and not God the Father, who had visually appeared to mankind throughout the pages of the Old Testament record. We know this because Scripture directly declares it to be so:

"No man hath seen God (the Father) at any time. The only begotten Son, which is in the bosom of the Father, He hath declared him." John 1:18

From Scripture we now know that the visible manifestations of God in the Old Testament are in reality manifestations of Jesus long before His physical Incarnation in Bethlehem. It was at Bethlehem that Jesus became the Unique Person of the Universe, becoming both God and Man at the same time. Prior to this, His existence dates back to times before the Creation of the Universe, back to eternity itself where He is identified as being, "the Word".

144

"In the beginning was the Word, and the Word was with God, and the Word was God." John 1:1

That "the Word" is another name for the 2nd Person of the Trinity is clearly asserted in John's first epistle, where we read:

"For there are three that bear record in heaven, the Father, the Word, and the Holy Ghost: and these three are one". I John 5:7

The important thing to remember is that in every instance in the Old Testament where God has visibly appeared to mankind as a person, it is God the Son and not God the Father who has been physically manifested.

The Alternate Names for Jesus in the Old Testament

Perhaps one of the most ironic aspects of the study of the life of Jesus Christ in the Old Testament is the fact that it most properly begins in the New Testament. For it is within the pages of the New Testament that we are directed by Scripture as to the true identity and historical record of Jesus Christ in the Old Testament.

In the 8th chapter of the Book of John, Jesus had brazenly declared to the religious leaders that His existence predated that of Abraham, and, by referring to Himself as "I Am" in John 8:58, had directly identified Himself as being the very same Person who had spoken to Moses from the "burning bush" on Mount Horeb:

"Verily verily I say unto you, before Abraham was, I Am." John 8:58

If we remember Moses' encounter with God at the burning bush on Mount Horeb in the 3rd chapter of the Book of Exodus, it was here that God had told Moses that His name was, "I Am" (Exodus 3:14).

145

So here in the New Testament, Jesus by referring to Himself as "I Am", was declaring Himself to be one and the same Person who had spoken to Moses from the burning bush on Mount Horeb, a fact that so infuriated the religious leaders that they wanted to stone Him (John 8:59).

To expand upon this new concept of Jesus being one and the same as the great "I Am" of the Old Testament, in the Book of John we are given 7 new distinct names for Jesus, each of which include the prefix "I Am", thereby solidifying the fact that it was the 2nd Person of the Trinity, Jesus Christ, who had visibly appeared to Moses on the mount, and not as is commonly believed, God the Father.

The fact that there are 7 specific instances in the Book of John denoting new names for Jesus is not an accidental occurrence, for 7 is the number that signifies completeness in Scripture. Whenever Scripture denotes 7 occurrences of anything, it is imploring the reader to pay special attention to that particular subject or matter. Some of the other important 7's in God's economy are as follows:

1) 7 days in a week.

2) God rested on the 7th day of Creation.

3) In the Book of Revelation there are 7 trumpets, 7 seals, 7 bowls, and 7 churches mentioned (actually, the number 7 occurs 55 times in the Book of Revelation).

4) Jesus spoke 7 different times on the Cross.

5) There are 7 major miracles listed in John's Gospel account.

6) There are 7 different theological dispensations listed in Scripture.

7) There are 7 listings of "I Ams" in the Gospel of John.

These 7 listings in John's Gospel clearly identify the relationship between the New Testament Jesus, with the Old Testament God known as "I Am". These references that Jesus makes concerning himself and to his true identity are as follows:

1) "I am the bread of life" John 6:35

2) "I am the light of the world" John 8:12

3) "I am the door of the sheep" John 10:7

4) "I am the good shepherd" John 10:11

5) "I am the resurrection and the life" John 11:25

6) "I am the way, the truth, and the life" John 14:6

7) "I am the true vine" John 15:1

These 7 declarations of "I Am" reveal not only personal attributes of Jesus, but they can also be construed as being titles for Jesus. In addition, these titles or new names given to Jesus may also be considered to be declarations of, and references to His Deity. For when Jesus stated, "I am the bread of life", he was in effect saying, "I Am, is the Bread of Life", or shortened, "I Am, the Bread of Life."

Again, these 7 new names for Jesus, which were all introduced by "I Am", are further confirmations of the fact that it was Jesus who had initially met with Moses at the burning bush on Mount Horeb. This identification of Jesus as the great "I Am" of the Old Testament is also brought to our attention later on in John's Gospel, in the Garden of Gethsemane.

The Garden of Gethsemane and Jesus as "I Am"

Perhaps the icing on the cake in terms of Scripture's presentation of Jesus as the "I Am" of the Old Testament comes at the time of Jesus' arrest in the Garden of Gethsemane. It is commonly believed that the "band" of men who had come to arrest Jesus were merely a handful of Roman soldiers, along with a few representatives of the Pharisees. This misconception has been reinforced throughout the years by films produced in Hollywood movie studios and stage productions of the Crucifixion story. Many New Testament scholars however believe that this "band" of men was much larger than a mere handful of soldiers. This is largely due to the fact that Matthew's Gospel directly declares that this "band" or contingency, consisted of "a great multitude" of men (Matthew 26:47). In addition, we must also remember that prior to this, Jesus had already avoided being captured by the religious authorities and their representatives on at least three separate occasions in Jerusalem (John 7:30, 8:59, 10:39). The Jewish religious authorities and their allies in the Roman military could ill afford to fail in capturing Jesus a fourth time.

Roman military experts maintain that there was an orderliness about conducting military business, and a set number of soldiers would have been sent to arrest this Person whom the Jewish religious leaders had deemed to be a threat to both their religious and Rome's political hierarchies. The largest military grouping of soldiers in the Roman Army would have been a Legion, which consisted of 6,000 soldiers. While some might maintain that the dispatching of 6,000 soldiers would seem to be a case of overkill, we must remember that during his arrest, Jesus told Peter to put his sword back in its sheath, because if he wanted to, he could have summoned 12 legions of angels to come to his aid (Matthew 26:53).

The next lower division of Roman soldiers would have been a cohort, which consisted of 600 men. The next delineation down from a cohort would have been a maniple, which was a grouping of 200 soldiers. Although it seems unlikely that 6,000 soldiers would have been dispatched, it is not altogether unlikely that this band of men had included either 200, or perhaps 600 soldiers. Again, we must remember that Matthew's Gospel informs us

148

that it was "a great multitude of men". The fact that Jesus had already escaped from the religious authorities in Jerusalem on three prior occasions made it incumbent upon both the religious and the secular authorities that there was to be no more botched opportunities to do away with Jesus. In either case, whether as a maniple of 200 soldiers, a cohort of 600 or a whole legion of 6,000, the group that came to arrest Jesus that night would not have been a mere handful, but rather, at least hundreds of men.

When this large contingency approached Jesus in the Garden, John's Gospel records that Jesus asked them, "Whom seek ye?", to which they replied, "Jesus of Nazareth." It is here that we have to dispel one of the other big misunderstandings of what actually occurred that night in the Garden of Gethsemane.

In the King James text, we read that Jesus answered, "I am *he*." However, when we closely examine the text, we see that the word "*he*", is written in italics. The reason that the King James translators wrote "*he*" in italics is because of the fact that the word "he" was not in the original text. It was added by the translators to make the sentence grammatically correct in English. So, in reality what we have here is Jesus forcefully answering the soldiers reply with a resounding, "I AM"!!!, after which Scripture informs us that hundreds of men were knocked over backwards to the ground, merely by the force of His words (John 18:6). This also explains the sudden bravado of an emboldened Peter who struck at the servant of the High Priest with his sword (John 18:10).

So, we see that this miracle in the Garden of Gethsemane, which is typically depicted as being a somewhat insignificant miracle, is in fact one of the major visual miracles to be found within the pages of Scripture. More importantly, it also clearly identifies the personage of Jesus as being one and the same as the all-powerful "I Am" who had appeared to Moses from the "burning bush".

Jesus and the Burning Bush

An interesting fact emerges when we carefully examine the 3rd chapter of Exodus. For here we have this revealed Personage of the Godhead, who we now know to be Jesus, also given 7 new names on Mount Horeb in the Old Testament, just as Jesus had acquired 7 new names in the Book of John in the New Testament. In the 3rd chapter of Exodus, these 7 new names attributed to the 2nd Person of the Trinity, Jesus Christ, are as follows:

1) The "Angel of the Lord", in Exodus 3:2.

2) The "God of Abraham", in Exodus 3:6. For it was Jesus who had appeared to Abram in the plains of Moreh to promise him the land (Genesis 12:7), after which Jesus had changed Abram's name to Abraham (Genesis 17:5), and then later Jesus had announced the destruction of Sodom and Gomorrah to Abraham in the plains of Mamre (Genesis 18:1).

3) The "God of Isaac", in Exodus 3:6. For it was Jesus who had appeared to Isaac in the plains of Beersheba (Genesis 26:24).

4) The "God of Jacob", in Exodus 3:6. For it was Jesus who had appeared to Jacob at Peniel (Genesis 32:30), and at Padanaram (Genesis 35:10).

5) As, "I Am", in Exodus 3:14.

6) The "LORD God of your fathers", in Exodus 3:15.

7) The "LORD God of the Hebrews", in Exodus 3:18.

A Closer Look at God's Name, "I AM"

It should be noted that the 5th name here listed for God, that of "I Am", also contains many misconceptions that were largely

150

initiated through the Hollywood film industry. If we remember the movie classic, "The Ten Commandments", in the passage where Moses asks God what His name is, He states, "I Am that I Am" (Exodus 3:14). In the movie version of this event, these particular words, "I Am that I Am", are spoken in such a manner as to convey the thought that God was being dismissive with Moses. God's tone of voice in the movie was in a sense to some degree indicating that "His name was none of Moses' business". We shall see however that this is not at all what Scripture is indicating here.

If we remember that at this juncture of Hebrew history, the Bible had not yet been written, and much of what was known by the Hebrew people about God had been passed on as an oral tradition. In the Hebrew language, the concept of "I Am" conveyed the meaning of God as being, "The one who is always existing in the present", or in a shortened form, "The pre-existing one."

When the Hebrew people talked of the God who had created the Universe, who had walked in the Garden of Eden with Adam, and had called their father Abraham, they would refer to Him as the "I Am", or "pre-existing one". So here at the burning bush, we have God telling Moses that, "He was that same "I Am", or "pre-existing one", who was indeed the same God of their oral tradition. The statement, "I Am, that I Am", can literally be interpreted as "I Am that pre-existing one", or when expanded, "I Am, that Creator God who had been present with Adam and Eve in the Garden of Eden".

Regarding the 6th and 7th listed names for this member of the Trinity, "The LORD God of your fathers", and "The LORD God of the Hebrews", we have a reference of the name of Jehovah, for as we shall soon see, the spelling of "LORD God" in Scripture is a designation for "Jehovah". The name "Jehovah" in Scripture carries with it the connotation of God as Savior. The Hebrew name "Joshua", literally means, "Jehovah saves." The name "Jesus" is a Greek transliteration of the Hebrew name of "Joshua".

It is of interest to note that when the angel had told Mary that the baby in her womb would "be called Jesus", the angel then immediately added these words to the commentary, "Because he shall save his people from their sins." (Matthew 1:21)

One of the other names given for Jesus at the burning bush besides "I Am", is that of "The Angel of the Lord" (Exodus 3:2). Long before it was revealed here to Moses that the great I Am was also the Angel of the Lord, we find Moses under guidance of the Holy Spirit making this same reference to Jesus during the days of Abraham. In the 16th Chapter of the Book of Genesis, we find Hagar fleeing from Sarai into the wilderness. We are told that the Angel of the Lord confronted Hagar, and had told her to return to Sarai, and to submit to her (Genesis 16:9). Hagar later remarks regarding the Angel of the Lord:

"... "You are a God of seeing", for she said, "Truly I have seen him who looks after me." Genesis 16:13 ESV

Hagar recognized that she had seen God. By simple inference, we know that she had seen none other than God the Son, Jesus Christ, for we know that His Old Testament name is also the Angel of the Lord, again, this is confirmed by the fact that, "No man hath seen God (the Father) at any time", and Hagar had clearly visually seen this manifestation of the Godhead.

This identification of the "Angel of the Lord" as being one and the same as Jesus is reaffirmed later in the Book of Genesis, not only at the burning bush, but also in numerous other occasions such as when Jacob had wrestled with this same Angel (Hosea 12:4). For we are told that Jacob also recognized that he had "seen God face to face" (Genesis 32:30). Therefore, we can establish the fact that Old Testament references to the "Angel of the Lord" are indeed references to the Pre-Incarnate Lord Jesus Christ.

Grammatical Nuances in the King James Text

In addition to the realization that the visible manifestations of God in the Old Testament were indeed appearances of the Pre-Incarnate Christ, there are also numerous instances in the Old Testament where statements and actions which we commonly attribute to having been made by God (the Father), were actually in fact performed by Jesus. We can know this because the translators of the King James Bible have included grammatical nuances in the text by changing the type-form in order to indicate to the reader which Person of the Trinity is actually speaking or engaging with mankind. While the Hebrew word for the Triune God is "Elohim", the Hebrew word for God the Father is "Adonai" and the name for God the Son is "Yahweh or Jehovah".

When the King James translators wanted to indicate the 1st Person of the Trinity, God the Father, God's name is spelled, "Lord GOD". When they wanted to indicate the 2nd Person of the Trinity, God the Son, God's name is then spelled, "LORD God".

L-o-r-d G-O-D = (Adonai), God the Father (upper case GOD, lower case Lord)

L-O-R-D G-o-d = (Jehovah), God the Son (upper case LORD, lower case God)

So, we see that "Lord GOD" is indicating a translation of the name Adonai, or God the Father, and that "LORD God" is an indication of the name Jehovah, or God the Son. Other spellings of God's name such as "Lord", "LORD", "God", or "GOD", are a little trickier to ascertain just which member of the Trinity is being singled out; be it the Father, Son, Holy Spirit, or the whole Godhead or Trinity as one. For these singular titles can often apply individually to all three members of the Trinity, or also to the complete Trinity or Godhead as a whole.

In many instances, we can determine which Person of the Trinity is being mentioned simply by the context. For example, in Isaiah 61:1 we read:

153

"The Spirit of the Lord GOD is upon me; because the "LORD" hath anointed me to preach good tidings unto the meek; he hath sent me to bind up the brokenhearted, to proclaim liberty to the captives, and the opening of the prison to them who are bound."

Here we have a passage of Scripture where each individual member of the Trinity is mentioned. "The Spirit" indicates the Holy Spirit, the "Lord GOD", points to God the Father, and "me" is an obvious reference to Jesus. When we come to "because the "LORD" hath anointed me", the name "LORD" is most likely an indicator of the whole Trinity, as Jesus came to the earth just as much by his own free will as by appointment of the Spirit and the Father (Hebrews 10:9,15). So here we have an example where LORD, with a large-capitalized L, and a smaller case capital O-R-D can also indicate the Trinity.

In Isaiah 48:17, we find the same term "LORD", all capital letters, as being an obvious reference to Jesus.

"Thus saith the "LORD", thy Redeemer, the Holy One of Israel; I am the LORD thy God which teacheth thee to profit, which leadeth thee by the way that thou shouldest go."

The titles "LORD God" and "Lord GOD" however, are clear indicators of which member of the Trinity the text is referring to, either to Jesus, or to God the Father, respectively.

Appearances of Jesus Christ in the Old Testament

When we approach the Old Testament with the knowledge that any visible physical manifestations of God have to have been physical appearances by the Lord Jesus Christ ("No man hath seen God the Father at any time" John 1:18), and that any references to God with the title of either "LORD God" or, "The Angel of the Lord", are also indicative of none other than the personage of Jesus, then the reading of the Old Testament becomes a whole new and exciting experience.

In the Book of Genesis, we first find Jesus as being the Creator of the Heavens and the Earth:

"These are the generations of the heavens and of the earth when they were created, in the day that the "LORD God" (Jehovah, or Jesus) made the earth and the heavens." Genesis 2:4

Next, we find that it was Jesus who had created Adam, "And the "LORD God" formed man of the dust of the ground" (Gen. 2:7). After this, it was Jesus who had literally planted the Garden of Eden, "And the "LORD God" planted a garden eastward in Eden" (Gen. 2:8). It was Jesus who had then formed Eve out of Adam, "And the rib, which the "LORD God" had taken from man, made he a woman, and brought her unto the man"(Genesis 2:22).

So, we see that it was Jesus who not only fashioned the bodies of both Adam and Eve, but who had also performed the world's first wedding ceremony (He "brought her unto the man" Genesis 2:22)!

It was also Jesus, who, "walked in the Garden with Adam and Eve" (for they certainly would not have hid themselves from an "ethereal cloud" Gen. 3:8), and later after the Fall, had promised to provide for mankind's redemption. In Genesis 3:15, we read:

"And "I" will put enmity between thee and the woman, and between thy seed and her seed; it shall bruise thy head, and thou shalt bruise His heal."

In many ways, Genesis 3:15 is one of the pivotal verses of Scripture. For here we find that it was Jesus Himself stating that it was He who was personally going to "put enmity between the serpent and the woman, between the serpent's seed and the woman's seed: and this enmity would bruise the serpent's head, and that the serpent would bruise His heel". This was a direct reference to His dying on the Cross. Therefore, in Genesis 3:15, it was the Pre-Incarnate Jesus who was personally promising to undo what Adam had done.

After Adam and Eve had been banished from the Garden of Eden, Scripture tells us that the whole earth had become corrupted, which necessitated the Flood. In God's Plan, mankind would get a fresh start through the family of Noah, whom God had instructed to build an ark in order that Noah, his family, and the animals of the earth would be saved from the coming Flood. When the appointed time was right for Noah and his family to go into the ark, quite interestingly, we find Jesus appearing unto Noah from within the ark, and beckoning Noah and his family to, "Come into the ark". In Genesis 7:1, we read:

"And the LORD said unto Noah, Come thou and all thy house into the Ark; for thee have I seen righteous before me in this generation."

In this instance, the term "LORD" is a direct reference to Jesus. For the wording of the passage necessitates a visual physical manifestation of God. For if the passage had been worded in a manner of, "And God said unto Noah go thou into the ark", it would have left the possibility open that it was simply the Voice of God talking to Noah. But the wording, "Come thou... into the ark", indicates two things:

1) That the voice was coming from a real Person.

2) That this Person was speaking to Noah from within the ark.

Later this same Person would also close the door of the ark ("And the LORD shut him in" Genesis 7:16).

If we put the whole scenario together, we first find Jesus Christ calling from within the confines of the ark out to Noah, and then telling him that it was time for both he and his family to come into the ark. Jesus would later close the door of the ark (quite

156

possibly also from the inside of the ark!). If this being the case, it is also a distinct possibility that Noah may have had an additional passenger in the ark, at least at the start of his journey! An incredible fact indeed!

After the call of Abraham, it was Jesus who then made numerous appearances to Abraham. As an interesting sidelight, because Noah did not die until Abraham was 58 years old (for Noah lived almost 350 more years after the Flood), it is therefore entirely possible that Noah may have personally related to Abraham this incredible encounter that he had with Jesus. Scripture is silent regarding this possibility, but it is more than likely that Abraham would have sought Noah out, as Noah probably would have enjoyed some worldwide celebrity status as the man whom God had chosen to build the ark and repopulate the earth. For all the peoples of the world would have known that they were ultimately related to Noah through one of his three sons. We must remember that Abraham was a direct descendant of Noah through Noah's son Seth, and it certainly would not be out of the question for Abraham at some point in his life to have wanted to go and visit his dear old great, great, ...grandfather.

So, long before Abraham physically encountered Jesus, he may have received a "first-hand account" of Him through Noah.

In Abraham's first encounter with God, we do not know if it was God the Father, Jesus, or the Holy Spirit who had approached him, for we are only told that, "The LORD had said unto Abram, Get thee out of thy country, and from thy kindred, and from thy father's house, unto a land that I will show thee" (Genesis 12:1). Soon thereafter however, when Abraham had come into Canaan, it is obvious which member of the Godhead had visually appeared unto him, as all visual appearances of God in the Old Testament are indeed appearances of Jesus (John 1:18):

"And the LORD appeared unto Abram, and said, Unto thy seed will I give this land: and there builded he an altar unto the LORD, who appeared unto him." Genesis 12:7

157

We know that it was God the Father (the "Lord GOD") who made the Abrahamic Covenant with Abraham ("And Abraham said, "Lord GOD", what wilt thou give me" Genesis 15:2). Soon thereafter however, Jesus physically appeared unto Abram again, to inform him that he was going to change his name from Abram to Abraham, and Sarai's name would now be Sarah (Genesis 17:5,15). He also promised Abraham and Sarah that although they were well along in age, they would have a son together (Gen. 17:16).

Soon thereafter, Jesus again appeared unto Abraham in the plains of Mamre, when Abraham was sitting at the door of his tent. In this encounter, Jesus had two angels with Him. Abraham prepared a meal for his three special visitors, after which Jesus informed Abraham of the coming destruction of Sodom and Gomorrah, in addition to reminding Abraham and Sarah that they were to have a son together (Genesis 18:10).

After Isaac was born, we find God ordering Abraham to take his son to Mount Moriah, and to sacrifice him there. When Abraham had lain Isaac on the altar of sacrifice on Mount Moriah and had raised his knife wielding hand to slay him, it was Jesus, as the Angel of the Lord, who stayed Abraham's hand, and then provided an animal sacrifice (Genesis 22:11).

After Abraham and Sarah had passed away, Jesus would once again appear unto Isaac during a time of great personal earthly struggles for Isaac, in order to comfort him and remind him of the blessings that were to come to him through his father Abraham:

"And the LORD appeared unto him the same night and said, I am the God of Abraham thy father: fear not, for I am with thee, and will bless thee, and multiply thy seed for my servant Abraham's sake." Genesis 26:24

Jesus would then later appear to Isaac's son Jacob in a dream, to remind him of the blessings that were to come to him through his grandfather Abraham:

"...I am the "LORD God" of Abraham thy father, and the God of Isaac: the land where thou liest, to thee will I give it, and to thy seed;

And thy seed shall be as the dust of the earth, and thou shalt spread abroad to the west, and to the east, and to the north, and to the south: and in thee and in thy seed shall all the families of the earth be blessed.

And, behold, I am with thee, and will keep thee in all places whither thou goest, and will bring thee again into this land; for I will not leave thee, until I have done that which I have spoken to thee of." Genesis 28:13-15

It was Jesus again who would later physically wrestle with Jacob at Peniel: "And Jacob was left alone; and there wrestled a man with him until the breaking of the day" (Genesis 32:24), "And Jacob called the name of the place Peniel: for I have seen God face to face, and my life is preserved." Genesis 32:30

Jesus did not appear again unto the sons of Abraham for the next 400 years, during which time they were enduring their time of bondage in Egypt. When the time was right, Jesus again reappeared on the stage of world history, this time at the calling of Moses to be the Deliverer of Israel out of Egyptian bondage.

For it was Jesus, as the Angel of the Lord, who met with Moses at the burning bush, and ordained him to be His agent for the deliverance of Israel from Egypt. Declaring His name to be "I AM":

"And God said unto Moses, I AM THAT I AM: and he said, Thus shalt thou say unto the children of Israel, I AM hath sent me unto you.

And God said moreover unto Moses, Thus shalt thou say unto the children of Israel, The "LORD God" of your fathers, the God

159

of Abraham, the God of Isaac, and the God of Jacob, hath sent me unto you: this is my name forever, and this is my memorial to all generations." Exodus 3:14,15

So again, we see in this passage of Scripture, a new name being introduced for Jesus, that of "I AM".

This brings about another interesting sidelight. When we read of Jesus during His Incarnation telling the religious leaders in the temple that He was alive before Abraham ("Your father Abraham rejoiced to see my day: and he saw it and was glad" John 8:56), the religious leaders challenged Him, saying, "Thou art not yet 50 years old, and hast thou seen Abraham?". This was stated either in an attempt to mock Jesus, or to see if He may have seen Abraham in a vision. To this, Jesus had famously replied, "Verily, Verily, I say unto you, Before Abraham was, "I AM." This brought an immediate affront to the religious leaders, for here Jesus was not only claiming to be the great "I Am" who had spoken to Moses at the burning bush, but in retrospect, Jesus was also claiming to be the member of the Godhead who had appeared numerous times unto Abraham ("who had rejoiced to see His day" John 8:56). Hence, they took up stones to kill Him, but Jesus safely passed through the midst of them (John 8:59).

Getting back to the narrative, soon after we have Jesus addressing Moses at the burning bush, we again find Him speaking to Moses, promising to personally deliver the Hebrew people out of the bondage of Egypt, and to bring them into the Promised Land:

"Go and gather the elders of Israel together, and say unto them, The LORD God of your fathers, the God of Abraham, of Isaac, and of Jacob, appeared unto me, saying, I have surely visited you, and seen that which is done to you in Egypt:

And I have said, I will bring you up out of the affliction of Egypt into the land of the Canaanites, and the Hittites, and the Amorites, and the Perizzites, and the Hivites, and the Jebusites, unto a land flowing with milk and honey." Exodus 3:16,17

"And God (Jesus) spake unto Moses, and said unto him, I am the LORD. And I appeared unto Abraham, unto Isaac, and unto Jacob, by the name of God Almighty, but by my name Jehovah was I not known to them." Exodus 6:3

Next, we find Jesus delivering Israel out of Egypt by the ten plagues foisted upon the Egyptian people. We know this was done by Jesus because Scripture clearly states:

"Thus saith the "LORD God" of Israel, I brought up Israel out of Egypt, and delivered you out of the hands of the Egyptians, ..." I Samuel 10:18

So, when we see references to the "LORD" in Scripture during the Exodus, they are indications of actions taken by the 2nd Person of the Trinity; Jehovah, or the Pre-Incarnate Jesus Christ.

It is of interest to note that when the Hebrew people had left Egypt on their journey to the Promised Land, that it was Jehovah (Jesus) who had hardened Pharaoh's heart, so that Pharaoh and his army followed the Hebrew people in hot pursuit:

"And the "LORD" hardened the heart of Pharaoh king of Egypt, and he pursued after the children of Israel ..." Exodus 14:8.

Next, we see Jesus as Jehovah parting the waters of the Red Sea (Exodus 14:21) by a strong east wind, and then later, after the Hebrew people had passed through to the other side, it was Jesus who caused the sea to return to its strength and drown the whole Egyptian army ("And the "LORD" said unto Moses, Stretch out thine hand over the sea, that the waters may come again upon the Egyptians..." Exodus 14:26).

Later, after the Hebrew people had made it to Mount Sinai, we again find Jesus coming down to Mount Sinai, in order to give the Ten Commandments and the Law unto Moses:

"And the LORD came down upon Mount Sinai, on the top

of the mount: and the LORD called Moses up to the top of the mount; and Moses went up." Exodus 19:20

Scripture then confirms that these actions of God were those of Jesus, because in Exodus 20, He announces, "I am the LORD thy God, which have brought thee out of the land of Egypt..."

It was Jesus who then later visibly appeared unto Moses, Aaron, Nadab, Abihu, and the 70 elders of Israel (Exodus 24:1) in Israel's First Communion with the Lord:

"And they saw the God of Israel: and there was under his feet as it were a paved work of a sapphire stone, and as it were the body of heaven in its clearness,

And upon the nobles of the children of Israel he laid not his hand: also they saw God, and did eat and drink." Exodus 24:10,11

It was none other than Jesus who had then led the Hebrews in their 40 years of Wilderness wanderings. This can be seen by comparing Exodus 17:2 with I Corinthians 10:9:

In the Book of Exodus, we read that when the people chided Moses, they were really chiding the Person who was actively giving Moses directions, "Why chide ye with me? Wherefore do ye tempt the LORD" (Exodus 17:2)? This Person was none other than Jesus, for we read in the New Testament, that in the Wilderness, when they had tempted the "LORD", that they had in fact "tempted Christ" (I Corinthians 10:9).

After the death of Moses, Jesus then appeared to Joshua under a new title, that of the "Captain of the Lord of Hosts". We know that this was Jesus, for He accepted the worship of Joshua, and declared the ground that Joshua was standing on to be "holy", in like manner that He had priorly done on the mount with Moses (Joshua 5:14,15). Jesus next discussed the battle plans for the assault upon Jericho with Joshua (Joshua 6:2-5).

After Joshua's death, Jesus personally appeared to the nation of

Israel to remind them that it was He who had brought them out of Egypt, and through the Wilderness (Judges 2:1).

Later, Jesus appeared unto Gideon as the "Angel of the Lord", to encourage him before the Battle with the Midianites (Judges 6:12).

Next, we find Jesus again as the "Angel of the Lord", appearing to Manoah and his wife to tell them about the birth of their son Samson (Judges 13:21).

Jesus then appeared twice unto Samuel in order to establish him as a prophet (I Samuel 3:10, 21).

After this, Jesus as the "Angel of the Lord" appeared unto David at Ornan the Jebusite's threshing floor (I Chronicles 21:16). David later bought the threshing floor from Ornan, and it eventually became the site where David's son Solomon, built the first Temple.

Later we find Jesus coming down to comfort and feed Elijah, after his bout with the priests of Baal on Mount Carmel. Jesus would then later feed Elijah again (I Kings 19:5,7), in order to prepare him for the road that lay ahead for him.

The prophet Isaiah also saw the Pre-Incarnate Jesus. In Isaiah 6:1 we read: "In the year that King Uzziah died I saw the LORD sitting upon a throne, High and lifted up, and his train filled the temple."

It was this same Jesus who would later save Hezekiah and the Jewish Nation, when He, as the "Angel of the Lord", would completely destroy the Assyrian army of 185,000 soldiers who had encamped round about Jerusalem:

"Then the angel of the LORD went forth, and smote in the camp of the Assyrians a hundred and fourscore and five thousand: and when they arose early in the morning, behold, they were all dead corpses." Isaiah 37:36

163

Next, in the Book of Daniel, we find Jesus joining Shadrach, Meshach, and Abednego in Nebuchadnezzar's fiery furnace!!!

"Lo I see four men loose, walking in the midst of the fire, and they have no hurt; and the form of the fourth is like the Son of God." Daniel 3:25

Jesus then later appeared unto the prophet Amos, who saw Him standing upon the altar, announcing His Judgment upon Israel:

"I saw the LORD, standing upon the altar: and he said, Smite the lintel of the door, that the posts may shake: and cut them in the head, all of them; and I will slay the last of them with the sword: he that fleeth of them shall not flee away, and he that escapeth of them shall not be delivered." Amos 9:1

Again, it is only when we recognize that these appearances of God in the Old Testament were in fact appearances of the Pre-Incarnate Jesus Christ, that we begin to realize the total significance of the verses found in the Psalms (Psalm 40:7), and in Hebrews (Hebrews 10:7):

"Then said I, Lo, I come (in the volume of the book it is written of me,) to do Thy will, O God."

The appearances of the Pre-Incarnate Jesus Christ literally fill the pages of the Old Testament record. As Arthur Custance remarked, "Where in the volume of the Book, is it not written of Him!". In addition to this, Custance also stated, "If one wants to get a more accurate grasp of who Jesus really is, one should substitute the name of Jesus for any references to God incorporating these preceding principles of interpretation while reading the Old Testament, and likewise substitute the title of God for any references to Jesus while reading the New Testament!"

The historical record of both the Old and the New Testaments is truly the story of the history of Jesus Christ. Which in turn

164

makes the written record of both the Old Testament and the New Testaments to literally be, "HIS-STORY".

Jesus Christ the Unique Person of the Universe

"Jesus, though born without a sinful nature, in his humanity was in essence, just like the rest of mankind"

Apart from being both God and man at the same time, in addition to being born in a sinless state, it is commonly believed that Jesus was just like any other human being who has ever been born into this world. This is a view however, that is not shared by Scripture. For Jesus in his humanity was not, "just another human being". For Scripture informs us that Jesus was uniquely related to the first human being created, Adam. In God's Word, Jesus is referred to as the "Last Adam" (I Corinthians 15:45).

We must remember that the First Adam, as created, was unlike all his eventual progeny. For the original Adam as created by God carried with him all the various traits and capabilities that would later be exhibited and expressed by all of mankind, both male and female.

When God made Eve from Adam as a helpmate to him, it is essential for us to remember that not only was a rib taken out of Adam to form the body of Eve, but a portion of the personage of Adam was also taken out of Adam in order to form Eve's psychological make-up as well. The fact that the personality traits that are typically found in males are quite different than the traits commonly exhibited by females is an open testimony to the fact that there are numerous personality differences between the sexes. Scripture tells us that the LORD God made Eve from out of Adam (Genesis 2:22). Unlike Adam however, Eve was not a distinct and separate creation. Everything that Eve was in her personage came out of Adam.

These many different personality traits that are typically found present in both males and females were at one time all present within the original Adam as created. After Eve was formed out of Adam, Adam would never be the same again either physically or psychologically. For what was once solely Adam, had now become Adam and Eve ("And God called their name Adam" Genesis 5:2).

The fact that the First Adam as originally created contained the personage of both male and female was not uniquely taught by the Hebrews in Old Testament times, but like the Scriptural accounts of the Garden of Eden and the Flood, had also become a part of other ancient cultural traditions. Plato in his Symposium wrote:

"Our nature of old was not the same as now. It was then one man-woman, whose form and name were common both to male and to female. Then said Jupiter, I will divide them into two parts."

After the Flood, humanity was again further fragmented into three separate and distinct races, with each race exhibiting their own peculiar and unique personality traits. We have already covered this phenomenon extensively in the 7th Chapter of this work regarding Noah's three sons, so there is no need to delve deeper into this matter here. What is important to recognize is that we as humans have become fragmented into beings who have lost many of the capabilities of man as originally created. Very seldom do we find humans that have both interests and talents in numerous aspects of life. It is rare indeed to find the philosopher, poet, musician, athlete, inventor, scholar, artist, tradesman, and compassionate nurturer of his fellow man, all rolled up into one person. When we do find such a person, he is often referred to as a "Renaissance Man.

This experience is still far from the total capabilities of Adam as first created, for Adam would have possessed all of the talents and abilities that would ever be exhibited in mankind, not merely a few. Most of us are "gifted" with one or two bents or talents, and do not relate to being multi-dimensional in either our interests or our capabilities.

We should always recognize that with the Fall, man also became much less than what he was in the First Adam as originally created. For the First Adam was like the Last Adam, Jesus Christ, being made after the power of an endless life (Hebrews 7:16). It was only after the Fall that Adam had become subject to death (Genesis 2:17). Before the Fall, Adam would have exhibited both amazing physical strength and intellectual capabilities. Adam would have possessed not only the athletic skills of Michael Jordan, the intellectual might of Albert Einstein, and the musical savvy of Wolfgang Mozart, but also the inventive genius of Tesla, the wit of Will Rogers, and the nurturing compassion of a Mother Theresa. Everything that we know about human abilities were all present in the First Man.

In the physical realm, while mankind erroneously believes that we are constantly getting better, "evolving" if you will, experience shows us that the Fall was down. Life expectancy for a short period of time after the Fall was often over 900 years, Adam himself living to the ripe old age of 930 years. After the passing of just 2,000 years, the life expectancy of man had been diminished to just 120 years, as was exhibited by the life of Abraham. One thousand years later, at the time of David, mankind's life expectancy had decreased to what it remains to be today, approximately 70 years (Psalm 90:10). Even with the cumulative advances and capabilities of modern medicine, 21st Century man still finds himself with not much more than the 3 score and 10 years of life expectancy that was prevalent at the time of King David.

These factors concerning both the fragmentation of abilities, and the loss of physical vibrancy, are likely what prompted Archbishop Richard Whately to state in the 19th Century, "An Aristotle was but the rubbish of an Adam."

169

Again, as was the case of the original Adam, the last Adam, Jesus Christ, was made after "the power of an endless life". It was only after the introduction of sin into his body at the time of the Fall that the first Adam had been made subject to death. The Last Adam, Jesus however, was never made subject to death. Were it not for his death on the cross, Jesus had the potential to live on endlessly, without ever having to experience death. Although he did die on the Cross, Jesus did not die because of the Cross. For on the Cross, we are told that Jesus willingly gave up his spirit, having accomplished his mission on earth (Matthew 27:50, John 19:30).

In order to better understand the relationship between the First and the Last Adam, it is necessary to examine the historical record of the opening passages of the Book of Genesis.

The Three Judgments upon Planet Earth

It is generally recognized within Christendom that there are two judgments that have been determined by God to be placed upon Planet Earth. The first Judgment being the Flood in the days of Noah, and the second being the Judgment at the end of time, which is mentioned by the Apostle Peter. In this Judgment, all of the elements will melt away with fervent heat (II Peter 3:10), after which there shall be the creation of a new heavens and earth (II Peter 3:13, Revelation 21:1).

There is however a third Judgment that is mentioned in Scripture, albeit in a more subtle way. This Judgment being the original judgment that was placed upon the Planet Earth at the time of Satan's Fall. This Judgment is often referred to in theological circles as "The Gap Theory", for it is believed to have taken place sometime between the original Creation mentioned in Genesis 1:1, and what many refer to as the Re-Creation or restoration of the Earth in Genesis 1:2.

170

The Gap Theory

We know that at the time of the original creation mentioned in Genesis 1:1, all was well within both the physical Universe and the angelic beings that God had created. For Scripture states that at the time of the original creation, "...All the sons of God shouted for joy" (Job 38:7). This perfect harmony however was interrupted at the time of Satan's Fall, a Fall in which he had declared his five famous, "I Wills", recorded in the Book of Isaiah (Isaiah 14:12-14). This was an attempt to usurp the Throne of God and become the Ultimate Ruler in the Universe. We are told in Scripture, that it was at this time that Satan also convinced one-third of the angels to join him in this rebellion against God (Revelation 12:4).

The following is the original account of Creation as written in Genesis 1:1,2 from the Authorized King James Version of the Bible. This will be followed by an expanded interpretive rendering of the same passages by Hebrew scholar Arthur Custance.

"In the beginning God created the heaven and the earth.

And the earth was without form, and void; and darkness was upon the face of the deep. And the spirit of God moved upon the face of the waters." Genesis 1:1,2

"Originally God brought into being and set in perfect order the heavens and the earth.

But the earth had become a ruin and a desolation: And a pall of darkness hung over this scene of disaster: And the Spirit of God moved mightily over the face of the waters." Genesis 1:1,2 (An expanded interpretive rendering)

From this examination of Scripture, we can see that something terrible had happened in the original Universe that God had created in Genesis1:1. For we know that when God creates something, He declares it to be good (Genesis 1:31).

171

In that this rebellion by Satan had prompted God to place Judgment upon the Planet Earth, it is a good indication that the overseeing of the Earth had been delegated by God to Satan, His Highest created Angel. Planet Earth had come under Judgment because it was Satan's domain.

That being said, it then follows that the subsequent account of Creation's story found in the Book of Genesis, from the third verse of Genesis 1 through Genesis 2:25, is not an account of the original Creation, but rather the six days of God's Re-Creation and restoration of Planet Earth after the Fall of Satan.

The Role of Adam in the Angelic Conflict

With the Fall of Satan and 1/3 of the Angelic Beings in the time gap between Genesis 1:1 and Genesis 1:2 began a drama in the history of God's Creation known as the "Angelic Conflict". God had to deal with this rebellion from within His created order in a just and judicious way. He had to demonstrate to the unfallen Angels that His Ways are Holy, Good, and Just. So, at this time God reconstituted the earth in Genesis 1:3-31 and brought Adam on to the world stage.

From Scripture, we know that God does not create anything in vain (Isaiah 45:18). Adam therefore could not have been created for the sole purpose of seeing whether or not he too would rebel against his Creator. We shall see that Adam as created probably had a far more noble calling. Scripture does not openly elaborate on what Adam's original calling was, for God in His wisdom and Omniscience knew that open direct knowledge of many aspects of His Plan would only lead to mankind making false interpretations. In addition, man would lose sight of the main issue at hand, that being his need for salvation from his newly acquired sinful condition. In this fact we see why some matters of Scripture are not openly discussed within God's Word ("The secret things belong to the Lord" Deuteronomy 29:29). We are
172

also told in Scripture that although God does conceal some things, He does leave the answers to many questions just below the surface and expects us to do a little digging in order to find these answers out.

"It is the glory of God to conceal a thing: but the honor of kings is to search out a matter." Proverbs 25:2

So we can see that we are given enough information throughout the pages of God's written Word to develop a more than reasonable explanation as to just what God's original purpose for the First Adam may have been.

After the six days of Re-Creation, we are told that God, observed all that He had made, "...and behold, it was very good" (Genesis 1:31). We are then told that God planted a Paradisiacal Garden, the Garden of Eden, and placed Adam within this separate earthly Paradise. Adam had been told that he was to be fruitful and multiply, and to replenish and subdue the earth (Genesis 1:28). From within the Garden, Adam was also told that he was to both "dress and keep" the Garden. Erich Sauer in his prodigious work, "The Dawn of World Redemption", stated that this dressing and keeping of the Garden carried with it the connotation of both "the guarding of the Garden, along with the expansion of its borders." When we couple this with the fact that everything within the borders of Eden was a Paradise, and everything physically outside of the borders of Eden was labeled as being merely "good", (as in not paradisiacal), we can ascertain that Satan still maintained a certain authority on Earth over everything that was outside of the Garden. Everything within the Garden was Adam's domain, and he was to not only "guard" it from outside attack, but he was also to expand its borders into the newly reconstituted Earth.

It was at this time that the First Adam was fragmented into two separate human beings. The male part was still known as Adam, and the female version of the First Adam became known as "Eve". This gave mankind the ability to reproduce and subsequently, an even greater ability to expand the borders of the Garden into Satan's domain.

From these Biblical accounts we can surmise that Adam was created for the purpose of resolving the Angelic Conflict. By remaining obedient to God and not partaking of the forbidden fruit, Adam and his progeny were to both protect and expand this Garden of Eden until it covered the face of the entire Earth. By so doing, Adam would have demonstrated to the Universe at large, "that obedience to God brings about an ever expanding and growing "circle of blessings", and therefore, we can assume that Adam would have then successfully resolved the Angelic Conflict.

How glorious the history of mankind would have been had Adam not fallen. When Satan had seen that God had split the First Adam into two beings, and therefore now had the ability to reproduce, he knew that the rapid expansion of the Garden into his territory was inevitable. That for him and his domain, the "writing was on the wall". Satan would then go to work on the first couple by tempting Eve with the same temptation by which he himself had fallen, that being that "she could be equal to or greater than God".

With the Fall, the innocence of Adam and Eve had been turned into corruption. Because Eve had been deceived, and Adam had knowingly chosen to reject God, the sinful nature they had acquired by ingesting the forbidden fruit would be passed on to their progeny through Adam's seed, and not Eve's. The woman's seed was preserved as the only non-corrupted cell in either a man's or a woman's body. This was necessary in order that the coming Savior could be born truly human, and yet without a sinful nature.

The Last Adam

When Jesus was born into the world, His primary mission was to be the Savior of mankind. He did however have another

174

matter of unfinished business to attend to, that being the resolution of the Angelic Conflict. While the First Adam had failed in his endeavor to "transfigure" the earth, it was now up to the Last Adam to exhibit to the Angelic Realms that a life lived in obedience to God would indeed result in a circle of blessings to all concerned.

In order to undo the works of the First Adam (I Corinthians 15:22), the Last Adam had to possess the full human potential of the unfragmented First Adam. At the risk of being mis-understood, Jesus in a sense had to be the reincarnation of the First Adam, as originally created. While in his physicality, Jesus was totally a male, in his personality and emotional make-up, he was both male and female.

While it is common to portray Jesus as being physically effeminate, this was hardly the case as evidenced by the incident in the 2nd Chapter of the Book of John, where he physically removed the money changers out of the Temple area. Jesus must have been an imposing physical force, for no one attempted to stop him from creating havoc and throwing over the tables. Jesus did however exhibit the feminine nurturing aspects of his personage, while making this statement in the Book of Matthew:

"O Jerusalem, Jerusalem, thou that killest the prophets, and stonest them which are sent unto thee, how often would I have gathered thy children together, even as a hen gathered her chickens under her wings, and ye would not!" Matthew 23:37

If we are honest with ourselves, it is hard for us to conceive of any man that we have ever known making such a nurturing statement. It is indeed a testament to the full scope of humanity, both male and female, that Jesus possessed in His role as the Last Adam.

God's Original Plan for Mankind as Revealed by the Last Adam

We know that in God's Plan for the life of the Last Adam, Jesus Christ, that He was maturing or perfecting Jesus in his humanity, for Scripture tells us that God was making "the captain of their salvation perfect through sufferings" (Hebrews 2:10). Both the First and the Last Adam came into this world in innocence. What we see here in this passage from the Book of Hebrews is that in the case of Jesus, this innocence was to be matured, perfected if you will, until it had become virtue. This must have been the case for the First Adam as well. For he was also created in innocence, and by enduring the conflicts of temptation, he too would have reached a point where his innocence would have matured into virtue. It would have been at this time that the First Adam could have been ushered into the heavens, having been perfected or matured through his resisting of Satan's temptations. The Earth as recreated, could then be seen to be in a sense a training school for mankind for eternity. A school in which innocence through trials would have been changed into virtue. Due to the First Adam's failure, we will never know the answer to this question on this side of heaven.

The Last Adam, however, did finish this maturation process. He did accomplish what the First Adam had failed to do, that being, He remained faithful unto God despite numerous temptations to do otherwise (Matthew 4:1-11, Matthew 16:21-23, Hebrews 4:15). In Jesus, innocence had been successfully matured into true virtue. Many Biblical scholars maintain that the celebration of the completion of this process of maturation occurred on the Mount of Transfiguration. That it was from the Mount of Transfiguration that Jesus could have potentially left the earth and gone into the eternal heavenly abode, having achieved virtue in his humanity.

While almost all Bible translations render Hebrews 12:2 as reading, "...who for the joy that was set before him endured the cross...", there are many Bible scholars such as Arthur Custance who state that the Greek clearly indicates that the verse should be rendered, "...instead of the joy that was set before him he endured the cross...". In other words, on the Mount of Transfiguration, Jesus as the Last Adam had been glorified in his humanity, and could have passed on into the heavens, not having to experience death. The process of his maturation had been completed, his innocence turned into virtue. He, as the Last Adam, had accomplished what the First Adam had failed to do. He had remained perfectly obedient unto God. This glorification of Jesus was clearly a glorification of his humanity. For we are told in the ninth Chapter of Mark that his "raiment became shining, exceeding white as snow; so as no fuller on earth can white them." This is in sharp contrast to the presence of the glory of Jehovah in the Old Testament, a presence by which no man can see and live (Exodus 33:18-20).

So, we see that on the Mount of Transfiguration, Jesus was presented with the opportunity to go on into Glory, having successfully demonstrated to the Angelic world that it is possible to remain loyal and obedient to God. That God was and is totally Holy, Righteous, and Good. There was one problem though with Jesus going on into Glory at this time, that being mankind's sin issue had not been resolved. So "instead" of entering into the eternal joy and glory that had been set before him, we are told by Scripture that from this time forward, Jesus set his face like a flint and marched on into Jerusalem and to the Cross (Isaiah 50:7).

It is interesting to note that the only other human being besides Jesus whom God had said that He was well "pleased" with, was Enoch. Enoch had been transformed out of this world into the heavens without experiencing death much the same as Jesus could have been on the Mount of Transfiguration. Just as Jesus went on to experience death, so must Enoch return to the Earth as one of the two witnesses from the coming Tribulation Period, and also experience death. "...as it is appointed unto man once to die, and after this the Judgment" (Hebrews 9:27).

It is also of interest to note that the two people who appeared with Jesus on the Mount of Transfiguration were Moses and

177

Elijah. This was by no means an accident. For Moses symbolizes the Law within Scripture, and Elijah the Prophets. So, we see that the Last Adam, Jesus, was the fulfillment of both the Law and the Prophetic Word. For we know that Jesus is the end of the Law for righteousness (Romans 10:4), being the fulfillment of the coming Messiah spoken of by the prophets (Isaiah 9:6,7; Matthew 2:23). God had also made sure that this important event was witnessed by at least three of the disciples, Peter, James, and John in accordance with Old Testament Law ("...in the mouth of two or three witnesses" Deuteronomy 17:6).

It should also be noted that if Jesus were simply "just another human being", under the legal principle of "an eye for an eye, and a tooth for a tooth" (Leviticus 24:20), then Jesus could have only died for one man. But in that Jesus as the Last Adam possessed the same non-fragmented humanity originally possessed by the First Adam, he could die as the legal representative of all of mankind.

The Last Adam was also unique in His life and death because it can be said that He was the only person who has ever lived who gave his life for someone else. All others who we credit with sacrificing their lives for others, be they soldiers or other heroes or heroines, sacrificed only what was left of their lives. For they were all destined to die as the result of the Fall. Jesus, on the other hand, need not to have died, for He was "made after the power of an endless life (Hebrews 7:16).

We see that Jesus Christ in His humanity, was far different than all others born into this world. For within Jesus, we find the full embodiment of all mankind: red, yellow, black, white or brown; male and female. With Jesus, we see who Adam really was in his original creation, and what it means to be fully and truly human.

Faulty Paradigm #12

Israel and the Error of Replacement Theology

"Israel has lost its place of favor with God, and the blessings that used to belong to Israel now belong to the church"

The above doctrine is often referred to as, "Replacement Theology". The basic tenet of Replacement Theology is that through their disobedience, Israel has permanently lost its place and position in God's Plan, and the blessings that were once promised to Israel now belong to the Church. This erroneous idea is directly refuted by Scripture. Paul writes in the Book of Romans that the Church should be careful not to boast against Israel, for the Church was grafted into God's Plan, and that God is able to (and will) regraft Israel back into a position of favor with Him (Romans 11:23).

In order to fully understand the position of permanence in God's Plan that Israel possesses, it is necessary to refer to the Abrahamic Covenant that God made with Abraham in the 15th chapter of the Book of Genesis.

The Abrahamic Covenant

In the ancient Orient, there were three basic kinds of covenants, or contracts, that people would engage in: 1) The salt covenant, 2) The sandal covenant, and 3) The sacrificial covenant.

In the arid climate of the Middle East, salt was not only used to season and flavor food, but it was also used to help one retain fluids during long stretches of travel. Salt was necessary for survival in this region of the world, and people would carry salt with them in a pouch. When two people would engage in a salt

179

covenant or contract, they would reach into their pouch and place a pinch of salt into the pouch of the person that they were making a contract with. It was more of a symbolic gesture than anything, much like in our Western Culture when people often "seal a deal", with a handshake.

When an agreement or a contract between two individuals required something more legally binding, then the participants in the covenant would provide a surety for the contract in the form of their personal sandals, where one person would take the other person's sandal as a form of collateral, to ensure that the contract would be honored.

When a contract required a solemn oath, the two participants would engage in a blood or sacrificial covenant. In this covenant, an animal would be sacrificed, and cut down the middle into two pieces. Then the two participants in the covenant would walk hand in hand through the middle of the two halves of the sacrificial animal. By so doing, they were both acknowledging that they were to fulfill the terms and conditions of the stated contract, under penalty of their own death, should they fail to do so. Each half of the dead animal symbolized their own deaths if they should fail to fulfill the demands of the covenant. We see that this form of covenant was very solemn and serious.

In the Abrahamic Covenant in the 15th Chapter of the Book of Genesis, we find that the Covenant between God and Abraham bequeathed the "land" of Israel to Abraham, and to his "seed". This aspect of the Covenant was not conditional on Abraham's part, for it was God alone who passed between the two halves of the sacrificial animal. Abraham was not in the Covenant. This therefore would signify that each half of the slain animal represented the death of God Himself, should He fail to permanently grant the land of Israel to Abraham and his progeny.

Although the Covenant was an unconditional Covenant as to these "land" and "seed" promises, the Covenant did contain conditional aspects to it regarding the possession of the land by Abraham and his seed. Abraham and his progeny could be removed from the land through disobedience to God, even though they were the rightful owners. A fact that we have witnessed twice in history. In 586 B.C., the Babylonians conquered a disobedient Israel and carried them away captive back to Babylon for 70 years. Then again, in 70 A.D the Romans removed Israel from their land in the 2nd dispersion, after they had rejected their Messiah. This removal from the land lasted until the year 1948, when once again the land became the residence of the Hebrew people, when the nation Israel was again reborn in a day (Isaiah 66:8)!

So, we see that God Himself has promised eternal ownership of the land of Israel to Abraham and to his descendants, under penalty of His own death should He choose to not uphold this Covenant with Abraham and his children! Although the nation of Israel through disobedience has been twice removed from their land, they will forever hold the deed to the land. This has been guaranteed by God Himself.

By believing that God has moved on from His relationship with the people of Israel, those who adhere to the tenets of Replacement Theology not only blind themselves to the many truths of the Jewish restoration in end time prophecy, but they also fail to recognize the fact that much of the dialogue that exists within the four Gospel accounts in the New Testament are not addressed to the Church at all, but rather to the Hebrew people specifically. For it was to the Jewish people that Jesus had been sent. Indeed, this fact is stated by Jesus Himself in the Book of Matthew:

"I am not sent but unto the lost sheep of the house of Israel." Matthew 15:24

God has never abandoned the Jewish people. Rather, He has set them aside so that ultimately the Church could be built up. In the Book of Romans, we read:

"I say then, Have they stumbled that they should fall? God forbid: but rather through their fall salvation has come to the Gentiles, for to provoke them to jealousy." Romans 11:11

Paul then goes on to write in Romans:

"For I would not brethren, that ye should be ignorant of this mystery, lest ye should be wise in your own conceits; that blindness in part is happened to Israel, until the fulness of the Gentiles be come in." Romans 11:25

We see that in the Plan of God, Israel was set aside in order that the Church might be grafted into the blessings of God. The Church is not to boast in any way against the Jewish people, which in fact is what those who adhere to the tenets of Replacement Theology are in essence doing. Paul writes:

"Boast not against the branches. But if thou boast, thou bearest not the root, but the root thee.

Thou wilt say then, The branches were broken off, that I might be grafted in.

Well; because of unbelief they were broken off, and thou standest by faith.

Be not highminded, but fear: For if God spared not the natural branches, take heed lest he also spare not thee." Romans 11:18-21

One day, Israel will once again find favor with God:

"And so all Israel shall be saved: as it is written, There shall come out of Zion the Deliverer, and shall turn away ungodliness from Jacob." Romans 11:26

To the adherents of Replacement Theology who may cynically claim that Israel has lost its birthright because God in the Person of Jesus did die, and thereby cancelling the Abrahamic Covenant, it must be noted that it was not the 2nd Person of the Trinity who had made the Covenant with Abraham in Genesis, but rather

God the Father. In Genesis 15:8 we read, that it was the "Lord GOD", or God the Father, who was the member of the Trinity involved in the Covenant. It is as if God in His Omniscience knew that in the future, there would be some who would try to write Israel off, and that He was effectively destroying any arguments that they might have in their attempt to justify this erroneous interpretation of Scripture.

To this we must again conclude with the Apostle Paul:

"O the depth of the riches both of the wisdom and knowledge of God! How unsearchable are his judgments, and his ways past finding out!" Romans 11:33

A New Look at Dispensations

"The ultimate purpose of the Theological Dispensations found within Scripture is a mystery known only to God"

Mankind typically regards the ultimate purpose of the various Dispensations or Ages found within Scripture to be a mystery, and considers them to be a part of the "unknowable things of God" as delineated in Deuteronomy 29:29 ("The secret things belong unto the Lord our God: but those things which are revealed belong unto us and to our children forever, that we may do all of the words of this law.").

Admittedly, there are no direct Scriptural references that explain God's Purpose in framing the history of mankind within these Theological Dispensations, but that does not mean that any attempt at understanding this Biblical framework of history will be fruitless and without merit.

God did give mankind the ability to reason, and hence would expect us to use that ability in our study of His Word. Although much of this particular chapter falls under the category of "Speculative Theology", it is the author's hope that it will be fruitful unto its readers and open up to them new avenues of understanding in their study of God's Word.

Dispensations

The Dispensations of Biblical human history are separate and distinct periods of time in the history of man, wherein God's dealings with mankind are accomplished within different formats. Each Dispensational time period begins with man operating within a new framework of conditions and responsibilities. After man has failed to live up to these responsibilities, each Dispensation then ends with a distinct judgment from God.

Dispensational Theology is often said to have originated in the 19th century with John Nelson Darby, but the early Church Fathers such as Irenaeus and Justin Martyr were also known to divide the Scriptures into periods of time, albeit not the same periods as proposed by modern day Dispensationalists.

Justin Martyr divided Biblical history into four distinct periods of time:

1) Adam to Abraham

2) Abraham to Moses

3) Moses to Christ

4) Christ to Eternity

Irenaeus also taught that there were four distinct time periods, but that these periods of time should be divided not by the lives of men, but rather by historical events. The Dispensational periods proposed by Irenaeus are as follows:

1) The Creation to the Flood

2) The Flood to the Law

3) The Law to the Gospel

4) The Gospel to Eternity

Dispensational Theology as a Branch of Theology goes far beyond interpreting Scripture through the lens of Dispensations. Although there are many disagreements amongst Dispensational-ists in their interpretation of God's Word, for the most part, they share a common outline of seven different Biblical Dispensations. In addition to this, at the core of their theological system, Dispensationalists hold to two main tenets:

1) All of Scripture is to be interpreted in a literal manner. Although there are many symbolic literary devices employed within Scripture, God's Word is to be interpreted from a literal perspective.

2) Israel's role within God's eternal plan is separate and distinct from that of the Church.

The seven Dispensational Ages that are commonly agreed upon by Dispensationalists are as follows:

1) The Age of Innocence (Genesis 1:1–3:7) The time period from the Creation of Adam until the expulsion of Adam and Eve from the Garden of Eden.

2) The Age of Conscience (Genesis 3:8–8:22) The time period from the expulsion from Eden until the Flood in the days of Noah.

3) The Age of Human Government (Genesis 9:1–11:32) The time period from Noah and his family leaving the Ark until the confusion of languages at the Tower of Babel.

4) The Age of Promise (Genesis 12:1–Exodus 19:25) The time period from the call of Abraham until the Exodus from Egypt.

5) The Age of Law (Exodus 20:1–Acts 2:4) The time period from the giving of the Ten Commandments on Mount Sinai until the Crucifixion.

6) The Age of Grace (Acts 2:4–Revelation 20:2,3) The time period from Pentecost until the 2nd Coming of Jesus Christ back to the earth.

7) The Millennial Kingdom (Revelation 20:4-6) The 1000-year

time period of the direct Rule of Christ on the earth, which is followed by the Great White Throne Judgment and the subsequent initiation of the eternal state.

As we have previously stated, for a theological time period to be considered a separate and distinct Dispensation, the time period must contain each of the following three criteria:

1) Man is given a new format to live in, with its own unique set of instructions to live by.

2) Man fails to live within the framework of these edicts.

3) God Judges man's failure and moves on to the next Dispensation.

Inherent Problems within Dispensational Theology

The seven Dispensations that are commonly recognized by Dispensationalists are not universally accepted by all students of Scripture. There are some inconsistencies in their selection of the different Dispensations, which this study will now attempt to address.

The first inconsistency of concern is to be found within the 4th Dispensation, the Age of Promise. When we carefully examine this Dispensation, there are two apparent problems in regarding the three criteria necessary for a time period to be deemed a Dispensation. For within the Dispensation of Promise:

1) There really is not a venue of new instructions by which man is to live. Rather, we have the calling of Abraham and his descendants into a special relationship with God.

2) The Judgment at the end of this Dispensation is inconsistent with the Judgments in the prior three Dispensations. For these Judgments are a series of ten judgments which are spread out

over an extended period of time, rather than a singular judgment.

First, let us address the issue of no new instructions for man to live by within this Dispensation. The initiation of the Dispensationalist's 4th Dispensation of Promise deals with the Covenant that God made with Abraham. Unlike the first three Dispensations, it does not contain a new format under which man must now live.

The second issue with the Dispensationalist's 4th Dispensation of Promise pertains to the Judgment that occurs at the conclusion of the Dispensation. For the Judgment that occurs at the end of the Age of Promise is very dissimilar to the Judgments that have occurred at the end of the prior three Dispensational Periods.

In the 1st Dispensation, the Judgment was declared and executed at one singular point in time. After the Fall, God declared that man would die from the poison that he had ingested (Genesis 2:17, 3:19), the ground would be cursed and require hard toil (Genesis 3:17-19), and the woman would be placed in subjection to the man in addition to having to now experience extreme pain in childbearing (Genesis 3:16). It was then that Adam and Eve received the Judgment of expulsion from the Garden (Genesis 3:23).

In the 2nd Dispensation, the Age of Conscience, the Judgment upon mankind also occurred at a singular point in time. All of mankind and nature who were outside of the Ark were destroyed by the Flood.

In the 3rd Dispensation, the Age of Human Government, Judgment was also carried out at a singular point in time. God confused the common language of the people into a multitude of languages, ensuring that man would have an extremely hard time uniting again in total opposition to Him. This Judgment also forced man to spread across the face of the earth, to "go forth and multiply", as they had been commanded to do at the start of the

Dispensation (Genesis 9:1,7).

When we come to the Judgment at the conclusion of the Age of Promise, we find an entirely different story. For the Judgment at the end of the Dispensationalist's Age of Promise is not a singular Judgment, but rather a series of ten Judgments placed upon Egypt over an expanded time period. These Judgments are completely "out of character" with the Judgments that had occurred at the conclusion of the prior three Dispensations. So, what do we make of this?

It is the contention of this study that the ten Judgments that were placed upon the nation of Egypt should not be considered as Judgments that signify an end to a Dispensational Age, for as we have seen, they are not "Dispensational" in nature. God is consistent in the methodology that He employs when executing His Judgments.

The purpose of the series of ten Judgments that were imposed upon Egypt was to punish Egypt for their mistreatment of the Hebrew people. For the better part of 400 years, the children of Abraham had been enslaved and mistreated by the Egyptians. That this enslavement would occur had been foretold to Abraham by God at the time of the initiation of God's dealings with Abraham (Genesis 15:13). At this time, God also told Abraham that He would Judge the nation that had enslaved them (Genesis 15:14). Hence, this Judgment should be considered as a fulfillment of God's Promise to Abraham, that He would, "Bless them that bless thee, and curse those that curse thee" (Genesis 12:3). The extended series of ten Judgments upon Egypt were not a Dispensational ending Judgment, but rather a fulfillment of God's oath to Abraham in the 12th Chapter of the Book of Genesis. Later, we shall see that at a future time in world history, God will once again employ an extended series of numerous Judgments to punish those who will have also engaged in the mistreatment of the Nation of Israel.

A Restructuring of Dispensational Periods

Now that we see that the period of the "Age of Promise" does not really constitute a separate and distinct Dispensational period, then we must conclude that this period of time from the call of Abraham until the giving of the Law must be included within what the Dispensationalists generally consider to be the 5th Dispensation, "The Age of the Law". This in turn would then make the 4th Dispensational Period to be more accurately and appropriately entitled, "The Age of Israel and the Law". In this change of venue, God would now speak to the world through a group of people, the nation of Israel. Through the nation of Israel, God would then give His strict and exacting moral Law by which mankind should ideally live.

In this restructuring of Dispensational Periods, we now have a total of six Dispensations. Knowing that in God's economy the number of completeness is seven, this calls for speculation as to just what the 7th Dispensation might be.

The most likely candidate for an additional Dispensation would be the 7-year period in which Israel will once again be God's representative upon the earth. This occurs after the removal of the Church at the time of the Rapture. This time period is often referred to as the "Time of Jacob's Trouble", or the "Great Tribulation Period". While traditional Dispensationalists typically include this 7-year Tribulation Period of time as part of the Church Age, or as a resumption of the "Age of the Law", we shall see that this 7-year period is within itself a separate and distinct Dispensational Period.

During the time period known as the 7-year Tribulation, man is placed under the direct rulership of Satan himself through his agents, the Anti-Christ and the False Prophet. This time period contains all three of the criteria needed to be a separate and distinct Dispensation. For in this period, man is given a new responsibility to live by, that being to decline to engage in an allegiance with Satan by refusing to accept the Mark of the Beast.

By taking the Mark of the Beast, men will be consigned to eternal damnation:

"And the third angel followed them, saying with a loud voice, If any man worship the beast and his image, and receive his mark in his forehead, or in his hand,

The same shall drink of the wine of the wrath of God, which is poured out without mixture into the cup of his indignation; and he shall be tormented with fire and brimstone in the presence of the holy angels, and in the presence of the Lamb:

And the smoke of their torment ascended up for ever and ever: and they have no rest day or night, who worship the beast and his image, and whosoever receiveth the mark of his name." Revelation 14:9-11

As in the days of Moses, there are a series of judgments that are carried out during the course of this Dispensation, but there is also a singular Judgment at the end of the 7-year period. This Judgment occurs after Jesus returns to the earth at the time of His 2nd Coming to set up His Millennial Kingdom. It is at this time that Jesus will gather together all of the survivors of the 7-year Tribulation period, and separate them into two groups, the sheep and the goats, to determine who will go with him into the Millennial Kingdom:

"When the Son of man shall come in his glory, and all the holy angels with him, then shall he sit upon the throne of his glory.

And before him shall be gathered all nations: and he shall separate them one from another, as a shepherd divideth his sheep from the goats." Matthew 25:31,32

The sheep shall be ushered into the 1,000-year reign of Christ, while the lives of the goats will be terminated until the end of the 1,000 years, at which time they shall be brought back to be judged at the Great White Throne Judgment.

It is of special interest to note that the 7-year Tribulation Dispensational Period shares a certain similarity with the 4th Dispensational age, the "Age of Israel and the Law". For within the Tribulation Period there is also a separate and extended series of Judgments. In the last 3 1/2 years of the 7-year Tribulation Period, we find God once again pouring out His wrath upon the world through a series of Judgments. In that these Judgments are numerous and carried out over an extended time period, they can be considered similar in nature to the series of ten Judgments that were brought upon Egypt in the days of Moses.

Therefore, this series of 21 Judgments that are initiated by the opening of the Seals (Revelation 5:1), followed by the blowing of the Trumpets (Revelation 8:2), and concluded by the pouring out of the Vials of God's Wrath (Revelation 15:1, 16:2), should be considered as a fulfillment of God's promise to Abraham within the Abrahamic Covenant, that He would "Bless those that bless thee, and curse those that curse thee" (Genesis 12:3).

Again, this series of Judgments that God brings upon the earth, are for the express purpose of judging the nations of the world for their mistreatment of the Jewish people.

There is also a degree of irony here regarding the adherents of Dispensational Theology. For although Dispensationalists have correctly recognized the "uniqueness" of Israel as being separate and distinct from the Church, they have failed to recognize the "uniqueness" of God's Judgments upon those who have wrongfully persecuted Israel. As we have seen, this in turn has caused Dispensationalists to make some severe errors in their delineation of the time periods that constitute the various Dispensational Ages.

The Judgment at the Conclusion of the Church Age

Another factor that must be considered is that some Dispensationalists would argue that if one makes the 7-year Tribulation Period a separate and distinct Dispensation, then the Church Age (Age of Grace) would not qualify as a Dispensation because there is no apparent Judgment meted out at its conclusion. However, when we consider the fact that when the Rapture occurs, not only is the Church removed from the earth, but so too is the restraining work of the Holy Spirit (II Thessalonians 2:7). This in and of itself will constitute a severe Judgment upon the earth. Not only will there be numerous driverless cars and pilotless airplanes creating havoc at the time of the Rapture, but even more damaging to the nations at large will be the fact that the world will be missing a large percentage of its hardest working and moral inhabitants. According to Jesus, this fact alone will render the world to be of little or no value:

"Ye are the salt of the earth: but if the salt have lost its savour, wherewith shall it be salted? It is thenceforth good for nothing, but to be cast out, and to be trodden under foot of men." Matthew 5:13

Without the presence of believers on the earth along with the restraining ministry of the Holy Spirit, the world will soon devolve into a full expression of the sinful nature of mankind. When we couple this with the fact that the world government system will be openly run by the Devil himself, we can then see that the Rapture of the Church will indeed be a massive Divine Judgment placed upon the earth and its inhabitants.

Given these facts, it would then seem to indicate that a more appropriate and accurate rendering of the seven Dispensations would be as follows:

1) The Age of Innocence (Genesis 1:1 – 3:7)

Adam and Eve were placed in the Garden of Eden and given one restriction, that they were not to eat of the tree of the knowledge of good and evil. After their failure which we know as the Fall, God judged them by expelling them from the Garden.

194

2) The Age of Conscience (Genesis 3:8 – 8:22)

After the expulsion from the Garden, mankind was left to live by the dictates of his own conscience. The results were disastrous. The whole earth became a place of corruption, and God had to destroy all of mankind excepting Noah, his family, and the old natural order by means of the Flood.

3) The Age of Human Government (Genesis 9:1 – 11:32)

After Noah and his family left the Ark to repopulate the earth (Genesis 9:1), God also ordained that men would have policing power over their fellow man (Genesis 9:6), thus instituting human government. The results of mankind living under less than a strict moral code however ended with mankind once again engaging in total rebellion against God. Instead of following God's command to go forth and repopulate the earth, mankind instead congregated together and constructed the Tower of Babel in blatant opposition to what God had commanded. God judged this effort by bringing upon them a confusion of speech. This in turn forced mankind to disband into separate groups and spread across the face of the earth.

4) The Age of Israel and the Law (Genesis 12:1 – Acts 2:4)

With the call of Abraham and the birth of the nation of Israel, God now had His nation of representatives to the world. With the trials they had experienced in Egypt, the Hebrew people had begun to develop their own national identity.

Soon after their departure from Egypt, God gave Israel and the world a strict moral code to live by, initiated by the giving of the Ten Commandments on Mount Sinai. History shows that neither Israel nor the world were successful in keeping the edicts of the Law. This Dispensational Period ended in 30 A.D., with the final Judgment of "The Age of Israel and the Law" suspended for a period of 40 years, at which time the Roman armies of Titus destroyed Jerusalem and scattered the Jewish people across the face of the earth in 70 A.D.

5) The Age of the Church (Acts 2:4 – I Corinthians 15:52)

The Age of the Church begins soon after the crucifixion of Jesus, at the Feast of Pentecost. While Dispensationalists call this period the "Age of Grace", this title is misleading, for God has always saved his people by means of His grace, "...Abraham believed God, and it was counted unto him for righteousness" (Romans 4:3). To name this period the "Age of Grace" is to wrongfully imply that salvation was accomplished by something other than God's grace in the prior Dispensational Ages.

In the Age of the Church, mankind is given instructions to, "Believe in the LORD Jesus Christ and thou shalt be saved...." (Acts 16:31), and was shown how one should best live their life by following the perfect example set by Jesus Christ, "He that saith he abideth in him ought himself also so to walk, even as he walked" (I John 2:6).

The Church Age Concludes with the Judgment of the Rapture of the Church

After the Rapture, the nation of Israel will once again be God's representatives to the world. Now for seven years, mankind will have to live under the direct rule of Satan through his agents the Anti-Christ and the False Prophet. No longer will the social fabric of the world enjoy the benefits of the restraining power of the Holy Spirit or of the moral presence of the Church.

6) The Age of the Rebirth of Israel and the Rule of Satan (I Corinthians 15:52–Revelation 20:3)

The Age of the 7-Year Tribulation begins with the Rapture of the Church. Since the time of Abraham, God has always had His own representatives to the world, either in the form of the Hebrew people, or the Church of Christ. The Rapture of the Church signifies that once again the nation of Israel shall be

God's representatives to the world. This Age is also referred to in Scripture as, "The time of Jacob's Trouble" (Jeremiah 30:7). During these seven years, man is instructed to refrain from swearing allegiance to Satan by taking the "Mark of the Beast" (Revelation 20:4). Man is also told that he must now endure the many trials and troubles that will come to him until the end of the 7-year time period (Matthew 24:13).

During the last 3 1/2 years of this 7-year period, the world endures a series of 21 horrendous Judgments for their mistreatment of the nation of Israel. This period then culminates with the 2nd Coming of Jesus Christ back to the earth.

After Christ arrives, there is a Judgment that marks the end of this Dispensation. In this Judgment, the sheep (those "who have endured to the end") will be separated from the goats (those who have taken the "Mark of the Beast"). The goats will be removed for a later Judgment which will occur at the Great White Throne, while the sheep shall enter Christ's Millennial Kingdom.

7) The Age of the Rule of Christ (The Millennial Kingdom)

In this age, mankind is ordered to live under the direct ruling domain of the LORD Jesus Christ. After 1,000 years of unprecedented prosperity and happiness, where the "plowman over takes the reaper" (Amos 9:13), and nature once again becomes Edenic as evidenced by the fact that, ".... The lion shall eat straw like the ox" (Isaiah 11:7), we find mankind once again rebelling against God. God judges this final rebellion by raining fire down upon the rebels (Revelation 20:9).

After this Dispensational ending Judgment, we then have the Great White Throne Judgment, wherein the deeds of men shall be examined from within the framework of these seven Biblical Dispensations.

The Ultimate Purpose of Dispensations

In order to better understand what Scripture is attempting to teach the believer by dividing history into seven different periods or Dispensations, it is necessary to answer the question, "What is the ultimate purpose of these different epochs of time that we refer to as "Dispensations"? While some Dispensationalists may argue that the purpose of the Dispensations is to show that man in his sinful nature is forever antagonistic towards God, it is the contention of this writer that God's Purposes in the various Dispensations go far beyond this simple but true assessment.

To begin, we know that God does nothing in vain (Isaiah 45:18), and that all things in history proceed along a path that is paved to accomplish His purposes.

"The LORD of hosts hath sworn saying, Surely as I have thought, so shall it come to pass; and as I have purposed, so shall it stand:" Isaiah 14:24

"...who worketh all things after the counsel of his own will." Ephesians 1:11

When we are reading a book and trying to ascertain what the message that the author is trying to convey to us, it is sometimes helpful to go to the back of the book and look for any possible clues or conclusions (anyone who has had to write a quick last minute book report in high school will attest to this fact!). The same often holds true when it comes to studying the Bible. When we go to the last actions of human history before the initiation of the eternal state, we find ourselves at the Great White Throne Judgment. Scripture tells us that at the conclusion of the Great White Throne Judgment, after all of mankind has witnessed the many mistakes and failures of all peoples throughout the ages within the framework of the seven Dispensations of world history, that all of mankind, both saint and sinner alike, will bow down and declare that, "Jesus Christ is Lord!". This fact is confirmed in both the Old and the New Testaments (Isaiah 45:23, Philippians 2:10,11).

When we examine the statement, "Jesus Christ is Lord", it is not a far stretch to say that the message this statement is conveying is, "Jesus Christ has the right to rule." From this it becomes obvious as to what God may indeed have been doing by dividing history into seven distinct time periods. For we can see that within each separate Dispensation, not only has man shown himself to be antagonistic towards God, but mankind has also been given the opportunity to successfully "rule himself" from within the context of seven different formats. History has shown and will show that no matter what Dispensational time frame or format that man finds himself in, he is incapable of successfully governing himself, hence the universal statement that is made by both saved and unsaved alike at the conclusion of the Great White Throne Judgment, that "Jesus Christ has the right to rule."

"Jesus Christ is Lord"

When we view Dispensations from the perspective that their purpose was to allow mankind an opportunity to successfully rule himself from within the context of seven different time frames, then the following explanation as to what was occurring during the seven Dispensational Ages comes into focus.

In the 1st Dispensation, man was given the perfect environment of the Garden of Eden, meaningful work (naming the animals and dressing and keeping the Garden, Genesis 2:15-20), in addition to enjoying a perfect love life (Genesis 2:22, 25). Yet he failed to properly govern himself and had to be expelled from the Garden.

Next in the 2nd Dispensation, man was given the opportunity to rule himself from the governance of his own conscience, which resulted in the total corruption of mankind, and the Judgment of the Flood in the days of Noah.

Now, in the 3rd Dispensation, God initiated the era of Human Governance (Genesis 9:4-6). Here man was given the chance to rule successfully through his own human government. This endeavor also failed as it found mankind disobeying God by refusing to spread out over the face of the earth and create self-governing societies. Instead, man chose to stay put and construct the Tower of Babel. God then judged mankind by confusing the common language of the time in order to force man to spread out over the face of the earth.

In the 4th Dispensation, God chose to speak to the world through Abraham and his descendants and provided a perfect Law under which man could successfully learn to rule over his own life. Again, this resulted time and time again in the failure of the Jewish people to follow this Law and ended with the Judgment of the destruction of Jerusalem in 70 A.D., after which the people of Israel were dispersed amongst the nations of this world.

In the 5th Dispensation, God chose to speak to the world through the Church, which was comprised of both Jewish and Gentile believers in Christ. The message of the Church was not only one of having a relationship with God in time by God's grace through faith, but also one of following the example of successful living set forth by God's Son, Jesus Christ. Again, mankind failed, as the majority of people of this age neither came to God for His free gift of Salvation, nor did they pay heed to the selfless example of a Perfect life, as exhibited by His Son Jesus Christ. The history of the Church age is a history of constant wars and selfish behavior exhibited by both the redeemed and unredeemed alike. The end of this age culminates with the Judgment of the Rapture of the Church.

In the 6th Dispensation, mankind will be given the opportunity to successfully rule himself under the reign of God's counterpart, Satan. Again, this venue will result in such chaos and failure that the Scripture states, "That unless those days be shortened, that no flesh would survive" (Matthew 24:22). This age will culminate with the Second Coming of Christ back to the Earth, at which time He will Judge the earth to see who amongst the living inhabitants of the earth will be brought into His Millennial Kingdom.

In the 7th and final Dispensation, man will again be afforded the opportunity to successfully rule himself under the Headship of the King of Kings, Jesus Christ. The curse against the environment will be removed, resulting in a tremendous prosperity wherein the "reaper will overtake the plower" (Amos 9:13). In addition to this, Nature will no longer exhibit hostility (Isaiah 11:6,7). Although righteousness, prosperity, and happiness will have prevailed for a period of 1,000 years, mankind will once again fail to successfully rule over his inclinations and will rebel against Jesus' authority at the end of the Millennium. This final rebellion will be quickly put down by the Lord (Revelation 20:9).

At this time, the rebels will be brought together with all the rebels from the prior Dispensations, at the Great White Throne Judgment of God. Again, it is here, after observing mankind's failed attempts at successfully ruling himself during the seven Dispensations, that all of mankind, both saint and sinner alike, will be forced to Universally proclaim that, "Jesus Christ has the right to rule over mankind", ("Every knee shall bow", and "every tongue confess that Jesus Christ is Lord" Philippians 2:10,11).

To these facts of human history, it must be asked, "Why was this grand display of seven Dispensations ultimately necessary?" If we appeal to Scripture, we read that, "All things are done for the sake of the believer in Christ" (II Cor. 4:15), and "All things are performed for the benefit of the believer" (Psalm 57:2). It can therefore be surmised that God, in His foreknowledge, knew that if He had created man and not given mankind every opportunity to successfully rule himself from within the various Dispensational scenarios and environments, that the Believer in eternity would have been forever nagged by the question, "Do we really need to have this Man, Jesus Christ, and the other members of the Godhead, the Father and the Holy Spirit, to rule over us? Could we be better served by being autonomous?"

With such a question at the back of a believer's mind during an eternal existence in Heaven, it can be ascertained that such an existence would be anything but "Heavenly". For without the experiences of the seven Dispensations, it is highly probable that a free will being such as man would be continually nagged by this question of whether the eternal Lordship of Christ over his life was totally necessary.

In the final analyses, the seven Dispensations were instituted within the framework of human history for the sake of the believer in eternity. God framed the history of the salvation of man into seven Dispensational Periods not only to expose the effects of sin, but more importantly, to fully exhibit to the believer in eternity, that Jesus Christ does indeed have, "The Right to Rule".

By incorporating the Seven Dispensations in His Plan for mankind, God the Father has freed believers from ever having to doubt the necessity of the Rule of Christ over their lives while living in the eternal state. What a truly Wonderful God He is that we serve!

What Occurs Between Death and Resurrection

*"What happens to a person in between the time of death and the
Resurrection"*

In Christendom, there is typically much confusion and
disagreement as to what happens to a person in the time lapse
between the moment they die, and when they are brought back
to life at the time of God's Resurrection. In the 4,000 years of
recorded history prior to the Coming of Christ into the world,
there were many different thoughts as to the whereabouts of the
departed souls from the earth. While some maintained that the
dead enter into a state of "soul sleep", others believed that they
either go to a "temporary heaven" or to special compartments in
the underworld known as "Sheol" ("Hades"), Abraham's Bosom,
or "Paradise".

"For thou wilt not leave my soul in Sheol (Hades), neither wilt
thou allow Thy Holy One to see corruption." Psalm 16:10 DBS

"And it came to pass that the beggar died, and was carried by
the angels into Abraham's Bosom; the rich man also died and was
buried;

And in hell he lifted up his eyes, being in torments, and seeth
Abraham afar off, and Lazarus in his bosom." Luke 16:22,23

"And Jesus said unto him (the thief on the cross), Verily I say
unto thee, Today shalt thou be with me in Paradise." Luke 23:43

In New Testament times, the whereabouts of the departed
are also believed to be in one of the priorly mentioned abodes,

excepting now the departed have the additional hope in the promise from Paul in his 2nd letter to the Corinthians, that wherever they are, they will be with Jesus: "To be absent from the body is to be present with the Lord" (II Corinthians 5:8).

However, all these dwellings of the departed as they wait for the emergence of the "eternal state", carry with them some form of logistical problem. Problems such as, "What kind of bodies do the departed possess while they are awaiting their new eternal resurrection bodies?" or, "What will happen to these temporal abodes when the eternal state begins?", in addition to, "What do the departed do with all of their time if they are not in a condition of soul sleep, but rather in limbo?"

There is another approach however, that can be taken in order to deal with these inherent resurrection problems, and that is the realization that these many varied and different heavenly abodes may not be intended to be taken as literal places. This takes a little explaining.

The Language of Accommodation

There are numerous occurrences in Scripture where God's Word uses figurative as opposed to literal examples in order to better convey His message to our finite way of thinking. This is called the "Language of Accommodation". One aspect of this "language of accommodation" is attributing human physical characteristics to God. These assignments of human physical characteristics to God are called "anthropomorphisms".

As an example, in II Chronicles 16:9 we read, "For the "eyes" of the LORD run to and fro throughout the whole earth ...". Obviously, there are not two literal eyeballs constantly scouring the face of the earth, as the statement is made in an anthropomorphic manner in order to convey in human terms, that God is aware of all that goes on in and around the earth.

204

As another example, when Scripture wants to express the fact that some aspects of God's efforts are more difficult for Him to accomplish than others, it again resorts to using anthropomorphic terms. We are told by the Psalmist that the work of Creation was a relatively easy thing for the LORD to perform, being merely the "work of His fingers", "When I consider thy heavens, the work of thy fingers, the moon and the stars, which thou hast ordained" (Psalm 8:3).

Judgment, however, necessitated the whole hand of God, "Remove thy stroke away from me: I am consumed by the blow of Thine hand" (Psalm 39:10).

We are then told that Salvation was a much more difficult thing for God to accomplish, requiring the use of His whole arm:

"Thou hast with thine arm redeemed thy people, the sons of Jacob and Joseph." Psalm 77:15

Another way that Scripture employs the language of accommodation is by anthropomorphically assigning to God some human emotion. This is done in order that we might better understand both God's Personage and His ways in dealing with man. An example of this would be when Scripture attributes the emotion of "anger" to God:

"For his anger endureth but for a moment; in his favor is life..." Psalm 29:5

Now we know from Scripture that there is nothing that man can do to spoil God's happiness:

"And it shall come to pass, that as the Lord rejoiced over you to do you good, and to multiply you; so the LORD will rejoice over you to destroy you, and to bring you to nought;..." Deuteronomy 28:65

"Who changed the truth of God into a lie, and worshipped

and served the creature more than the Creator, who is "blessed forever". Amen." Romans 1:25

In other words, there really is nothing that mankind can do, that would spoil God's happiness by making Him angry in the human sense. So why does Scripture assign to God this human emotion? God's Word ascribes the human emotion of anger to God in order to better convey to mankind, using human terms, that they have in some way violated God's System of Justice.

So, one might ask, "Why would God find it necessary to employ figurative concepts of heaven within Scripture? The answer to this question is that presently there are two separate and distinct worlds or realities that are existing simultaneously. These realities are the world of the spirit, where God resides, and the world of the physical, where we as humans reside. While God can certainly understand the physical world where time exists as a 4th dimension, we as humans typically have a difficult time relating to God's reality wherein the past, present, and future are all experienced as one. For in God's reality, there is no need of incorporating time in the same sense that we as humans experience it. There is no past, present, and future as we know it in the world of eternity or spirit.

Albert Einstein, when discussing the relationship between the physical temporal and the spiritual eternal worlds regarding his well respected Theory of Relativity, stated, "If you don't take my words too seriously, before the Theory of Relativity, if you removed all of the physical matter from the Universe, then time would still exist. But now after the development of the Theory of Relativity, if you removed all the physical matter from the Universe, then time would no longer exist, for it would have no function."

As the great theologian Augustine stated with remarkable insight, "God did not create the Universe at some point in time, but rather He created the physical Universe along with time."

So again, we see that there are two separate and distinct worlds that are existing simultaneously, the spiritual world and the physical world, with each world possessing its own reality. In the spiritual world, time as we know it here on earth in the physical world, does not exist. Scripture tells us that, "...all things, (including the past, present, and future), are naked and opened unto the eyes of him with whom we have to do" (Hebrews 4:13). With God, past, present, and future are experienced as an ongoing "present" event. This is how Scripture can state that the realities of the Crucifixion were known immediately unto God from the moment of the Creation of the Universe:

"And all that dwell upon the earth shall worship him, whose names are not written in the book of life of the Lamb slain from the foundation of the world." Rev. 13:8

While we as humans need to wait for time to unfold in order to know the future, in God's reality, past, present, and future all meld into one. In the Book of Ecclesiastes, we are told that with God:

"That which hath been is now; and that which is to be, hath already been..." Ecclesiastes 3:15

The reality in which we as humans live is quite different from God's reality. For we live our lives encased within a strict consciousness of the present. The future is totally unknown to us, and the past oftentimes is merely a fading memory. With God in the spiritual world, the totality of the physical world, both the past, present, and future, are in a sense, "one event".

On numerous occasions, Scripture recognizes the existence of both of these two worlds in addition to their differences when it comes to their concepts of time. In John 4:23, where Jesus is talking to the woman at the well, we read:

"But the hour cometh, and now is, when the true worshippers shall worship the Father in spirit and in truth: for the Father seeketh such to worship him."

207

Here we have Jesus explaining to the woman at the well, that from her perspective, there will be a future time wherein the true worshippers of God the Father will worship Him in both spirit and in truth ("the hour is coming"). But from the eternal perspective, or world of the spirit, that reality already exists ("and now is").

Later, in the Book of John, we find Jesus talking with Martha soon after the death of her brother Lazarus. After Martha had in a sense scolded Jesus for allowing her brother to die ("Lord if you hadst been here, my brother had not died" John 11:21), Jesus, always the gentleman, had informed Martha that death was merely a matter of perspective. He comforts her by telling her that from her point of view, that though her brother has died, he shall one day again live, "...... he that believeth in me, though he were dead, yet shall he live" (John 11:25). He then goes on to say that from the perspective of Lazarus, that he is still fully alive and conscious, "Whosoever liveth and believeth in me shall never die" (John 11:26).

In other words, when Lazarus or any other believer dies, they experience no loss of consciousness, but rather step out of this temporal world and go immediately into the eternal world. Stated another way, "When a believer leaves the reality of this world, he or she steps out of this reality of the physical (which is bound and limited by time), and immediately goes into the reality of the eternal world, where time is no longer a limiting factor."

The Apostle Paul addressed this issue when he stated in II Corinthians 5:8, "that to be absent from this body is to be present with the Lord". When one steps out of this present world, which is governed and limited by time, we step into a world or existence of "timelessness".

From the perspective of eternity, we can see that all New Testament believers in a sense die simultaneously, the only difference being a matter of "sequencing". Paul addresses this fact in I Thessalonians 4:16, 17:

208

"For the Lord himself shall descend from heaven with a shout, with the voice of the archangel, and with the trump of God: and the dead in Christ shall rise first:

Then we which are alive and remain shall be caught up "together" with them in the clouds, to meet the Lord in the air: and so shall we ever be with the Lord."

Here Scripture clearly indicates that during the Church Age (the time between Christ's Crucifixion and the Rapture of the Church at the time of Jesus' invisible 2nd Coming), all believers at the moment of their death will be immediately transported in time to meet the Lord in the air. Although all New Testament Saints die over an extended period of time, from the perspective of eternity, they in essence all die at the same time. That the dead in Christ are said to "rise first" is merely a matter of sequencing.

To this, one might ask, what about the Old Testament Saints? Are there any verses in Scripture that would indicate they too go through this experience of immediate "time travel" to their appointed place in the Resurrection? The answer to this question is a resounding "Yes", for the book of Job also states that, "all flesh shall perish together..." (Job 34:15). Again, to better understand how this works, we must realize that the "Resurrection" is not a single moment in time event, but rather a "program" or series of events.

God's Resurrection Program

When we study Scripture, we find that "The Resurrection" occurs over a period of time, and more accurately should be called, "God's Resurrection Program".

We are told in Scripture that the initiation of this program or first phase is Jesus' resurrection from the dead:

"But every man in his own order: Christ the firstfruits; afterward they that are alive at his coming." I Corinthians 15:23

The second phase of the resurrection is the Rapture of the Church. This occurs at the end of the Church Age and immediately before the Tribulation Period. At this time, all Church Age believers, both those who have died since the time of Jesus and those who are still alive, will be simultaneously caught up into the air and brought to Heaven by Jesus. Then in heaven, while the inhabitants of the earth are experiencing the 7 Year Tribulation Period, the Church Age believers will be judged at the Judgment Seat of Christ. After this they shall be formally wed to Jesus Christ at the Marriage Supper of the Lamb, before returning to the earth with Jesus at the time of His physical Second Coming back to the earth.

Next comes the third phase of the Resurrection Program, the resurrection of the Old Testament Saints at the time of Jesus' 2nd Coming at the end of the Tribulation Period.

This will then be followed by a fourth phase of the Resurrection Program at the end of the Millennial Reign of Christ on the earth, at the Great White Throne Judgment. It is here that all the unbelievers throughout all the ages will be brought before the Great White Throne to be judged. Those who have been born into the Millennial Kingdom and come to faith in Christ shall also be judged at this time.

So, we see that there are at least four points in time where those who have died will be transported into God's Resurrection Program.

Time Travel

Scripture does indeed address the issue of time travel for both Old Testament and New Testament believers. In Jude 1:14, we have the vision of Enoch: "Behold, the Lord cometh with ten thousands of his saints." In that Enoch was an Old Testament Saint (just the seventh generation since Adam), his vision fits perfectly with the initiation of the third phase of God's Resurrection Program, the resurrection of the Old Testament Saints at the time of Christ's 2nd Coming back to the earth. It is not altogether unlikely that Enoch's vision was a vision of when and where he would one day be transported to after his final departure from earth.

In the New Testament, Jesus demonstrated His ability to "eclipse time" in the sixth chapter of the Book of John. Here we read that after Jesus had shown His power over nature by first walking on the water, after which He had also exhibited His ability to bypass the passage of time. For we are told that after He had entered into the disciple's boat, the boat and its inhabitants were "immediately" transported safely back to land, although the boat had been three to four miles out to sea (John 6: 19-21).

This being said, it is not at all a stretch to consider that the places of habitation that the Old Testament Saints are said to reside in while awaiting their place in the Resurrection Program of God (Paradise, Abraham's Bosom, Hades, et al), could merely be examples of the language of accommodation. These compart-ments may well be fictional places that Scripture uses to assuage the concerns of believers for their departed loved ones, rather than attempt to explain to ancient man concepts of physics which they would have extreme difficulties in relating to. Today, with all the advances that Science has made in the understanding of the Universe, our modern mindset really has a much easier time understanding the concept of "time travel". Before Einsteinian Physics however, time travel would have been almost completely foreign to the minds of almost all people(s).

In the final analyses, the aforementioned compartments for the dead in the afterlife may indeed be literal existing places, but due to the fact that we know from New Testament Revelation that God has the ability to eclipse time ("Then they willingly received him into the ship: and immediately the ship was at the land whither they went" John 6:21), there certainly is no apparent necessity for the existence of these places or compartments. They may in fact function solely for the purpose of easing the minds of both Old and New Testament believers in their concern for their departed loved ones from this earth.

A New Look at the Book of Job

"The Book of Job is primarily concerned with the unsolved mystery as to why there is so much suffering in the world"

The Book of Job is probably one of the most misunderstood Books of the Bible. Many Biblical commentators view the book as a treatise on the unjust sufferings of life in general, Job's life in particular. The editors of the Encyclopedia Britannica state: "The theme of the Book of Job is the eternal problem of unmerited suffering."

Halley's Bible Handbook also states that the subject of the Book of Job is:

"The problem of human suffering. Very early in history men began to be troubled over the awful inequalities and injustices of life: how a good God could make a world like this, where there is so much suffering, and so much of the suffering seems to fall on those who least deserve it."

To this, Pastor Greg Boyd adds, "The point of the Book of Job is to teach us that the mystery of evil is a mystery of a war-torn and unfathomably complex creation, not the mystery of God's all controlling will."

In almost all commentaries on the Book of Job, we find these references to the "mystery" of "unmerited human suffering". Pastor Boyd even implies that the interpretation of the Book of Job is too difficult for us as humans to understand, as Job's sufferings were due to the extreme complexities of evil within God's creation and are in no way to be attributed to the sovereign will of God.

What these commentaries appear to have in common is the fact that they fail to recognize that evil is just as much a part of God's Plan for our fallen world as is good.

In the Book of Isaiah, we read:

"I form the light and create darkness: I make peace, and create evil: I the LORD do all these things." Isaiah 45:7

The Book of Amos states:

".... Shall there be evil in a city, and the LORD hath not done it?" Amos 3:6

Evil is often equated with sin in the pages of Scripture. Some prime examples of this include the following verses:

"So shall ye say unto Joseph, Forgive, I pray thee now, the trespass of thy brethren, and their sin; for they did unto thee evil: ..." Genesis 50:17

"And after all that is come upon us for our evil deeds, and for our great trespass, seeing that our God hast punished us less than our iniquities deserve, and hast given us such deliverance as this;" Ezra 9:13

"Be not wise in thine own eyes: fear the Lord, and depart from evil." Proverbs 3:7

However, as we have learned in a prior study, evil is also often to be viewed within the framework of God's Word from a historical perspective. Within a historical perspective, an action is deemed to be either "good" or "evil", simply by the effect that the action has upon the recipient of the action. There are really no moral implications involved.

In this context, it can be observed that God often uses "evil" to accomplish His purposes. In the Book of Exodus, we find Moses pleading with God not to chastise Israel with evil (Exodus 32:12).

214

Later in the Old Testament, we find Joshua warning the Hebrew people that the LORD would bring "evil" upon them should they choose to ignore His ways and live in sinful rebellion against Him:

"Therefore it shall come to pass, that as all good things are come upon you, which the LORD your God promised you; so shall the LORD bring upon you all evil things, until He has destroyed you from off this good land which the LORD your God has given you." Joshua 23:15

In the Book of Judges, we find the LORD chastising the Hebrew people with evil when they had forsaken Him:

"Whithersoever they went out, the hand of the LORD was against them for evil, as the LORD had said, and as the LORD had sworn unto them: and they were greatly distressed." Judges 2:15

In the Book of Samuel, we even find God sending an evil spirit upon Saul (I Samuel 18:10).

Later in the Book of Nehemiah, we read, "... did not our God bring all this evil upon us, and upon this city? ..." (Nehemiah 13:18).

The prophet Micah brought these words of condemnation towards God's chosen people: "For the inhabitant of Maroth waited carefully for good: but evil came down from the LORD unto the gate of Jerusalem." Micah 1:12

In the case of Job, Scripture informs us that all of the evil that had befallen Job, had come directly from the hand of God:

"Then came unto him all his brethren, and all his sisters, and all they that had been of his acquaintance before, and did eat bread with him in his house: and they bemoaned him, and comforted him over all the evil that the LORD had brought upon him..." Job 42:10

As we have learned in a prior chapter, good and evil in God's Word are typically to be considered as events viewed from a historical perspective, while righteousness and wickedness are terms that are used when actions are viewed from a moral perspective. While Scripture teaches that God uses evil to accomplish His ends, the Word of God never states at any time that God ever engages in wickedness (Job 34:12).

Contrary to common opinion within Christendom, not only does God use evil to accomplish his ends, but He also maintains sovereign control over all the events of human history. Romans 11:36 tells us, "That of Him, and through Him, and to Him, are all things...", that God is indeed sovereign over all that occurs in the world around us.

The "evils" that God brings upon his chosen people are to be regarded as chastisements or sufferings that He brings in order to refine and purify them. David states in Psalm 119:71, that, "It is good for me that I have been afflicted, that I might learn thy statutes." It is through suffering that God first gets the attention of the believer, and then through the work of the Holy Spirit, refines and purifies the believer to be more like Jesus. According to Scripture, suffering is an integral aspect of the Christian life. The Book of Hebrews states:

"For whom the Lord loveth he chasteneth, and scourgeth every son whom he receiveth." Hebrews 12:6

The writer of the Book of Hebrews then goes on to say:

"If ye endure chastening, God dealeth with you as sons; for what son is he whom the father chasteneth not? But if ye be without chastisement, whereof all are partakers, then are ye bastards and not sons.

Furthermore, we have had fathers of our flesh which corrected us, and we gave them reverence: Shall we not much rather be in subjection unto the Father of spirits and live?

For they verily for a few days chasteneth us after their own pleasure: but He for our profit, that we might be partakers of his holiness.

Now no chastening for the present seemeth to be joyous, but grievous: nevertheless afterward it yieldeth the peaceable fruit of righteousness unto them which are exercised thereby." Hebrews 12:7-11

Christendom it seems, needs to be reminded that everything that comes into the life of God's children, be it good or evil, comes through His loving and caring Hands. God's chastisements are not solely for eternal benefits, but are also meant to increase the believers' happiness while here on earth "...happy is the man whom God correcteth" (Job 5:17).

An Overview of the Book of Job

While the Book of Job is one of the most misunderstood books of the Bible, it is at the same time one of the most respected books in the history of literature. It is held in high regard in many literary circles for the depth of thought that it contains. Victor Hugo called the Book of Job "...perhaps the greatest masterpiece of the human mind."

Tradition tells us that the setting for the Book of Job, the Land of UZ, is in a fertile area east of the Sea of Galilee. The exact time period of Job's life is not known, but many believe that Job was an early descendant of Abraham. Job was an extremely wealthy and prosperous person in his day and age. In addition to having seven sons and three daughters, we are told that Job also possessed 7,000 sheep, 3,000 camels, 500 yoke of oxen, and 500 she asses and a large house of attendant servants. Job was recognized as being "the greatest of all men of the east" (Job 1:2,3). This however, was soon about to change.

We are told that one day in heaven, Satan had returned from roaming about the earth, and had presented himself to the LORD. God asked Satan if he had, "considered his servant Job, that there is none like him in the earth, a perfect and upright man, one that feareth God, and escheweth evil?" (Job 1:8). Satan replied to God that if He would remove the hedge of protection that He had built around him, and take away his wealth and possessions, that Job would curse God to His face. God then gave Satan leave to destroy all of Job's wealth excepting his person. Soon thereafter, the Sabeans came and stole Job's 500 yoke of oxen and 500 she asses, killing their attendant servants. Next a "fire of God" came down and burned up Job's 7,000 sheep along with their attendants. In the same day, news came to Job that the Chaldeans had come and stolen his 3,000 camels, and in the process had also killed Job's servants who had been attending them.

Finally, immediately after Job had received the news about his camels, he got word that a great wind had come up and brought down the house in which his ten children were enjoying a meal, killing them all (Job 1:19). We are then told that Job's reaction was to fall to the ground, and worship God. That he did not sin by making charges or accusations against God (Job 1:22).

The main body of the rest of the Book of Job is largely concerned with discussions between Job and his three friends; Eliphaz, Bildad, and Zophar, and a man named Elihu. Job's three friends all argue that suffering is sent to men as a punishment for their sins. They then infer that there must be some secret sin in Job's life. Job's reactions to the arguments of his three friends is one of disdain, declaring, "Miserable comforters are ye all" (Job 16:2).

Job then pleads his case, stating that he had not placed his wealth above God in his life (Job 32:24,25), that he had not rejoiced at the destruction of those who had hated him (Job 32:29,30), and he had always shown hospitality to those in need (Job 32:32). In Job's mind, there was seemingly no reason for the numerous tragedies that had befallen him.

Later Elihu argues that these calamities that have plagued Job should be seen not so much as a punishment for his sins, but rather as a means to keep Job from sinning. That Job's calamities were sent by God to be corrective rather than punitive.

Finally, after all of the human reasoning seeking to understand Job's sufferings had been exhausted, God steps in at the end of the book, and confronts Job, declaring:

"Who is this that darkeneth counsel by words without knowledge?

Gird up now thy loins like a man; for I will demand of thee, and answer thou me.

Where was thou when I laid the foundations of the earth? Declare, if thou hast understanding." Job 38: 2-4

God then continues with a whole litany of remarks to Job indicating that men with their finite minds should neither question God's ways, nor should they totally expect to understand all that He is doing in His governance of the Universe.

To this a now repentant Job replies to God:

"I know that Thou canst do every thing, and that no thought can be withholden from Thee.

Who is he that hideth counsel without knowledge? Therefore have I uttered what I understood not; things too wonderful for me, which I knew not.

Hear, I beseech Thee, and I will speak: I will demand of Thee, and declare Thou unto me.

I have heard of Thee by the hearing of the ear: but now my eye seeth Thee.

Wherefore I abhor myself, and repent in dust and ashes." Job 42:2-6

Next, we are told that after Job had prayed for his friends, that God had not only restored all of Job's possessions, but indeed had doubled them (Job 42:10). Now Job had 14,000 sheep, 6,000 camels, 1,000 yoke of oxen, and 1,000 she asses, in addition to seven more sons and three more daughters.

As an interesting aside, many have claimed that Scripture is in error here reasoning that if God had truly doubled all that Job had, then Job would have been granted twenty more offspring, and not ten. However, because the spirit of man is not the same as the spirit of animals (Ecclesiastes 3:21), it should be recognized that God had indeed doubled Job's offspring, because his original 10 children still existed in the heavens ("To be absent from the body is to be face to face with the Lord." II Corinthians 5:8). A wonderful Biblical truth indeed!

The Real Lesson of the Book of Job

Now we must ask the question, of what sin was Job guilty of, that it should require such severe chastisement in his life? When we examine the life of Job, there does not immediately appear to be any overt sin that he was engaging in.

We see from Job's statements that he was a true student of God's Word and Ways. After all his sufferings had come upon him, and Job's wife had told him to "Curse God and die" (Job 2:9), his response showed that he completely understood the theological concept of Good and Evil, for Job replied to his wife, "Thou speaketh as one of the foolish women speaketh, What? Shall we receive good at the Hand of God, and shall we not receive evil" (Job 2:10)? Unlike many of our modern theologians, Job knew that the concept of evil was often to be viewed from a historical rather than a moral perspective. That God is perfectly just in employing evil in the perfecting of His children.

We also see that in his calamities, Job correctly understood the

220

Sovereign Hand of God in his life, for Job stated, "...Naked came I out of my mother's womb, and naked shall I return thither: the LORD gave, and the LORD hath taken away; blessed be the name of the LORD" (Job 1:21).

Finally, long before Paul wrote the Book of Romans, we see that Job also understood the Biblical principle of Romans 8:28, that God works all things in the life of believers together for their eventual good, for we are told that when his troubles befell him, Job fell face down on the ground and worshipped God (Job 1:20).

We now can see that:

1) Job was not engaged in any overt sins.

2) Job was a real student of God's Word and Ways, that he was fulfilling the admonition that Paul had later spelled out in II Timothy 2:15, that is, to "Rightly divide the word of truth, that he might be a workman that needeth not to be ashamed."

So why, we must now ask, was Job coming under such severe discipline in his life? Again, often times, the answer to understanding the mysteries found within a book, are spelled out at the end of the book. This certainly is the case in the Book of Job. For when we "go to the back of the book", we are told that God does not take His Hand of Judgment off of Job until Job had "prayed for his friends" (Job 42:10). It is only when Job finally exhibited a heartfelt care and concern for his friends that we can begin to see what God was doing by bringing all of these afflictions into Job's life.

Although Job was outwardly an exemplary believer, (not engaging in sinful acts, and was a keen student of God and His ways), there was an area in his life in which he had been "weighed and found wanting." This was in the area of true love and compassion for others. The Apostle Paul deals with this issue in his first letter to the Corinthians where he writes:

"Though I speak with the tongues of men and of angels, and have not charity, I am become as sounding brass, or a tinkling bell." I Corinthians 13:1

According to God's Word, that if we follow all aspects of the Christian walk to a "T", and have not true love and compassion for others, then our lives have been a waste of time, and of no heavenly value. When we observe Job in his dealings with his friends, his response to their erroneous charges against him was a curt, "Miserable comforters are ye all" (Job 16:2). Jesus on the other hand, when he had suffered wrongfully at the hands of his friends, the Jewish people, graciously stated, "Father forgive them, for they know not what they do" (Luke 23:34).

What God was doing by bringing these afflictions upon Job, was perfecting Job in love. God's Word commands the Christian to, "Let all your things be done with charity" (I Corinthians 16:14). When we find Job praying for his friends, we see that Job's afflictions had caused him to become more Christlike. It was only after Job had prayed for his friends that God had lifted His disciplinary hand off Job. God then doubled all the wealth that Job had possessed prior to the initiation of God's refining process in Job's life (Job 42:10).

To those who maintain that it was Satan who had afflicted Job, and not God, one might ask the question, "Who started the proceedings against Job?" For it was God who had asked Satan, "Hast thou considered my servant Job" (Job 1:8)? God in His Omniscience knew how Satan would react. Satan was a mere tool in the Hand of Almighty God.

Again, we must remember that Good and Evil are not always events that are to be viewed from a moral perspective. God is able to use both Good and Evil to accomplish His purposes. There are numerous events in world history where God employs Evil to accomplish His ends, the Crucifixion being the prima facie example. For Scripture informs us that Jesus was crucified by not only the foreknowledge of God, but also by God's "determinate council" (Acts 2:23). While there are numerous occasions in Scripture where God is said to use evil to accomplish His ends, there is no place in Scripture where God is ever said to act "wickedly", in fact, the Word of God specifically declares that God never engages in wickedness in any form:

"Yea, purely God will not do wickedly, neither will the Almighty pervert judgment." Job 34:12

While God through Satan did indeed bring great evil events into the life of Job, He did so only to refine Job. To perfect Job in love.

The Budding of God's Fig Tree

"The re-birth of the nation of Israel in 1948 constitutes the Biblical "budding of the fig tree" (Matthew 24:32-35) and is a direct sign that the generation that witnessed this event would also witness the 2nd Coming of Jesus Christ back to the earth"

This faulty paradigm could well be the principal cause for the lack of interest in Bible Prophecy that is currently being exhibited by the 21st Century Church. Rather than rejoicing in the almost daily recurring signs of Jesus Christ's imminent return, the Church at large has exhibited a fair amount of indifference to His 2nd Coming.

In the years immediately following the rebirth of the nation of Israel in 1948, many teachers of Bible Prophecy had a field day in proclaiming that this was indeed the "budding of the fig tree" that Jesus had referred to in the 24th Chapter of Matthew's Gospel, the event which would signify that He would soon be coming back to the earth to set up His Millennial kingdom. The passage in question reads as follows:

"Now learn a parable of the fig tree; When his branch is yet tender, and putteth forth leaves, ye know that summer is nigh:

So likewise ye, when ye shall see all these things, know that it is near, even at the doors.

Verily I say unto you, This generation shall not pass, till all these things be fulfilled." Matthew 24:32-34

Numerous books were written during the 1960's-80's

proclaiming that the time of the end of the age was near, based largely upon this so called "budding of the fig tree" and the fact that Scripture proclaims that the generation that had witnessed this event would also witness the 2nd Coming of Jesus Christ back to the earth. Because a Biblical generation is often considered to be 40 years (Hebrews 3:9,10), one book by Colin Deal went so far as to proclaim in its title, "Christ Returns by 1988". Making the same judgmental error, Edgar Whisenant entitled his book, "88 Reasons Why the Rapture Will Occur in 1988".

After the year 1988 had come and gone, many recognized "experts" on Biblical Prophecy still kept insisting that the end of the Age would soon occur based largely upon this concept of the "budding of the fig tree". They reasoned that a Biblical generation may indeed be slightly longer than the commonly accepted 40 years. Evangelist Jack Van Impe is known to have predicted numerous possible end-time scenarios for the 2nd Coming, as had noted Christian leader Pastor Jerry Falwell. With each passing of these time frames, a new possible time period for the 2nd Coming of Jesus back to the earth was developed. In 1999, Falwell stated that the 2nd Coming would probably occur by the year 2009. Again, at the core of these predictions was the so called "budding of the fig tree" which had occurred in 1948.

The deleterious effect that these failed prognostications have had upon the Church at large is more than understandable. The Body of Christ grew tired of the many erroneous predictions, and for decades now has by and large paid little attention to the study of end-time Bible Prophecy.

This study will attempt to show where so many Christian teachers and leaders have gone astray in their interpretation of the meaning of "the budding of the fig tree", a teaching that is not only contained within Matthew's Gospel, but in the other Synoptic Gospels of Mark and Luke as well (Mark 13: 28-31, Luke 21: 29-33).

We will see that the key to understanding what Scripture

means by "the budding of the fig tree" lies in understanding how God views the history of the nation of Israel. In order to do this, it will be helpful to first briefly examine how the secular world analyzes the history of nations.

Theories of Secular History

Throughout the years, mankind has developed many theories as to how the history of nations should be viewed or analyzed. One of the most popular theories of history is commonly known as the "organic theory of history". The organic theory of history goes back at least to the time of the early Greek Philosophers.

Aristotle believed that nations or societies were in a sense, similar to human organisms. Just as a body has many functioning parts (arms, legs, ears, eyes, etc.), so do societies. Aristotle taught that the state itself is like a body, and the various talents of the individuals within the body are the organs that serve to perform the many functions needed by the state to be successful in its operation. This organic theory was later redefined by Vico, Spengler, Arnold Toynbee and many others, who also stated that all societies or nations are organic in nature. These newer versions of organic history tended to emphasize the fact that nations, like individual organisms, all go through a cycle of birth, growth, and then eventual death.

Through the years there have been numerous other concepts as to how history should be viewed, such as the perspective of Karl Marx, who considered history to be an accounting of economic class warfare, with the middle-class tradesman bourgeoise, abusing the wage working lower class proletariat.

Many of these secular views of history tend to be one-dimensional in scope. It is not uncommon for our schools to still teach that "taxation without representation" was the cause for the American Revolutionary War, and slavery was the cause of our American Civil War.

While in recent years there has emerged more multi-dimensional theories of history, many theories of history still approach the analyses of history from only one or two angles or perspectives.

We have observed during the course of these studies on Faulty Paradigms that God's methodology in analyzing matters pertaining to mankind tends to be multi-dimensional, typically incorporating a 3-sided approach. We have seen how God not only created man as a 3-part being composed of body, soul, and spirit (I Thessalonians 5:23), but that He also structured human civilization to reach its highest levels through incorporating the unique capabilities and contributions of the three races of mankind; the Semitic, Hamitic, and the Japhetic peoples. It should therefore come as no surprise to us that God would also analyze and view the history of nations, Israel's in particular, from a 3-dimensional approach.

God's View of Israel's History

Throughout the pages of Scripture, we find that the Word of God consistently views the history of the nation of Israel through three separate viewpoints. The first viewpoint being that of Israel's physical history as a nation, the second viewpoint being concerned with the history of Israel's religious life, and the third historical viewpoint being that of the spiritual history of Israel's true believers. Each of these three aspects of Israel's history is symbolically represented by incorporating the use of one of three trees, respectively the vine, the fig tree, and the olive tree.

Throughout the pages of Scripture, the vine is used to represent Israel's physical existence as a nation. The fig tree represents Israel's formal cultural religious life, and the olive tree, the spiritual history of Israel's true believers. That these symbolic references are consistently incorporated by the many different authors of the Books of the Bible is a testament to the fact that, although there were numerous human agents used in the writing of God's Word, the message itself originated from one single source.

The Vine

The vine is a tree that is often referred to as a horizontal tree, as it tends to spread parallel to the ground instead of upward. This can also be seen to be true regarding the physical existence of nations, for they too have a tendency to constantly expand outward until they are met with some impediment to their growth. While the vine is referenced numerous times within the Book of Genesis and the other Books of the Torah, it is not until the Psalms that we find a direct symbolic reference of the vine in relation to the existence of Israel as a nation.

"Thou hast brought a vine out of Egypt: thou hast cast out the heathen, and planted it." Psalm 80:8

Here we see the physical emergence of the nation of Israel as symbolized by the vine. For 400 years Israel had been developing their national identity while being enslaved in Egypt, and here they are, finally appearing on the world stage as an independent nation of people, ready to spread its wings at the time of the Exodus.

It is also of interest to note that when Israel was on the doorstep of entering the Promised Land, that the spies Moses had sent out to search the land of Canaan brought back clusters of grapes (the fruit of the vine) as evidence of the land's bounty (Numbers 13:23,24). It was as if God was symbolically commemorating the arrival of the new nation of Israel on to the world's stage. For without the possession of land, a group of people are not truly a nation. Although through their rebellious spirit, this generation of the Hebrew people were not allowed to come into the land at this time, the offer to become a true nation as symbolized by the vine, was indeed legitimate on God's part.

After their 40 years of wandering in the wilderness, the children of Israel finally became a legitimate nation through their conquering and possession of the Promised Land under the leadership of Joshua. They continued on as a nation until their disobedience towards God brought about their captivity in Babylon in 586 B.C. While in Babylon, they still existed as a people, but the nation itself had disappeared. No longer did they possess either their land or their king. Ezekiel wrote about the loss of their national identity by symbolically likening it to a vine being plucked up out of the ground:

"Thy mother is like a vine in thy blood, planted by the waters: she was fruitful and full of branches by reason of many waters.

And she had strong rods for the scepters of them that bare rule, and her stature was exalted among the thick branches, and she appeared in her height with the multitude of her branches.

But she was plucked up in a fury, she was cast down to the ground, and the east wind dried up her fruit: her strong rods were broken and withered; the fire consumed them.

And now she is planted in the wilderness, in a dry and thirsty ground.

And fire is gone out of a rod of her branches, which hath devoured her fruit, so that she hath no strong rod to be a scepter to rule. This is a lamentation, and shall be for a lamentation." Ezekiel 19:10-14

Later in the New Testament, we find Jesus again likening the nation of Israel to a vineyard:

"Hear another parable: There was a certain householder, which planted a vineyard, and hedged it round about, and digged a winepress in it, and built a tower, and let it out to husbandmen, and went into a far country:

And when the time of the fruit drew near, he sent his servants to the husbandmen, that they might receive the fruits of it.

And the husbandmen took his servants, and beat one, and killed another, and stoned another.

Again, he sent other servants more than the first: and they did unto them likewise.

But last of all he sent unto them his son, saying, They will reverence my son.

But when the husbandmen saw the son, they said among themselves, This is the heir; come let us kill him, and let us seize on his inheritance. And they caught him and cast him out of the vineyard, and slew him.

When the lord therefore of the vineyard cometh, what will he do unto those husbandmen?

They say unto him, He will miserably destroy those wicked men, and will let out his Vineyard unto other husbandmen, which shall render him the fruits in their seasons.

Jesus saith unto them, Did ye never read in the Scriptures, the stone which the builders rejected, the same is become the head of the corner: this is the Lord's and it is marvelous in our eyes?

Therefore I say unto you, "The kingdom of God shall be taken from you, and given to a nation bringing forth the fruits thereof." Matthew 21:33-43.

In this parable of the Lord, God the Father is the obvious householder, the servants are the Old Testament Prophets, the husbandmen the peoples of Israel, and the vineyard a symbol of the nation of Israel in their role as God's representatives to the world. Jesus in essence was forewarning the people of the nation of Israel, that if they rejected God's son, they would once again be stripped of their nationhood, and the duties of the nation of Israel as God's representatives to the world would be taken from them and meted out to be fulfilled by other nations.

We have seen the fulfillment of this prophecy amongst the Christianized nations of the world, most notably after the Protestant Reformation of the 16th Century. In the 18th Century, we find the nation of Germany leading the way in worldwide missionary activity through the efforts of Nicolas Zinzendorf. In the late 18th century, in addition to the 19th and 20th centuries, the role of being God's chief emissaries to the world was taken over by the nations of England and the United States of America. As spreaders of the Gospel, both of these nations enjoyed a high level of worldwide status, a testament to the fact that, "Righteousness does indeed truly exalt a nation" (Proverbs 14:34).

Jesus as the True Vine

Another point of interest when studying the symbolism of the vine in Scripture is that Jesus referred to himself as the true vine (John 15:1). When he stated this, he was likely referring to the fact that he was the "true representative" of the nation of Israel. If we remember that the literal meaning of the word Israel is, "governed by God", we can see how Jesus could make such a claim. For He is the only person in the history of mankind who has remained faithful to being fully "governed by God" throughout the course of his entire life.

In addition to this, we know that the ultimate representative of every nation is that nation's king, so by referring to himself as the true vine, Jesus not only declared his right to be the true representative of the nation of Israel, but he also claimed the right to be the nation of Israel's True King (Mark 15:2). So, we see within this parable of the vine in the 21st chapter of the Book of Matthew that when the nation of Israel destroyed their True King, they once again also destroyed their nationhood.

The Fig Tree

The symbolic meaning of the fig tree emerges within the opening chapters of the Book of Genesis. The first thing that Adam and Eve did after the Fall was to try and clothe themselves by means of their own righteousness, that is, by covering their nakedness with fig leaves (Genesis 3:7). This first expression of man's newly acquired sin nature would reveal that thereafter, mankind would be driven by an innate desire to "be religious". For the word "religion" itself, can often be simply defined as, "The attempt to make oneself righteous through one's own efforts, and under one's own terms." The Biblical narrative then informs us that the 2nd Person of the Trinity, Jehovah (Jesus Christ), immediately stepped in and demonstrated unto man that "without the shedding of blood, there is no remission of sins" (Hebrews 9:22). He did this by making Adam and Eve proper clothing through the slaying of an innocent animal (Genesis 3:21).

This is not to say that all of what we call, "religious activity" is wrong. For the Jewish Temple sacrifices and worship along with the Church's sacraments of baptism and communion are ordained by God and are recognized as not only being valid, but also necessary within their proper respective times and places. It must always be remembered that true Judaism and true Christianity are not religions as the world views religions, but rather relationships in time between the individual believer and God.

The fig tree in Scripture can therefore be seen to represent the religious life, both good and bad, of the people of Israel.

One of the distinguishing characteristics of the fig tree itself is that the fruit of the tree appears long before its leaves. Such is the nature of religious institutions, for they typically start out with the fruit of true spirituality, only to devolve into a dead religious formality. The history of the Post Reformation Protestant Church is a stark testament to this fact. For what started out as true spiritual revival, over the course of many years became little more than uninspired congregations filled with layers of religious ceremonial traditions.

This certainly was the reality of the religious cultural climate of Jesus' day. Time and time again we find Jesus chastising the religious leaders of the Jewish people for their erroneous beliefs and misinterpretations of Scripture. For not seeking God from their hearts, but rather, engaging in what amounted to be religious lip service.

"Ye hypocrites, well did Esaias prophesy of you, saying,

This people draweth nigh unto me with their mouth, and honoureth me with their lips; but their heart is far from me.

But in vain they do worship me, teaching for doctrines the commandments of men." Matthew 15:7-9

Religious pretense as symbolized by the fig tree, as opposed to true spirituality, had overcome the Jewish people. This of course was most poignantly expressed in the parable of the fig tree:

"He (Jesus) spake also this parable; A certain man had a fig tree planted in his vineyard; and he came and sought fruit thereon, and found none.

Then said he unto the dresser of his vineyard, Behold, these three years I come seeking fruit on this fig tree, and find none: cut it down; why cumbereth it the ground?

And he answering said unto him, Lord let it alone this year also, till I shall dig about it and dung it:

And if it bear fruit, well: and if not, then after that thou shalt cut it down." Luke 13:6-9

Here we find Jesus referring directly to his own life, for it was he who had visited the Temple (as represented by the fig tree), located in the nation Israel (as represented by the vineyard), for three straight years, and had found no fruit growing thereon.

234

It was then determined by the dresser of the vineyard (the Holy Spirit) that he would attempt for one more year to prod the fig tree into producing fruit, after which time, judgment would be pronounced upon the fig tree.

Soon after the third visit to the Temple by Jesus, He was crucified. According to this parable in the Book of Matthew, the offer of accepting the message of Jesus was still open to the religious leaders for a period of one year after the Crucifixion. This offer was withdrawn at the end of one year, likely at the time that the religious establishment had ignored the pleas that Stephen had made to them for repentance (Acts 7: 1-54). When the Jewish religious establishment made Stephen the Church's first martyr, the fate of the Temple and the Jewish priestly hierarchy was sealed. The fig tree was now doomed. Although the judgment of the fig tree was suspended for 40 additional years, there would be no more apparent nurturing and dressing of the fig tree made by God from the time of Stephen's death onward.

The Olive Tree

The olive tree in Scripture represents true spirituality. The first reference to the olive tree in God's Word occurs in the Book of Genesis. After Noah sent forth a dove from the Ark to see if the waters of the Flood had yet receded, the dove had returned with a leaf from an olive tree in its mouth (Genesis 8:11). This was a symbolic notification to Noah that not only had the waters of the Flood receded, but that the Flood had indeed accomplished its purpose. For after the destruction of the corrupt old world, the olive leaf represented the fact that the earth was now a place where true spirituality could once again flourish.

The olive tree is a vertical tree. Its growth goes straight upward towards heaven. It is a slow growing tree, requiring a lot of special attention by its owner before it can truly deliver its fruit. The most productive of olive trees are grown on dry rocky ground. In like fashion, so too is the spiritual growth of the 235 believer. For true spiritual growth is also a long and arduous process, requiring many difficulties and much pruning by the Holy Spirit before real fruit appears in the life of the believer.

The olive tree itself had many uses, its oil for anointing (Exodus 30:24,25; Psalm 23:5), for illumination (Leviticus 24:2), and as an ointment (Psalm 104:15). The wood of the olive tree was used for both fuel and in the building of the Temple (I Kings 6:31,32). The leaves of the olive tree have been used for medicinal purposes at least since the days of the Hebrews in Egypt, and have been scientifically proven to contain antibacterial, anti-fungal, anti-inflammatory, and antioxidant properties.

Like the life of a truly loving spiritual person, the olive tree is also said to represent true beauty (Jeremiah 11:16; Hosea 14:6).

The Apostle Paul informed the believers in his day, that the Church had its roots in the Jewish faith as represented by the olive tree. That although many Jewish branches of the tree had been pruned off, and the Gentile believers grafted in, the Church still owed its life to the remaining Jewish root of the tree, and Christians were not to boast against the Jewish people. For one day in the future, they will once again be grafted back into true spirituality as represented by the olive tree (Romans 11:17-26).

Unlike the national history of the Jewish people as symbolized by the vine, and their religious history as represented by the fig tree, the spiritual history of the true believer as represented by the olive tree is a history that is typically known only by God. It is a history that occurs behind the scenes, its secrets unknown to the viewing public. The only times that the manifestations of the history of the olive tree are openly shown, are during times of great revival, but then only for a short season. The fact that the true spiritual history of both individuals and of the nation of Israel is known only by God is illustrated in Scripture in the days of Elijah. For when Elijah was bemoaning the fact that "it was only he" who had been left to single-handedly engage against the forces of evil, God had pulled Elijah aside and informed him

236

that He still had a remnant of 7,000 believers who had not bowed their knee to Baal (I Kings 19:18).

In more recent years, the evangelist D.L. Moody reaffirmed the existence of this secretive spiritual history that is known only by God, when he stated, "When you get to heaven, there will be three things that are going to surprise you. One, the people who are there; two, the people who aren't there; and three, that you're there!"

The Three Trees in the Garden of Eden

As an interesting sidenote, could it be possible that the three trees that God uses to symbolize the various aspects of the history of the nation Israel, could also be the same three trees that are mentioned as existing in the Garden of Eden? We know that within the Garden, there had to be a fig tree, for Adam and Eve had used the leaves of this tree for a covering. We also know that the Tree of Life mentioned in the Book of Revelation, whose leaves were, "for the healing of the nations" (Revelation 22:2), shares the same medicinal qualities as the olive tree, whose leaves are also used for healing. This in turn would leave the possibility open that the remaining tree mentioned as being in the Garden of Eden, the Tree of the Knowledge of Good and Evil, could very well have been the vine. While common folklore attributes the fruit of this tree as being an apple, there is no Scriptural basis for this conjecture. The fruit of the vine however, the grape, would somehow make more sense as being the agent of the poison of sin that Adam and Eve ingested. For this poison of sin would eventually be the cause of both of their deaths. Because grapes are commonly associated with wine, which in turn is commonly associated with alcohol, we can see that the Tree of the Knowledge of Good and Evil may well indeed have been a vine. For alcohol itself is a known and often deadly poison.

In that Scripture is not specific on the matter, this conjecture certainly falls under the umbrella of speculative theology, but it is an interesting possibility, nonetheless.

Conclusion

Getting back to the correct interpretation of "the budding of the fig tree" as depicted in Matthew 24:32, it is apparent that most interpreters of Biblical Prophecy have really missed the mark. For if the rebirth of the nation of Israel in 1948 in and of itself was to carry any significance regarding a possible end times prophetic timetable, then Jesus would have indicated that, "the generation that witnessed the re-emergence of the vine, would be the same generation that would also experience the end of the age".

Since we have seen that the fig tree represents aspects of Israel's open religious history, we might expect that the budding of the fig tree would be something pertaining to Israel reinstituting an aspect of their former religious life. Something such as the rebuilding of their Temple, the restoration of their daily sacrificial system, or anything that would indicate the Jewish people were once again engaging in the practice of their religious system or rituals. These would certainly qualify as elements that would fall under the symbolic banner of the re-emergence of the fig tree.

The rebirth of Israel as a nation in 1948 only signifies that once again, God's vine has started to flourish. While this fact has certainly paved the way for the possibility of the fig tree's budding, it really holds no other significance regarding the generational prophecy which is mentioned in the 24th Chapter of the Book of Matthew.

We can rest assured however, that the generation that does witness the rebuilding of the Temple, or some other major aspect of the Jewish religion, will likely be the generation that will witness the 2nd Coming of Jesus Christ back to the earth.

238

There are Two Separate Gods revealed in Scripture

"There are two separate Gods revealed in Scripture. The mean, angry, and judgmental God of the Old Testament, and the kind, loving, and gracious God as revealed in the Person of Jesus Christ in the New Testament"

Of the many faulty paradigms that we have examined within the body of this work, the idea that there are two separate Gods revealed in Scripture is certainly one of the more common misconceptions in Christendom regarding the interpretation of God's Word. This study is an attempt to show how the idea of the God of the Bible possessing two different personalities is not in line with the clear teachings of Scripture. The faulty paradigm that the God of the Old Testament is overly harsh and judgmental, while the God of the New Testament is primarily concerned with love and grace, should be considered as being a "false dichotomy", one that stems from a lack of proper understanding of God's Word.

The Unchanging God

Throughout the entirety of Scripture, we are told that God does not change. In the Book of Numbers, we read that unlike mankind, God is not fickle, His Personage not being subject to change:

"God is not a man that he should lie; neither the son of man, that he should repent: hath he said, and shall he not do it? Or hath he spoken, and shall he not make it good?" Numbers 23:19

239

Later we find the Psalmist echoing the same sentiment. That while everything we see in the world around us is constantly changing, God by His very nature, is not:

"Of old thou hast laid the foundation of the earth: and the heavens are the work of thy hands.

They shall perish, but thou shalt endure: yea, all of them shall wax old like a garment; as a vesture shalt thou change them, and they shall be changed:

But thou art the same, and thy years shall have no end." Psalm 102:25-27

The Prophet Isaiah also testified of the stable unchangeable nature of God and His Word:

"The grass withereth, the flower fadeth: but the Word of our God shall stand forever." Isaiah 40:8

At the closing of the Old Testament record, Malachi reaffirms the fact that God is not subject to change.

"For I am the LORD, I change not: therefore ye sons of Jacob are not consumed." Malachi 3:6

In the New Testament record, we are again reminded of the unchangeable nature of God. In the Book of Hebrews, we read of the 2nd Person of the Trinity, Jesus Christ:

"Jesus Christ the same yesterday, today, and forever." Hebrews 13:8

Later, in the Book of James, we find James testifying about the consistency of God's character:

"Every good gift and every perfect gift is from above, and cometh down from the Father of lights, with whom is no variableness, neither shadow of turning" James 1:17.

The Gracious God of the Old Testament

Rather than predominantly being a capricious and overly strict God of vengeance in the Old Testament, as the faulty paradigm suggests, we find that the Old Testament record abounds with indications of God's expressions of goodness, grace, and love towards mankind. Right from the beginning of God's Word, in the Book of Genesis, we find God revealing His boundless grace towards Abraham, declaring him to be righteous not because of any virtue or great works that he had done, but simply on the basis of his faith:

"And he (Abraham) believed in the Lord; and he counted it to him for righteousness." Genesis 15:6

Later in the historical record of Scripture, we read that Moses also referred to this goodness and graciousness of God:

"And the LORD passed by before him, and proclaimed, The LORD, The LORD God, merciful and gracious, long suffering, and abundant in goodness and truth." Exodus 34:6

The Book of Psalms is also filled with numerous references to the goodness, mercy, and loving kindness of God:

"Because thy loving kindness is better than life, my lips shall praise Thee." Psalm 63:3

"Blessed be the Lord, who daily loadeth us with benefits." Psalm 68:19

"...O God, in the multitude of thy mercy hear me, ..." Psalm 69:13

"...Thou hast holden me by my right hand." Psalm 73:23

"O satisfy us early with thy mercy; that we may rejoice and be glad all our days." Psalm 90:14

"The LORD is merciful and gracious, slow to anger, and plenteous in mercy." Psalm 103:8

"He hath not dealt with us after our sins; nor rewardeth us according to our iniquities.

For as the heaven is high above the earth, so great is his mercy toward them that fear Him." Psalm 103:10,11

"O give thanks unto the LORD, for he is good: for his mercy endureth forever." Psalm 107:1

"Oh that men would praise the LORD for his goodness, and for his wonderful works to the children of men!" Psalm 107:8,15,21,31

"The LORD is gracious, and full of compassion; slow to anger, and of great mercy.

The LORD is good to all: and his tender mercies are over all his works." Psalm 145:8,9

All throughout the Old Testament record, we find numerous examples of the writers of Scripture declaring that God is kind, caring, gracious, and loving. A God who after delivering the Hebrew people from their bondage in Egypt, made sure to attend to their every need in their 40 years of Wilderness wanderings. He provided not only food and water for them to eat, but also miraculously did not allow the clothes on their backs, or the sandals on their feet, to wear out during this extended period of sojourning (Deuteronomy 29:5).

We must also remember that the God of the Old Testament, in addition to providing for the Hebrew people, also exhibited His love and kindness by making provision for the foreigner in the Land (Leviticus 19:34, Ezekiel 47:23). In the Book of Deuter-

242

onomy, God implores the Hebrew people to "Love the stranger" (Deuteronomy 10:19). A prime example of God's concern for all, be they Hebrew or not, is to be found in the Book of Ruth, where we find the Gentile Ruth being taken care of providentially by God through Boaz (Ruth 2:1-23).

Nowhere is the loving and forgiving heart of God so exhibited in Scripture as it is in the Book of Hosea. After Hosea had married a prostitute named Gomer, we find Gomer leaving Hosea and returning to her former life as a prostitute. Nonetheless, God told Hosea to forgive her, and buy her back from her new consort (Hosea 3:1,2).

As these examples from Scripture clearly indicate, the God of the Old Testament is not a Person who is preoccupied with performing vengeance on the disobedient. Ezekiel affirms this fact regarding this attribute of the character of God when he writes:

"Have I any pleasure at all that the wicked should die? Saith the Lord GOD: and not that he should return from his ways and live?" Ezekiel 18:23

This brings us to the point of examining the acts of judgment that God did indeed bring about against whole groups of people such as Sodom and Gomorrah (Genesis 19:28) and the Canaanites (Joshua 6:21) in the Old Testament record.

Sodom and Gomorrah

When we think about God destroying the entire population of Sodom and Gomorrah, excepting Lot and his extended family, it is natural for us to assume that there were numerous people living there who were law-abiding citizens, who were much like our own friends and neighbors. This however was not the case, as Scripture tells us that after much pleading by Abraham to not destroy the city ("Wilt thou destroy the righteous with the wicked?" Genesis 18:23), it was clearly established that there were indeed no righteous people to be found within the entire area of Sodom and Gomorrah, apart from those in the family of Lot.

In fact, Sodom and Gomorrah had become so degenerate, that even the righteous Lot himself had become corrupted through his being constantly exposed to the great wickedness of the area. Evidence of this can be seen by the fact that Lot offered to give up his own two young virgin daughters as sexual substitutes to the men of the city, homosexual men who had come to Lot's house to rape the two angels who were visiting Lot at the time (Genesis 19:8). Now if the righteous Lot had become so corrupted from living in Sodom and Gomorrah that he was willing to subject his own children to sexual abuse, then one can only imagine the deviancy that the children of the unrighteous in the city had to endure. One can justly assume that not only was the sin of homosexuality openly accepted in Sodom and Gomorrah, but the sins of incest and pedophilia were also likely practiced there. When a society sinks so low that its children are automatically exposed to physical and sexual abuse upon coming into the world, then at this point there is no turning back for that society. For what people see being done, they tend to do. Sins such as homosexuality and pedophilia are no different than other sins, for all sin tends to perpetuate itself in the offspring of those who commit such atrocities (Exodus 34:7). The abused become the abusers.

When such sexual immorality becomes commonplace throughout any society, and its people are hardened to the idea of repentance, then the only way for God to stop gross sexual perversions and the generational abuse of children, is to bring judgment upon that group of people. God was perfectly just in destroying Sodom and Gomorrah. In so doing he was saving future generations of children from being born into a world in which they would be subjected to certain physical and sexual abuse.

The reason that God did not send a prophet to warn the

people of Sodom and Gomorrah of their pending judgment, is that God knew that this group of people were not open to repentance. Make no mistake, God has not only known the total history of the Universe from the moment of its conception (Revelation 13:8, Hebrews 4:13), but He also knows all potential and/or "iffy" history:

"Woe unto thee, Chorazin! Woe unto thee Bethsaida! For if the mighty works, which were done in you, had been done in Tyre and Sidon, they would have repented long ago in sackcloth and ashes." Matthew 11:21

When we see God judging and removing from the earth whole groups and nations of people, it is safe to assume that there was no turning back for these societies, as they were not open to repentance. For God to have allowed for their continuance would have been consigning innocent children to being brought into a world in which they would have had no hope for a happy and moral existence.

Scripture clearly teaches that children have a special place in the heart of God: "But whoso shall offend one of these little ones which believe in me, it were better for him that a millstone were hanged about his neck, and that he were drowned in the depth of the sea." Matthew 18:6

"But Jesus said, Suffer little children, and forbid them not, to come unto me: for of such is the kingdom of heaven." Matthew 19:14

By destroying Sodom and Gomorrah and other wicked groups of people in the Old Testament record, God was ending not only their wickedness in general, but quite likely also the generational perpetuation of their gross sexual immorality and abusive exploitation of children.

The Case of Ancient Nineveh

In like manner of Sodom and Gomorrah, in the days of Jonah, God had pronounced judgment upon the ancient Assyrian city of Nineveh. Instead of sending angels to Nineveh to inform any righteous people to flee, God chose rather to send Jonah to warn the entire population of Nineveh of their impending judgment, for God knew that there existed the possibility that Nineveh might indeed repent. We are all familiar with the story of how Jonah had refused to do this task that was assigned to him of warning Nineveh of their forthcoming destruction, and instead, he had chosen to flee in the opposite direction to Tarshish. Even though Jonah had refused to do the known will of God, God in His sovereignty, was determined to have Jonah do His bidding. In God's Providential ways, He had a great fish swallow up Jonah, and then spew him out on the shores of Assyria.

Nineveh was an extremely large city in the ancient world. A city whose geographical expanse was so vast that it took three days to walk throughout its entirety (Jonah 3:3). Scripture informs us that there were 120,000 children living in Nineveh, so we can assume that the total population of Nineveh was well over a quarter of a million people.

After Jonah had reluctantly preached to the people of Nineveh of a coming Judgment from God, the people had indeed repented, which in turn caused God to refrain from destroying this wicked city:

"And God saw their works, that they turned from their evil way; and God repented of the evil, that he had said that he would do unto them; and did it not." Jonah 3:10

An interesting thing then occurred. Rather than rejoice over the fact that he had just conducted the most successful evangelistic campaign in the Old Testament record, one in which God had spared this vast number of people from destruction, Jonah instead become angry that God had not destroyed the city.

246

It is here that we get an insight into the depths of depravity inherent in the sinful heart of man.

Scripture goes on to record the prayer that was then spoken by the enraged Jonah:

"...I pray thee O LORD, was not this my saying, when I was yet in my country? Therefore I fled before unto Tarshish: for I knew that thou art a gracious God, and merciful, slow to anger, and of great kindness, and repentest thee of the evil.

Therefore now, O LORD, take, I beseech thee, my life from me; for it is better for me to die than to live." Jonah 4:2,3

Here we find Jonah declaring that the reason that he had tried to escape from God to Tarshish, and thereby avoid warning Nineveh of their coming destruction, was that he knew that God was kind, gracious, and merciful. Jonah did not want to participate in any way in the potential sparing of the city of Nineveh by God. When God did indeed remove His hand of Judgment away from Nineveh after their repentance, Jonah had become so angry that he wished that he himself would now die.

Ironically, here it is clearly illustrated that it is not the God of the Old Testament that is angry, harsh, and overly judgmental, but rather it is the heart of man that is shown to be totally lacking in both grace and compassion towards his fellow man.

Judgment in the New Testament

The idea that the God of the New Testament is strictly a God of love, and not concerned with Judgment, is also totally inaccurate. For there is no person in Scripture who warned more of the existence and perils of hell than Jesus Christ himself. In fact, Jesus spoke more about the realities of hell than he did about the glories and wonders of heaven.

Jesus taught that people should remove anything from their life that might cause them to be subjected to the horrors of hell:

"And if thy right hand offend thee, cut it off, and cast it from thee: for it is profitable for thee that one of thy members should perish, and not that thy whole body should be cast into hell." Matthew 5:30

That hell is a place of great suffering and regret: "But the children of the kingdom shall be cast into outer darkness: there shall be weeping and gnashing of teeth." Matthew 8:12

Jesus also taught that hell is a place that should be greatly feared by mankind: "And fear not them which kill the body, but are not able to kill the soul: but rather fear him which is able to destroy both soul and body in hell." Matthew 10:28

That hell is a place of great darkness and despair: "Then said the king to the servants, Bind him hand and foot, and take him away, and cast him into outer darkness; there shall be weeping and gnashing of teeth." Matthew 22:13

Hell is a place of everlasting torment that was not originally created for mankind, but rather for Satan and his demons. When Adam fell however, hell became a place where all unrepentant mankind would also have to eternally suffer alongside Satan and his fallen angels:

"Then shall he say also unto them on the left hand, Depart from me ye cursed, into everlasting fire, prepared for the devil and his angels." Matthew 25:41

In addition to this, Jesus taught that part of the hellishness of hell is that those who go there will have to eternally observe the glories of heaven, while those who are in heaven will not be aware of either their existence, or their sufferings:

"There shall be weeping and gnashing of teeth, when ye shall see Abraham, and Isaac, and Jacob, and all the prophets, in the

248

kingdom of God, and you yourselves thrust out." Luke 13:28

"And beside all this, between us and you there is a great gulf fixed: so that they which would pass from hence to you cannot; neither can they pass to us, that would come from thence." Luke 16:26

Not only did Jesus preach a strong message of Judgment in the New Testament, but in like manner, so did His disciples. Paul wrote in the Book of Acts:

"Because he hath appointed a day, in the which he will judge the world in righteousness by that man whom he hath ordained; whereof he hath given assurance unto all men, in that he hath raised him from the dead." Acts 17:31

To the Romans, Paul wrote:

"For as many as have sinned without the law shall also perish without law: and as many as have sinned in the law shall be judged by the law:" Romans 2:12

"In the day when God shall judge the secrets of men by Jesus Christ according to my gospel." Romans 2:16

Peter wrote of the coming Judgment that will be placed upon the entire physical Universe, when God shall destroy the whole sin cursed Creation by fire, after which He shall create a new heavens and earth:

"But the day of the Lord will come as a thief in the night; in the which the heavens shall pass away with a great noise, and the elements shall melt with fervent heat, the earth also and the works that are therein shall be burned up.

Seeing then that all these things shall be dissolved, what manner of persons ought ye to be in all holy conversation and godliness." II Peter 3:10,11

The Apostle John also clearly warned of the coming Judgment of mankind:

"And I saw a great white throne, and him that sat on it, from whose face the earth And the heaven fled away: and there was found no place for them.

And I saw the dead, small and great, stand before God; and the books were opened: And another book was opened, which is the book of life: and the dead were judged out of those things which were written in the books, according to their works.

And the sea gave up the dead which were in it; and death and hell delivered up the dead which were in them: and they were judged every man according to their works.

And death and hell were cast into the lake of fire. This is the second death.

And whosoever was not found written in the book of life was cast into the lake of fire." Revelation 20:11-15

We see that the New Testament record is not a story that is devoid of Judgment. On the contrary, when we compare the coming Judgment that will occur with the burning up of the entire Universe as expressed by Peter in comparison to the Judgment of the Flood, Judgment within the New Testament is seen to be far more severe than it was within the Old Testament record!

Jesus in the Old and New Testaments

Rather than there being a polarity between the Gods of the Old and the New Testaments, we must remember that the manifestations of God in the Old Testament were indeed appearances of the 2nd Person of the Trinity, God the Son, and not of God the Father, "For no man hath seen God (the Father) at any time, the only begotten Son, who is in the bosom of the Father, he has
250

declared him" (John 1:18). In the Old Testament record, this 2nd Person of the Trinity was known not only as Jehovah, but also by a host of other names such as the "God of Abraham", "I Am", the "Angel of the Lord" amongst others.

In the New Testament, this same Jehovah, after becoming both God and man, took on a new name, that being the Lord Jesus Christ. The actions of Jesus within the New Testament are perfectly consistent with His actions in the Old Testament.

In the Book of Matthew, we find Jesus making reference to His Old Testament activities:

"O Jerusalem, Jerusalem, thou that killest the prophets, and stonest them which are sent unto thee, how often would I have gathered thy children together, even as a hen gathereth her chickens under her wings, and ye would not." Matthew 23:37

In this passage of Scripture, Jesus is referring to the fact that it was He, when he was known as Jehovah, who had from Old Testament times protected the nation of Israel under His wings:

"As an eagle stirreth up her nest, fluttereth over her young, spread abroad her wings, taketh them, bareth them on her wings." Deuteronomy 32:11

"Keep me as the apple of thy eye, hide me under the shadow of thy wings." Psalm 17:8

"How excellent is thy lovingkindness O God! Therefore the children of men put their trust under the shadow of thy wings." Psalm 36:7

"He shall cover thee with his feathers, and under his wings thou shalt trust: his truth shall be thy shield and buckler." Psalm 91:4

In the Old Testament, it was in fact the Lord Jesus who had promised to always be present with the Hebrew people:

251

"And the LORD (Jehovah), he it is that doth go before thee, he will not fail thee, neither forsake thee: fear not, neither be dismayed." Deuteronomy 31:8

"Have not I commanded thee? Be strong and of a good courage; be not afraid, neither be thou dismayed: for the Lord thy God is with thee whithersoever thou goest." Joshua 1:9

"Nevertheless I am continually with thee:..." Psalm 73:23

In like manner in the New Testament, we find Jesus making the same reassuring promise to his followers, to be always at their side throughout the entire course of their earthly existence:

"...and, lo, I am with you always, even unto the end of the world." Matthew 28:20

In terms of judgment, it's important to remember that it was the meek loving Jesus of the New Testament who had made a scourge of cords and drove the money changers, sheep, and cattle out of the temple. In the process, He had also turned over their tables of merchandise (John 2:14,15). We must never forget that it was this same Jesus, as the "Angel of the Lord" in the Old Testament, who had destroyed the entire Assyrian army of 185,000 men in the days of King Hezekiah (II Kings: 19:35).

The actions of Jesus/Jehovah are consistent throughout both Testaments:

1) Jesus referred to his disciples not as his servants, but rather as his friends, for "a servant knoweth not what his Lord doeth" (John 15:15). In like manner, Jehovah referred to Abraham and Moses as being His friends (Exodus 33:11, II Chronicles 20:7), in addition to stating, "Shall I hide from Abraham that thing which I do?" (Genesis 18:17).

2) Jesus declared himself to be the Rock upon which the Church was to be built (Matthew 16:18), while in the Old Testament, David had declared that it was Jehovah who was his Rock

(Psalm 18:2).

3) In the New Testament, on a large scale, we find Jesus feeding 5,000 people (Matthew 14:19-21), and on a smaller scale, Jesus fed his disciples an intimate meal on the shoreline (John 21:9). In the Old Testament, on a large scale, we find Jehovah feeding the entire Hebrew people manna in the Wilderness (Exodus 16:4), and on a smaller scale, we find Jehovah feeding Elijah, the widow, and her son (I Kings 17:14-16).

4) Jesus in the New Testament demonstrated to the disciples his ability to control not only nature, but also the 4th dimension of time, by His eclipsing of time on the Sea of Galilee ("immediately the ship was at land" John 6:21). In the Old Testament record, we find Jehovah controlling the passage of time by first suspending it during Israel's battle with the Amorites at Gibeon ("the sun stood still" Joshua 10:12,13), and later, by reversing the passage of time in the days of Hezekiah, when He had caused the sundial to go 10 degrees backwards (Isaiah 38:8).

5) In the New Testament, we have Jesus bringing the young damsel back to life by physically holding her hand (Matthew 9:25). In the Old Testament, Jehovah brought life back to the widow's son after Elijah had physically stretched his body over the child's body three times (I Kings 17:21,22).

6) In the New Testament, we find Jesus "saving the day" at the wedding feast in Cana, by "turning the water into wine." (John 2:1-11) In the Old Testament record, we find Jehovah "saving the day" for the Hebrew people during the Exodus, by "turning the water into a wall", after Pharoah's Army had backed them into a corner with seemingly no means of escape (Exodus 14:21)!

Incredibly, the miracles that Jesus performed in the New Testament were often in a sense, "repeat performances" (with slight variations), of what He had already done in the Old Testament as Jehovah! While the revealed God of the New Testament goes by a different name than the God of the Old Testament, it is still the same wonderful, loving, good, and

253

gracious Person throughout the entirety of Scripture.

God is no more a typically "angry God" of the Old Testament, than He is a constantly "warm, kind, and loving God" in the New Testament. The God consistently revealed throughout Scripture is the 2nd Person of the Trinity, who we now refer to as Jesus Christ.

In the written record of both the Old and New Testaments, God the Father usually remains behind the scenes. His main function amongst the members of the Trinity is that of being the Master Planner of history. God the Son on the other hand, is openly visible throughout the pages of both the Old and the New Testaments. His primary function being that of the implementer of the Father's Plan. Paul reveals this succinctly in his first letter to the Corinthian Church:

"But to us there is but one God, the Father, "of whom are all things", and we in him: and one Lord Jesus Christ, "by whom are all things", and we by him." I Corinthians 8:6

The Personage of God as revealed throughout the pages of Scripture is never changing or "evolving". In both the Old and the New Testaments records, it is the Lord Jesus Christ, "the full visible expression of the Godhead bodily" (Colossians 2:9), who is not only implementing the Plan of God the Father, but is also revealing to mankind the true character of the Triune God.

There are not two separate and distinct God's exhibited in Scripture, the one being "judgmental", and the other "kind and loving". The openly revealed God of both the Old and the New Testaments never changes:

"Jesus Christ the same yesterday, and today, and forever." Hebrews 13:8

All Scripture is not Created Equal

"No Scripture is of more importance than any other Scripture", or in other words, "All Scripture is created equal"

Although this faulty paradigm is seldom openly taught, the evidence that this belief exists is found throughout the Christian Church. Christians typically approach their study of God's Word from the standpoint of, "If all Scripture is inspired by God and is profitable (II Timothy 3:16), then all of Scripture must be of equal importance." The problem with taking such a stance is that it serves to promote a lack of proper focus in the life of the individual Christian.

All around us we observe believers whose focus in life is in a constant state of flux or change. In recent years we have observed many Christians going from concentrating on being a "promise keeper" (The Promise Keeper Movement), to becoming "Seeker Sensitive" (The Mega Church Movement), and then on to being more "Purpose Driven" (The Rick Warren-Saddleback Movement), only to later find themselves believing that they will somehow come to a more meaningful relationship and understanding of God by following the edicts of "The Prayer of Jabez"! This is all driven by a legitimate desire to feel a moment by moment closeness to God, to walk in the realization that all is well between ourselves and our God.

By not acknowledging the fact that some aspects of Scripture are of more importance than others, many believers in Christ end up flitting from flower to flower, going from concentrating on one theological topic to another, hoping to find the ever-elusive proper focus of the Christian life.

Sadly, many televangelists and popular preachers of the gospel make merchandise of this common condition, often subtly insinuating to their congregants, "that they have an inside track with God", and whatever Scriptural topic they are currently pushing is "the Christian's ultimate key to attaining the proper focal point for the Christian life".

Thankfully, this malady of feeling disenfranchised from God can be cured through a deeper understanding of God's Word. Scripture informs us that, "My people are destroyed for lack of knowledge" (Hosea 4:6). To this writer's experience, one of the most neglected areas of Christian study is what Scripture refers to as, "the weightier matters of the Law."

Not All Scripture is Created Equal

Again, because we fail to acknowledge that some aspects of Scripture are of more importance than others, Christians often fail to place their attention on the things that are of the most importance in their daily walk with the Lord. As we have already stated, Christians tend to center their attention on whatever the latest fad in the current Christian Pop Culture may be rather than seeking to acquire the proper Biblically centered focus that God would have them possess in their daily walk with Him.

We should recognize that while some of the aforementioned Christian pursuits such as Promise Keepers, the Purpose Driven Topics, and the latest "Fad Christian Book" do indeed have some spiritual value in and of themselves, this value however is secondary, and should never be a replacement for what the true focus of the individual Christian's life should ideally be.

This examination of faulty paradigms within the Church will now attempt to exhibit from Scripture what the center of the Christian life should be. This can only be accomplished by acknowledging the fact that, "there are indeed some aspects of

Scripture that are of more importance than others." That the "weightier matters of the law" that Jesus referred to in the 23rd Chapter of the Book of Matthew form not only the foundation of the structure of the normal Christian life, but also provide for the appropriate day to day focus that Christians should have during their pilgrimage here on earth. This in turn allows the believer in Christ to come into a greater understanding of the Personal love and care that God has individually for each one of His children.

The Weightier Matters of the Law

Jesus directly and succinctly addressed the fact that some aspects of Scripture are of greater significance than others in the 23rd Chapter of the Book of Matthew, where we read:

"Woe unto you, Scribes and Pharisees, hypocrites! For ye pay tithe of mint and anise and cummin, and have omitted "the weightier matters of the law", judgment, mercy, and faith: these ought ye to have done, and not to leave the others undone." Matthew 23:23

Here we find Jesus chastising the Jewish religious leaders of his day for not recognizing that there are some components of Scripture that are of more importance than others. By failing to emphasize the truly important aspects of God's Word, both the ancient Jewish religious leaders and likewise many of our current church leaders can be seen to be guilty of "majoring in the minors". When issues and topics of secondary importance are treated as if they were of primary importance, the end result can only be that of confusion and disarray amongst those who are subjected to them. The utter simplicity of the Gospel becomes lost, as does the believer's sense and awareness of God's individual personal love and care for them.

This is part and parcel to why Paul admonished Timothy to "rightly divide the word of truth". For Scripture clearly teaches that without the correct categorization of God's Word, believers not only run the risk of missing out on God's best for them while here on earth, but also of being "ashamed" as to how they have conducted their lives when they eventually come to stand before Him in judgment.

"Study to show thyself approved unto God, a workman that needeth not to be ashamed, rightly dividing the word of truth." II Timothy 2:15

To the serious student of Scripture, it is commonly acknowledged that there is nothing random contained within God's Word. Hence, that of the three topics that Jesus lists in Matthew 23:23 as comprising the most important aspects of Scripture: "Judgment, Mercy, and Faith", the fact that Judgment is listed first is no accident. It is obviously meant to be the starting point of any serious study of the weightier matters of the law, and unless proven otherwise, is to be considered the topic of the Christian life that is of the greatest significance.

Judgement

Every person who has ever been born into this world, believers and non-believers alike, have one thing in common, and that is that each and every one of our lives will be judged or assessed by God at the time of their completion (Hebrews 9:27). The believer in Christ shall be judged at the Judgment Seat of Christ (II Corinthians 5:10), while non-Church Age believers, and all unbelievers, shall be judged either at Christ's 2nd Coming, and/or at the Great White Throne (Revelation 20:11).

While there are many aspects involved in God's assessment of the individual lives of believers, it is the contention of this study that Scripture teaches that the overriding issue in God's assessment of our lives will be, "Did you accomplish the purpose that God created you to perform?" This of course leads us back to our examination of the "Ultimate Purpose of Man" found in Chapter Five of this book. Here we addressed the fact that man's ultimate purpose in life is not as is commonly taught by the Westminster Confession, "To glorify God, and to enjoy Him forever", but rather as a more theologically viable and less ambiguous alternative, man's ultimate purpose in life is quite simply to "Please God" (Revelation 4:11).

In order to better understand the significant role that "the pleasing of God" plays in the matter of Judgment, it is now necessary to review some of the issues that have been priorly discussed in our study of faulty paradigms while building upon some additional perspectives.

The author apologizes for any perceived redundancies related to prior chapters of this book, but they were deemed necessary in order to rightly convey the full importance and proper under-standing of the three "weightier matters of the law" within the confines of the chapter.

Future ministers are often taught during their training in seminaries to preach 3-part sermons. It has been said that this is due to the fact that, "Two parts in a sermon would not be enough, and that four parts would be too many! The basis by which God shall judge man is so important however, that we will now violate the 3-part sermon rule and incorporate some additional approaches to the subject matter of "pleasing God". The first new approach will be accomplished through incorp-orating the use of analogy.

The Purpose for Which Man was Created

One of the best ways to better understand a subject is through the use of analogy. Analogies allow us to "think outside of the box" by letting us approach a subject from different angles or perspectives. Philosophy 101 teaches that, "Truth is not reality, but rather, truth is a perception of reality." It is not that there are not ultimate truths, but "truth is often multifaceted". The use of analogy allows us to better view the diamond of truth through the reflection of its many different facets.

Let's say hypothetically that we have a Christian friend named Joe, who has a lovely wife named Kathy. Now Joe and Kathy decide that they want to go on a mission trip to Haiti. On this trip, they will be working with a team of fellow mission people who will be both constructing new homes in addition to repairing existing housing. Joe is told before he leaves on the trip that his job will primarily be that of framing new houses. In addition to this, he will also be doing some remodeling, along with some finish carpentry work. Due to Haitian government rules and regulations, Joe will only be allowed to bring one hammer with him into the country. So, Joe goes to the local hardware store and buys a multi-purpose hammer that he will use primarily to frame houses.

To Joe's frustration, he finds that the hammer which he has purchased is too light weight for framing houses. Instead of being able to strike each 16-penny nail four or five times in order to drive it into the framing members, he has to hit each nail eight or nine times in order to secure it. Throughout the course of a typical workday, this causes Joe to have to exert a lot of undue extra effort.

During the course of the mission trip, Joe also uses the hammer on occasion to tear down portions of existing structures. This hammer has a nice claw to it, making the pulling out of nails, both big and small, quite easy. It also has a long handle which functions as a powerful lever for prying apart well secured boards. For the purposes of demolition, the hammer works quite well.

Joe also engages in some finish carpentry work. The hammer that he bought for the primary purpose of framing also has a nice crown in its head, making it ideal for finish work. Joe finds that he does not even need a nail set to do most of the basic finishing work.

One night an intruder with dubious intent came into the mission camp where Joe and Kathy were staying. Kathy picked up the hammer and shook it at the potential perpetrator. The sight of the nasty looking claw on the hammer caused the intruder to immediately flee from the camp in abject terror.

At the end of the mission trip, when all was said and done, when Joe makes his final assessment of the hammer, will he be totally happy with his purchase? I think not. Although the hammer performed more than adequately in the secondary functions that Joe used it for, and even worked well for Kathy as a potential weapon, it did not properly perform the primary function for which it was purchased, that of framing houses.

This is why it is so important for the Christian to fully understand what God's primary purpose for mankind is. We are not talking about one's personal individual vocational calling, but rather what God's general calling or ultimate purpose is for all of mankind. It can be argued that how we fulfill this general calling will also be the ultimate and primary focus of God's assessment of our individual lives. From our previous study we know that man's ultimate purpose is that of "pleasing God". As in the case of Joe's hammer, all the other aspects of the Christian life such as prayer, giving, the glorification of God, fidelity, church attendance, etc., must be considered as issues of secondary importance in matters of Judgment. We must always remember that God is more concerned with the motivations of our heart than He is with our outward works (I Samuel 16:7, Proverbs 4:23), and that the "pleasing of God" is accomplished primarily through the proper condition of our hearts before Him. The Apostle Paul tells us that throughout our lives, God is constantly working in us to not only do the actions that He has fore-ordained we should do (Isaiah 26:12), but more importantly, God is working in us to "will His will" in our lives. This, as we have previously exhibited, is the primary way in which we please God.

"For it is God which worketh in you both to will and to do His good pleasure." Philippians 2:13

261

A Contextual Re-Examination of Isaiah 43:7

While a significant percentage of the Church believes in the edict from the Westminster Confession, "That man was created for the purpose of glorifying God and enjoying Him forever", as we have already shown in chapter five, this is based upon what many consider to be an erroneous interpretation of Isaiah 43:7, which reads:

"Even every one that is called by my name: for I have created him for my glory, I have formed him; yea I have made him."

"I have created him for my glory" demands a far different interpretation than that proposed by the writers of the Westminster Confession, which is, "I have created man to glorify me". For in Isaiah 43:7, we clearly see an instance in which God is being glorified by His own actions. This passage of Scripture in no way implies that His glorification is the primary duty of mankind, nor does it request for, or demand any action on the part of mankind.

When this verse is examined on a broader book wide contextual basis, we find this same theme of God bringing glory to Himself by his own actions in other passages within the Book of Isaiah. In chapter 25 of Isaiah we read:

"For thou hast made of a city an heap; of a defenced city a ruin: a place of strangers to be no city; it shall never be built.

Therefore shall the strong people glorify thee, the city of the terrible nations shall fear Thee." Isaiah 25:2,3

Here we see God bringing glory to himself through His own actions. Later in the 26th chapter of Isaiah, we again find God glorifying himself by his own actions:

"Thou hast increased the nation, O LORD, thou hast increased the nation: Thou art glorified: thou hadst removed it far unto all the ends of the earth." Isaiah 26:15.

Later in the 44th chapter of Isaiah, we find God once again glorifying Himself through His own actions, with no hint of responsibility to glorify God being placed upon man:

"Sing, O ye heavens; for the LORD hath done it: shout, ye lower parts of the earth: break forth into singing, ye mountains, O forest, and every tree therein: for the LORD hath redeemed Jacob, and glorified himself in Israel." Isaiah 44:23

We thus see that within the context of the Book of Isaiah, Isaiah 43:7 should more properly be interpreted as an action performed by God (the creation of man) which results in God's own glorification. It implies no responsibility on the part of man.

Mankind is to glorify God, for he is instructed to do so numerous times throughout Scripture. It can be argued that these calls to glorify God are issued primarily in the interest of truth. For God is Wonderful (Isaiah 9:6), and mankind is not. The glorification of God is important and is not to be taken lightly, as is indicated by the severe judgment placed upon Herod for failing to give God His due glory (Acts 12:21-23).

In addition to this, when we say that God created man to glorify Himself, we are also subtly implying that God somehow has a need or desire to be glorified by man. God's Word however clearly states that God in no way "needs" anything from man:

"If I were hungry, I would not tell thee: for the world is mine and the fulness thereof." Psalm 50:12

God is completely happy within Himself, and in no way does He need to be glorified by man or any other creature of His Creation in order to be fulfilled. The Apostle Paul acknowledges this fact in the Book of Romans, where he writes that, God is "blessed for ever." (Romans 1:25, 9:5).

Pleasing God in the Old Testament

Perhaps the best example of mankind being created for the purpose of pleasing God as opposed to glorifying Him can be found in the Old Testament Book of Psalms. In Psalm 50 we read:

"Whoso offereth praise glorifieth me: and to him that ordereth his conversation aright will I show the salvation of God." Psalm 50:23

Here we find the Psalmist indicating that the act of "praising God" is synonymous with that of "glorifying God". When we substitute the word "praise" with "glorify" in Psalm 69, an interesting facet of theology emerges:

"I will praise (and therefore glorify) the name of God with a song, and will magnify him with thanksgiving.

This also shall please the LORD better than an ox or bullock that hath horns or hoofs." Psalm 69:30,31

If the praising of God is indeed synonymous with the glorification of God as is indicated in Psalm 50, we can then assume that the glorification of God is subordinate to the pleasing of God as is indicated in Psalm 69. For in Psalm 69 David teaches that we "praise" (or "glorify") God in order that we might ultimately "please" Him, and not the other way around.

Scriptural Anomalies

Not only is it helpful to better understand Judgment through the use of "analogy" and "interpretive context", it can also be beneficial to better understand Judgment by means of "anomaly". This requires some explanation. Oftentimes Scripture calls attention to matters of importance by presenting them in ways that appear to be either unique, or seemingly out of place. In other words, anomalies are items that jump out at the reader due to their unexpected existence within certain segments of God's Word. Scriptural anomalies can also be theological teachings that are often "hidden within plain sight".

A case in point can be seen in the Old Testament, in the 2nd tablet of the Ten Commandments. All the sins listed in this 2nd tablet are sins of actions, except for one, that being the mental attitude sin of jealousy or covetousness (Exodus 20:17). By including this mental attitude sin of covetousness within this 2nd tablet, it is as if God is calling special attention to this particular sin.

The need for the believer to give special attention to covetousness was also taught by Jesus in the New Testament. In the 12th chapter of Luke, Jesus states:

"…Take heed and beware of covetousness; for a man's life consisteth not in the abundance of the things he possesseth." Luke 12:15

It is important to note that the sin of covetousness is the one and only sin that Jesus warned his followers, "to be wary of". This in turn begs the questions:

1) "Why does Scripture single out the sin of covetousness in both the Old and the New Testaments?" and,

2) "Why is the sin of covetousness such a dangerous sin?"

The answer to these questions lies in the fact that Scripture shows us by example that the sin of covetousness is to be considered a "gateway sin", or in other words, a sin that leads to more and greater sins. This is why the Apostle Paul also sternly warns against coveting, declaring that "The love of money is the root of all evil" (I Timothy 6:10). If we remember that Israel's best king, David, and Israel's worst king, Ahab, both started out by coveting, then went from coveting to stealing, and after becoming thieves, both men eventually ended up becoming murderers (The difference between the two of them of course was that David repented of his sins).

Regarding Scriptural anomalies relating to Judgment within the New Testament, it is of particular importance to note that in the entire New Testament, God the Father only makes two "personal appearances" in the form of public verbal proclamations. While God the Father did speak privately to Peter, John, and James on the Mount of Transfiguration, on only two occasions does He speak to the public at large in the New Testament. Of interest regarding our present debate between whether man's highest calling is to glorify God or to please God, one of the said proclamations is concerned with the "glorification" of God, while the other proclamation is focused on the "pleasing" of God. It is as if God knew that in the future this theological matter would arise and had decided to resolve the issue through the declaring of these two unique public proclamations in His Word.

In the proclamation concerning the glorification of God, in the Book of John we read:

"Now is my soul troubled; and what shall I say? Father, save me from this hour: but for this cause came I unto this hour.

Father, glorify thy name. Then came there a voice from heaven saying, I have both glorified it, and will glorify it again." John 12:27,28

In this passage of New Testament Scripture, we find God the Father bringing glory to Himself, just as He had often done within the Old Testament record (Psalm 19:1, Proverbs 25:2, Isaiah 25:2,3, 26:15, 43:7). It is important to note that in this public declaration, there is again no hint of any action or responsibility in the glorification of God placed upon man.

In the only other public proclamation made by God the Father in the New Testament, the declaration regarding the

266

pleasing of God however, this is not the case. In the Book of
Matthew we read:

"And lo a voice from heaven, saying, This is my beloved Son, in
whom I am well pleased." Matthew 3:17

Here we find God the Father declaring that the manner in
which Jesus lived his life was pleasing unto Him. In essence,
this proclamation is an admonition to the followers of Jesus
to follow His exemplary lifestyle, so that they too might live a
life that is found to be "pleasing unto God". Unlike the public
proclamation regarding the glorification of God in John 12:27,28,
this proclamation concerning the pleasing of God places strict
responsibilities upon mankind. So that there is no doubt as to the
importance of man living to please God, this public proclamation
found in the Book of Matthew is also included in the Books of
Mark (1:11) and Luke (3:22), whereas John's public proclamation
concerning the glorification of God is only to be found within
John's Gospel.

The importance of mankind being "Pleasing to God" is also
brought forth in the only other statement made by God the
Father in the New Testament, that being His private declaration
to Peter, James, and John at the Mount of Transfiguration. Here
we again find God the Father not only imploring these three
disciples to listen to the things that Jesus had to say to them, but
also reiterating the fact that Jesus was indeed His Son, and that
He Himself was indeed "well pleased with how Jesus conducted
his life":

"While he yet spake, behold, a bright cloud overshadowed
them: and behold a voice out of the cloud, which said, This is my
beloved Son, in whom I am well pleased, hear ye him." Matthew
17:5

It is interesting to note that God the Father in the entire New
Testament only issues a total of three proclamations, all of which
are concerned with either the "pleasing", or the "glorifying" of

Himself. The instances of the pleasing of God are recorded five times in God's Word by four different authors (Matthew 3:17,17:5, Mark 1:11, Luke 3:22, II Peter 1:17), and implies a strict responsibility on the part of mankind to live one's life in a manner that would be "pleasing unto Him".

The glorifying of God however that is spoken of by God the Father, is only found in one passage of Scripture, and implies no responsibility on the part of man, being concerned solely with God the Father glorifying Himself (John 12:28).

Jesus also affirmed the importance of living a life that was pleasing unto God, when in making what appears to be His personal assessment of His own life in John's Gospel, where He significantly states:

"And he that sent me is with me: the Father hath not left me alone; FOR I DO ALWAYS THOSE THINGS THAT PLEASE HIM !!!" John 8:29 (emphasis mine)

The Things that Scripture does NOT State

Another approach that we can take to further establish the fact that God created man for the primary purpose of "pleasing Him" as opposed to "glorifying Him", is through showing that, "Scripture says as much by what it doesn't say, as by what it does say."

For example, Scripture DOES NOT state that Enoch found favor with God because he had properly "glorified" God, but rather because of the fact that he had "pleased" God:

"By faith Enoch was translated that he should not see death; and was not found, because God had translated him: for before his translation he had this testimony, that he "pleased" God." Hebrews 11:5

God's Word DOES NOT pronounce His pleasure in how His

Son conducted his life in Matthew 3:17 by saying:

"This is my beloved Son who doth always "glorify" me."

But rather God's Word DOES declare in Matthew 3:17:

"This is my beloved Son, in whom I am well "pleased".

When Jesus wanted to state what the overriding principle by which He lived His life was, He DID NOT say:

"...For I do always those things that "glorify" Him." John 8:29

Rather, He DID state:

"For I do always those things that "please" Him." John 8:29

Neither does the Apostle Paul insinuate that man's ultimate aim and purpose should be to "glorify God". For Paul DOES NOT state in Romans 8:8:

"So then they that are in the flesh cannot "glorify" God."

Rather, Paul DOES make the declaration:

"So then they that are in the flesh cannot "please" God."

In so doing, Paul effectively implies that "the pleasing of God" should be the issue of the utmost importance in the life of a Christian regarding Judgment.

In addition to these factors, on a purely rational theological basis, the action of glorifying God could never be the primary factor in God's judgment of mankind. This is because there are numerous instances in Scripture where the Christian is commanded to glorify God (Isaiah 42:12, Matthew 5:16, I Corinthians 6:20, 10:31, Revelation 14:7). According to the 17th Chapter of the Book of Luke, man is not to necessarily expect any reward for doing those things that are commanded of him, for they are a part of what Scripture calls man's "reasonable service", or "duty", unto God:

"Doth he thank that servant because he did the things that were commanded Him? I trow not.

So likewise ye, when ye shall have done all those things which are commanded you, say, We are unprofitable servants: we have done that which is our duty to do." Luke 17:9,10

This fact alone disqualifies "the glorification of God" as being the primary basis of judgment for mankind, for it is one of the things that the Christian has definitely been commanded to do (I Corinthians 6:20, 10:31). To make the glorification of God mankind's highest purpose in terms of Judgment is in direct contradiction to the clear teachings found in the 17th Chapter of the Book of Luke.

To this we must add that there is never an occurrence in God's Word where the Christian is commanded to "please God." This makes the pleasing of God uniquely qualified amongst Christian works to be the ultimate basis of Judgment and rewards for faithful service to the Lord, as it works in perfect harmony with the parable of the obedient servant found in the 17th Chapter of Luke's Gospel.

All other aspects of the Christian life such as loving others, giving, glorifying God, prayer, and worship are effectively ruled out as candidates for the primary basis of God's assessment of our lives, as the Christian has been "commanded" at some point in Scripture to perform each and every one of these other functions.

So again, we see that the singular most important thing for a Christian should be that of "living a life that is pleasing unto God". This is the ultimate purpose for which mankind was created and should therefore be the focus of the Christian's walk with the Lord.

Scripture tells us: "Thou art worthy, O Lord, to receive glory and honor and power: for Thou hast created all things, and for thy pleasure they are and were created." Revelation 4:11

Every man, woman, and child shares this same general calling, and it will be the basis of God's assessment for each and every one of our lives. Scripture informs us that the pleasing of God is not only accomplished by doing God's will (I John 3:22), but more importantly, by "willing God's will" in one's life (Philippians 2:13).

A person's vocational calling is of secondary importance in God's Economy. The Apostle Paul stated that it was of necessity that he preached the Gospel (I Corinthians 9:16). It was a job from which he could not escape. During the course of his vocational calling, Paul had been beaten, stoned, and left shipwrecked on numerous occasions (II Corinthians 11:25). He likely was growing tired of the abuse. The temptation to engage in self-pity was always there for Paul. Paul recognized this fact and knew that he would only be rewarded for his service, if he would perform his duties "willingly", and not begrudgingly (I Corinthians 9:17). Paul knew that the essence of pleasing God was to be found in our "willing God's will" throughout all of the circumstances of our lives, whether those circumstances were pleasant or unpleasant.

Non-believers do not know God, so they can never be motivated out of a personal love for God to will God's will in their lives. It only follows then that they cannot please Him, a fact that Paul brings to light in Romans 8:8:

"So then they that are in the flesh cannot please God."

The Christian, however, has the moral option of "living to please God" as opposed to "living to please himself". The non-believer does not have this option. In that he does not know God, his only ultimate motivation can be the various ways in which he chooses to "please himself". Although a non-believer may lead

271

an exemplary life in terms of how people and society at large view him, in God's eyes, there is always a hint of selfishness in even the good things that non-believers do, for apart from saving faith, the non-believer can never be motivated by what God considers to be truly righteous motives.

"But we are all as an unclean thing, and all our righteousnesses are as filthy rags; and we all do fade as a leaf; and our iniquities, like the wind, have taken us away." Isaiah 64:6

So not only should the pleasing of God be the focus and goal of the Christian's life, it should also be the backbone of the Christian's study in matters pertaining to Judgment in Scripture. We are commanded by God to be serious students of His Word (II Timothy 2:15). To cease to be a student of His Word is not an option. It is a life-long endeavor. The proper recognition and categorizing of the most important aspects of Scripture, those aspects which Jesus referred to as the "weightier matters of the law" in Matthew 23:23, is part and parcel to "rightly dividing the word of truth." Again, this is all to be done in order that the Christian may be found to be a workman that needeth not to be ashamed" when his life is assessed by God (II Timothy 2:15).

Not only is the issue of Man's Ultimate Purpose an essential part of Judgment, but so too are many of the other faulty paradigms that we have addressed during the course of this book. Understanding the differences in God's perspective of time and eternity compared to man's (FP #1), the Biblical teachings of free will (FP#2), the moral issues pertaining to good and evil (FP #3), God's basis of judgment being more concerned with motives as opposed to actions (FP #4), and the differences between "sin" and "sins"(FP#8), are all integral for our understanding of what Scripture teaches concerning the topic of Judgment.

When we remove the numerous faulty paradigms concerning the above-mentioned Biblical topics, it is then that we see how these Biblical topics augment and complement one another, intertwining and weaving into a beautiful mosaic that expresses an uncomplicated and simple explanation into the ways of God in His dealings with mankind in the matter of Judgment.

If we were to compare our understanding of Judgment with that of a well-ordered closet, it could be argued that the doctrinal supporting bar in the closet upon which all of the other doctrines and topics concerning God's Judgment should hang, would be that of Man's Ultimate Purpose (that of being "Pleasing to God"). For all matters pertaining to Judgment are ultimately concerned with and related to this purpose. Without this supporting bar in our spiritual closets, our study of Scripture will not fit neatly together, and the various topics and doctrines that pertain to Judgment would likely end up in disorderly random piles upon the floor.

Again, through a better understanding of the many issues involved in Judgment, the Christian becomes far more capable of attaining proper focus in his or her walk with the Lord, thus freeing them from living a life that "majors in the minors".

Mercy

The second item of importance that Jesus mentions in the "weightier matters of the Law", is that of Mercy. Now, when we talk about mercy, we are in reality talking about love, for mercy and love are synonymous. A merciful heart is a loving heart, for God's love is revealed in His mercy by sending Jesus to die for our sins.

It is likely that God used the word "mercy" as opposed to simply incorporating the word "love" in this listing of the weightier matters of the law in order to convey to believers that He desires them to be "non-judgmental" in their expressions of love towards others.

We know from our earlier study of the Book of Job, that in

273

God's eyes it is not enough for the believer to simply possess a proper understanding of Biblical Doctrine. For the study of Scripture must also be consciously mixed with a loving and merciful heart towards our fellow man: "Thou shalt love thy neighbor as thyself" (Matthew 22:39), and "Forgive in order that you might be forgiven" (Matthew 6:14,15).

As we have seen, Job had a good understanding of Biblical Doctrine. He understood God's Sovereignty, the fact that all things come into the life of the believer through God's Hands ("The Lord gave, and the Lord hath taken away." Job 1:21). Job also understood the concept of Good and Evil, of how God uses both Good and Evil to accomplish His ends ("Shall we receive good at the hand of the Lord? and shall we not receive evil" Job 2:10)? In addition to this, long before Paul had written Romans 8:28 ("All things work together for good to them that love God, to those who are called according to His purpose"), Job understood the principles of this particular passage of Scripture. This is evident because when all the evil had befallen Job, and he had lost his wealth, health, and his children, Job's response was to fall face down to the ground and worship the Lord (Job 1:20)! Job knew that in the end, God was faithful, and that He was going to work out these calamities that came into Job's life into something that was both good and necessary for him, which prompted Job to declare:

"Though he slay me, yet will I trust in him." Job 13:15

Although Job possessed great understanding of God and His ways, he was still lacking in one area of his life, that of being a loving and merciful person. When Jesus was treated unjustly by His fellow man, He reacted by saying, "Father forgive them, for they know not what they do" (Luke 23:34). When Job was treated unfairly by his friends, he replied to them in disgust, "Miserable comforters are ye all" (Job 16:2). He was anything but merciful and loving in his attitude towards them. It was not until Job had seen the error of his way, and had prayed for these same friends, that God pulled His Disciplinary Hand away, and restored unto

Job twofold the wealth that he had possessed before the initiation of the severe discipline that had been meted out from the Sovereign Hand of God (Job 42:10).

Perhaps Job's dilemma has been best described in the words of John Wesley, who stated, "Beware ye be not swallowed up in books, for an ounce of Love is worth a pound of Knowledge."

If the experience of Job is any indication, it can be said that in addition to faithfully studying God's Word, the Christian must also be faithfully vigilant in assessing the condition of his or her own heart in order to be found consistently walking in a state of true love towards both God and mankind. Evidence of this fact can be found in God's Word when it implores the believer to, "Keep your heart with all diligence, for out of it are the issues of life" (Proverbs 4:23).

While the many aspects and actions of the Christian's life such as prayer, giving, worship, service, etc., are indeed important and of great value, apart from pleasing God, none of these other facets of the Christian life are as important as love. When Jesus was asked which commandment was the greatest, He answered:

"Thou shalt love the Lord thy God with all thy heart, and with all thy soul, and with all thy mind.

This is the first and great commandment.

And the second is like unto it, Thou shalt love thy neighbor as thyself.

On these two commandments hang all the law, and the prophets." Matthew 22:37-40

The Apostle Paul addresses this same issue in his first epistle to the Church at Corinth, when he states:

"Though I speak with the tongues of men and of angels, and have not charity, I am become as sounding brass, or a tinkling cymbal." I Corinthians 13:1

Without love, all of our efforts can be considered to be in vain. Later in his epistle to the Corinthians Paul reiterates the importance that God places upon love when he writes:

"Let all your things be done with charity." I Corinthians 16:14

Peter also acknowledges the importance of love in the life of a Christian when he states:

"And above all things have fervent charity among yourselves: for charity shall cover the multitude of sins." I Peter 4:8

From this verse we can understand that when a Christian's life is motivated by a loving heart, it causes God to overlook many of his other shortcomings!

Of course, the greatest exhibition of love in human history was exhibited on the cross by the Lord Jesus Christ, who took upon himself the full weight of the sins of all of those who would come to Him for forgiveness.

It is at this point that the first two items in our study of the weightier matters of the law, justice and love (judgment and mercy), come together and require some additional elaboration on the mechanics of justice.

God's Standard of Justice

When it comes to Law, God's standards take a back seat to no one. Within the western legal system there is a commonly known principle called "double jeopardy". Essentially, double jeopardy is a procedural legal defense that prevents an accused person from being tried more than once on the same or similar charges, and on the same essential facts in cases following a prior valid acquittal or conviction. In like manner, if Jesus' death on the

276

cross had been for the "sins of ALL of mankind", then also under the principle of double jeopardy, God would not have a legal basis to try those who have rejected His plan for redemption at a later date and time. For if the full penalty for ALL the sins of mankind had already been paid for at the cross, then the "Great White Throne Judgment" which occurs at the close of the Millennial Age would in essence be, an "invalid trial".

For God to have the ability to try unbelievers at the Great White Throne, Jesus' death on the cross could not have been merely a symbolic death that potentially covered all of mankind's sins, but rather would had to have been accomplished specifically for each person who would ever come to him through faith, and for each one of those particular individual's sins which they had committed during the course of their lives.

In addition to having to experience the literal guilt, shame, and punishment for every sin that His followers had ever committed during their earthly lives, Jesus would also have to experience a separation between Himself and God the Father and Holy Spirit during the time in which He was taking upon Himself all those individual sins. For we know that God can neither look at sin or be a part of sin in any way (Habakkuk 1:13).

We also know that from our study regarding God's perspective versus man's perspective, in God's world, time can not only be eclipsed (John 6:21, Jude 1:14), but it can also be stretched out into indeterminable lengths ("And the sun stood still, and the moon stayed, until the people avenged themselves upon their enemies..." Joshua 10:13). When God the Father poured out the individual sins that every believer throughout the ages had either committed, or would ever commit, the time that it would have taken to do such a large accounting from our human perspective would have been seemingly endless. We simply cannot fathom how this amount of judgment involving the sins of millions of believers could have been accomplished in the matter of three hours. We must remember however that the passing of one day to the Lord is akin to the passage of 1000 years of time to us as human beings (Psalm 90:4, II Peter 3:8). When we realize by extrapolation that the three hours that Jesus spent on the cross would be to us an expanse of time of 125 years (three hours being 1/8th of a 24-hour day, 1/8th of 1000 years being equal to 125 years), then it becomes much easier to fathom how such a vast undertaking could have been accomplished by the Lord during the three hours that He was under Judgment on the Cross.

In addition to this, when we consider that Jesus Christ as the 2nd Person of the Trinity had always known perfect fellowship with God the Father and Holy Spirit for all eternity, it follows that from Jesus' perspective, this break in fellowship between Himself and the Father and Holy Spirit must have amounted to what was in His reality, an "eternity of time" (oxymoron intended) while He endured the sufferings of the cross. While our human clocks meaninglessly clicked on for three hours, His internal (and eternal) clock must have slowly clicked on for what may have amounted for Him to be an indeterminable and experientially endless period of time!

It is quite apparent that the love Jesus Christ has for believers is so strong that He would experience a seemingly endless separation from God (hell) for their sakes. Such magnitude of love is hard for us to imagine. If we are honest with ourselves, we all know that our immediate thoughts for our fellow man are all too often, "anything but loving." Rather than being merciful towards others in their human frailties, we are often quick to judge and condemn our fellow man.

The lack of love and concern towards others that we commonly exhibit is in stark contrast to the love of Christ. Thankfully, through the inner workings of the Holy Spirit in the life of Christians, God changes our hearts to become more like His. While some may say that the Christian life is "a changed life", the fact is that the Christian life is "an exchanged life."

"I am crucified with Christ: nevertheless I live; yet not I, but Christ liveth in me: and the life which I now live in the flesh I live by the faith of the Son of God, who loved me, and gave himself for me." Galatians 2:20

Through our "dying daily" to self (I Corinthians 15:31), the Holy Spirit interjects the heart of Christ into the Christian in order that he or she may be more and more like Him.

While the growth to become Christlike can be a slow and arduous process, in the end, in eternity, Scripture states that all believers shall fully possess the love of Christ:

"Beloved, now are we the sons of God, and it doth not yet appear what we shall be: but we know that, when He shall appear, we shall be like Him; for we shall see Him as He is." I John 3:2

This possession of the Love of Christ is not merely a "pie in the sky" hope. For Scripture records two instances, one in the Old Testament and one in the New Testament, where individual believers have possessed the Love of Christ during the course of living out their individual lives while still here on earth.

The first person in Biblical history to possess the Love of Christ was Moses, the man whom God chose to communicate with, "face to face" (Exodus 33:11). When the nation of Israel sinned in the wilderness by making a golden calf, and God had brought harsh judgment upon them, Moses attempted to intervene on Israel's behalf, by offering to have God's judgment fall upon him for an eternity in lieu of his brethren, the Hebrew people. Scripture records Moses' words as follows:

"Yet now, if thou wilt forgive their sin; and if not, blot me, I pray thee, out of thy book which thou hast written." Exodus 32:32

Here we have Moses offering to receive eternal separation from God if God would only lift His hand of judgment off Moses' brethren, the Hebrew people.

Paul later in the New Testament would also display this same Love of Christ in the Book of Romans, when he too offered to be eternally separated from God for the sake of his Jewish brethren in order that they might be saved:

"For I could wish that myself were accursed from Christ for my brethren, my kinsmen according to the flesh:" Romans 9:3

So, we see that possessing the Love of Christ is not beyond the realm of our earthly existence. It is possible for the Christian to experience it while still in one's mortal body.

Faith

The last topic mentioned by Jesus concerning "the weightier matters of the law", is that of Faith. It is important to realize that Biblical saving Faith is far different than simple human faith, for human faith requires one's own personal reasoning abilities. Scripture tells us that Biblical saving Faith is not a product of human reasoning, but rather it is a belief and trust in God that comes to the believer as a gift from God at the time of the believer's salvation:

"By grace are you saved through faith; and that not of your-selves: it is the gift of God, and not of works, lest any man should boast." Ephesians 2:8,9

While there are many facets to Biblical Faith, for the purposes of this discussion, we will concern ourselves with the aspects of faith as they relate to the everyday life of the believer in Christ, and how faith relates to the other two weightier matters of the law, Judgment and Mercy (love).

In our study of the Faulty Paradigm of "God helps those who help themselves", we learned that according to Scripture, quite the opposite is true. The Bible states that God is in the business of helping the helpless.

"He giveth power to the feint; and to them that have no might he increaseth strength." Isaiah 40:29

We've also come to understand that God matures believers through the mechanics of what many have termed as, "The Faith Rest Life". In this life, believers learn to rest by faith in the fact that God has sovereign control over their lives and will supply all their individual needs during the time of their individual pilgrimage here on earth.

In practice, the Christian life mirrors that of the Hebrew people during their wanderings in the Wilderness after their deliverance from Egypt. In the Wilderness, God continually brought the Hebrew people to places of need where their only hope was to trust in Him. The Hebrew people constantly failed in these times of testing that God had brought to them. Instead of trusting in God's care and promises to supply all their needs by faith, the Hebrew people instead chose to rebel and complain to both God and Moses. They faithlessly rejected the idea of God's sovereign control over their lives. Instead of learning to will God's will, they instead chose to will their own wills. They hardened their hearts against God (Hebrews 3:8), even though they had observed God's faithfulness in first delivering them from Egypt, and then in His providing for their daily needs for 40 years in the Wilderness (Hebrews 3:9).

We see then that the essence of the spiritual life of Old Testament believers was that of learning by faith to rest in the promises of God, a lesson that the majority of the Hebrews had failed miserably at accomplishing.

"Wherefore I was grieved with that generation, and said, They do always err in their heart; and they have not known my ways.

So I sware in my wrath, they shall not enter into my rest." Hebrews 3:10,11

Just as God had started the process of spiritual growth for the Hebrew people by first delivering them out of slavery in Egypt, so God initiates the spiritual growth of the individual Christian in the New Testament through first delivering them from the slave market of sin at the time of their salvation. Thereafter, the Christian's life mirrors that of the Hebrews in the Old Testament. For after trusting in God for the big thing in life (salvation), the Christian must then learn to trust in Him for the little things, the daily needs of life. By this resting in God, the Christian is displaying to the Universe that God is not only good and faithful, but He is also sovereign over all aspects of life. As He did with the Hebrews in the Wilderness, God now leads Christians into circumstances where the Christian's only hope is to be found in relying upon God and His faithful provisions for their life.

"But my God shall supply all your need according to his riches in glory by Christ Jesus." Philippians 4:19

Like the ancient Hebrews, the Christian is implored to trust in the promises of God, and by faith, to enter into this rest.

"There remaineth therefore a rest to the people of God.

For he that is entered into his rest, he also hath ceased from his own works, as God did from His." Hebrews 4:9,10

Entering into this faith-rest life is counter-intuitive to the normal ways of mankind. Sarah Young, in her book "Jesus Calling", writes:

"In a world characterized by working and taking, the admonition to rest and receive seems too easy."

The Christian must always remember however that God's ways are not man's ways:

"For my thoughts are not your thoughts, neither are your ways my ways, saith the LORD.

For as the heavens are higher than the earth, so are my ways higher than your ways, and my thoughts than your thoughts."

Isaiah 55:8,9

Scripture acknowledges that the life of learning to rest in God is not easy. This is why the writer of Hebrews implores the Christian to "...Labor therefore to enter into his rest, lest any man fall after the same example of unbelief." Hebrews 4:11

Paul tells us that the failures of the Hebrew people to enter into the faith-rest life are recorded in Scripture to admonish the Christian in this present age to be careful not to do the same thing and thereby fail to enter into the life of resting by faith in the faithfulness of God.

"Now all these things happened unto them for examples: and they are written for our admonition, upon whom the ends of the world are come." I Corinthians 10:11

Like the Hebrews, the Christian is not to live in overt sins (I Corinthians 10:5-10). The Christian is also to recognize that all of the events of his life come to him through the Sovereign Hand of God:

"For of Him, and through Him, and to Him, are all things..." Romans 11:36

Through all the events of his or her life, both good and evil, the Christian is to accept by faith that God is working all things together for good" (Romans 8:28). The believer is therefore called to give thanks to God for all things and in all circumstances of life.

"In everything give thanks, for this is the will of God in Christ Jesus concerning you." I Thessalonians 5:18

"Giving thanks always for all things unto God and the Father in the name of our Lord Jesus Christ." Ephesians 5:20

By living with less than a thankful attitude, the Christian makes the same mistake that the Hebrews made in their Wilderness wanderings, that of faithlessly harboring a complaining attitude towards God and His Sovereign ways. When a Christian constantly spends his days with less than a thankful and trusting attitude towards God, he is in essence repeating the same mistakes of the Hebrews of old, and in his own way is "constantly complaining to God". Anything short of living with a spirit and attitude of joy and thankfulness is in God's reality, living a faithless life that is a public display of rejecting the goodness of God and the truthfulness of His promises. The Christian is to pay heed to Paul's warning, "That whatsoever is not of faith, is sin" (Romans 14:23).

Pastor Bob Mumford once told the story of a fellow pastor who had asked one of his parishioners, "How are things going?" The parishioner replied, "Fine, under the circumstances." To this the pastor then remarked, "What are you doing under there?"

The faith-rest life demands a thankful spirit that by faith, takes God at His Word. A life in which the believer rises above negative circumstances, knowing that God is working all the events of his life together for his eventual good.

In summation, the Christian's new life in Christ is a life of growing in the knowledge of the Lord and of His ways. True love can never come from anything less than true understanding. Starting out with the basic doctrines or milk of the Word (I Peter 2:2), the Christian must then steadfastly continue on in growth until he or she is able to receive the deep "meat of the Word" (Hebrews 5:13,14). The Christian life is an extreme educational quest into understanding God and His Ways, especially in the realm of what Jesus termed as being "the weightier matters of the law": Judgment, Mercy, and Faith.

As we have seen throughout the course of this book, Christian theology is relatively simple, requiring no more intellectual sophistication than what is possessed by the average high school student. Christian theology only becomes difficult when one develops faulty understandings of the basic doctrines found within God's Word. These "faulty paradigms" serve to blind the believer's ability to successfully integrate Scripture into an easy to comprehend, composite whole.

After the Christian has become versed in their understanding of the various aspects of God's Judgments, especially of the fact that the primary focus of one's life should be that of "pleasing God", the 2nd "weightier matters of the law" comes in to play, that being the matter of Mercy or love. As we have seen in the case of Job, and reaffirmed by the Apostle Paul, without love, all the knowledge of God and His Ways in Judgment are without benefit. Christian love is not just a sentimental feeling but should be born out of the fact that the believer now has the love of Christ within him, and that they are to be constantly aware of whether he or she is being ruled by the love of Christ, or by their old sinful nature. The Spirit of Christ has a genuine concern for others, the sinful nature does not. When a Christian becomes aware of a lack of concern for others, it is then that they should come to the realization that they are not being led by the Spirit, but rather by their own flesh:

"For the flesh lusted against the Spirit, and the Spirit against the flesh: and they are contrary the one to the other: so that ye cannot do the things that ye would." Galatians 5:17

"But the fruit of the Spirit is love, joy, peace, longsuffering, gentleness, goodness, faith,

Meekness, temperance: against such there is no law." Galatians 5:22,23

The 3rd aspect of the "weightier things of the law", Faith, is the vehicle by which the first two aspects (Judgment and Love) are transported. This is spelled out beautifully in Scripture by the fact that God's Word is careful to bind Faith together with both Judgment and Love.

In the Book of Hebrews, we find Faith joined to Judgment:

"But without Faith, it is impossible to Please him…" Hebrews 11:6

In his letter to the Ephesians, Paul unites Faith with Love:

"That Christ may dwell in your hearts by Faith; that ye, being rooted and grounded in Love, May be able to comprehend with all saints what is the breadth, and length, and depth and height; And to know the Love of Christ, which passeth knowledge, that ye might be filled with all the fulness of God." Ephesians 3:17-19

The Apostle Paul also wrote of this intimate relationship between Faith and Love on numerous other occasions. In the Book of Galatians, Paul ties Faith to Love, "…faith which worketh by love" (Galatians 5:6). Throughout the New Testament, Paul is careful to constantly show this intimate relationship between Faith and Love:

I Thessalonians 1:3 "Remembering without ceasing your work of Faith, and labour of Love…"

I Thessalonians 3:6 "…Timotheus came from you unto us, and brought us good tidings of your Faith and charity (Love), …"

I Thessalonians 5:8 "… putting on the breastplate of Faith and Love: …"

II Thessalonians 1:3 "… your Faith groweth exceedingly, and the charity (Love) of every one of you all toward each other aboundeth."

I Timothy 1:14 "And the grace of our Lord was exceeding abundant with Faith and Love which is in Christ Jesus."

I Timothy 2:15 "… if they continue in Faith and charity (Love) …"

I Timothy 4:12 "… in charity (Love), in spirit, in Faith, in purity."

I Timothy 6:11 "… follow after righteousness, godliness, Faith, Love, patience, meekness."

II Timothy 1:13 "Hold fast the form of sound words, which thou hast heard of me, in Faith and Love which is in Christ Jesus."

II Timothy 2:22 "… follow righteousness, Faith, charity (Love), peace, with them that call on the Lord out of a pure heart."

Titus 2:2 "That the aged men be sober, grave, temperate, sound in Faith, in charity (Love), in patience.

Titus 3:15 "… Greet them that Love us in the Faith. Grace be with you all. Amen."

Philemon 5 "Hearing of thy Love and Faith, which thou hast towards the Lord Jesus, And toward all saints."

Again, it is the introduction of the Holy Spirit by God into the life of the believer at the time of salvation that simultaneously brings saving Faith (Ephesians 2:8,9), and equips the believer with the ability to understand the aspects of Judgment (I Corinthians 2:14). It is also through this channel of Faith that the Holy Spirit also brings the Love of Christ into the heart of the newly reborn believer. So, we see that it is through Faith that both Judgment and Love are introduced and made alive in the heart of the believer. It is also through Faith that the believer fully understands that the union of Judgment and Love reach their ultimate expression in the Cross of Christ.

Finally, at the end of each and every day, the Christian can assess their behavior in their faith walk with the Lord by not only reflecting upon their actions of the day, but more importantly, by considering if their attitude had been one of constant thankfulness and gratitude towards the Lord or not. For when the Christian is exhibiting less than a thankful and loving attitude, it is a clear indication that they are not fulfilling their primary duty in life, that of "willing God's will", and in so doing, living life in a manner that is found to be "pleasing unto God".

We can now easily recognize how the matters of Judgment, Mercy, and Faith work in perfect unity and harmony with one another to form the essence of the Christian life. For all three are woven together in Scripture to form a beautiful tapestry that is both simple, and easy to comprehend. An outline that provides the proper Spiritual guide and focus for the daily Christian life and affirms the reason why Jesus put so much importance on these three, "weightier matters of the law".

Epilogue

Throughout the course of studying some of the faulty paradigms that afflict the Church, it has been the author's hope that the reader would not only come to a better understanding of many of the more challenging aspects of Scripture but would also come to see the utter simplicity of basic Christian Theology. When we as believers have our understanding of the various doctrines and topics of Scripture tainted by the many faulty paradigms that have been generated through the years, then the simplicity of the Gospel breaks down and becomes obscured.

In God's Economy, the Truthfulness of His Word ranks high in the hierarchy of God's own values. The Psalmist tells us:

"...For thou hast magnified thy word above thy name." Psalm 138:2

In other words, God regards the veracity of His Word above His own Personage. He has ordained that there will be strict punishment for those who would change His Word in any way:

"For I testify unto every man that heareth the words of the prophecy of this book, if any man shall add unto these things, God shall add unto him the plagues that are written in this book:

And if any man shall take away from the words of the book of this prophecy, God shall take away his part out of the book of life, and out of the holy city, and from the things that are written in this book." Revelation 22:18,19

Scripture also teaches that there shall be strict discipline imposed upon those who would misrepresent Him or His Word. When the Hebrew people had no water to drink in the Wilderness, God instructed Moses to take his rod and strike a large rock, after which streams of water poured out of the rock (Exodus 17:6). Later in their wanderings, they once again ran out of water, and God then instructed Moses to merely "speak to the rock" in order to supply the people with water (Numbers 20:8).

What God was doing here was setting up a Biblical type. The Rock, which represented Jesus Christ, who was once smitten, "once offered" (Hebrews 9:28), in order to provide the waters of salvation, was now to be simply spoken to in order to supply the true "living waters" (John 4:10, Revelation 7:17). Rather than merely speaking to the rock, Moses had instead struck the Rock twice with his rod (Numbers 20:11), thus obscuring God's intention of establishing a Biblical Type in His Word. God was still faithful, he did supply the people with water from the Rock, but for this sin of disobedience in his misrepresenting God to the people, Moses was not allowed to enter the Promised Land (Numbers 20:12).

How careful then should we as believers be in our representations of God and His Word to the world around us. The many faulty paradigms that have developed throughout the history of the Church have by and large come down to us by means of well-intentioned people. Unfortunately, these people were seemingly guided more by their feelings and/or cultural traditions than they were by God's Holy Word. According to Jesus, these misrepresentations and misunderstandings of God's Word only serve to drive one's heart further away from the Lord:

"This people draweth nigh unto me with their mouth, and honoureth me with their lips; but their heart is far from me.

But in vain they do worship me, teaching for doctrine the commandments of men." Matthew 15:8,9

If we were asked to hypothetically envision in our minds what we would imagine to be a picture of the perfect Peace of the Lord, many of us would conjure up an image of a person lying on a couch or bed, the fingers of his (or her) hands interlocked and placed upon their chest, with a contented smile upon their face. Now imagine if you will, if each of the fingers of this person's hands were individually representative of the many topics within this study (Free Will, Good and Evil, Man's Ultimate Purpose, etc.). If one's concept of the numerous afore-mentioned doctrines and topics were accurate, then their fingers would naturally be straight, allowing for them to easily interlock together, and thus enabling the believer to view Scripture as a simple and integrated composite whole. However, should one's concepts of some or many of these theological topics be found to be in error, then the fingers representing those topics would not be straight, but rather gnarled and crooked. These fingers could never be successfully integrated with one another should the believer attempt to clasp his hands together. In like manner, we can surmise that there would be little harmony between the various topics and doctrines of Scripture, when the believer's understanding of these topics and doctrines are clouded by faulty paradigms. Not only do faulty paradigms inhibit the believer from successfully integrating the various topics of Scripture into a composite whole, but they can also serve to prevent the believer from experiencing the complete Peace and Contentment that is to be found in the LORD and His Word.

A Caveat

We have observed throughout the course of this study that one of the leading misconceptions within Christendom is the failure of the Church to recognize the dominating role that Jesus Christ plays within the pages of the Old Testament record. While these truths can be exhilarating to learn, they do present a problem in the form of potentially creating another faulty paradigm, that being, "God the Father is distant and aloof from His Creation."

The believer in Christ can easily see the demonstrated love and care that the 2nd Person of the Trinity has for him or her, and the indwelling of the Holy Spirit is a constant reminder of the love, presence, and comfort of the Trinity's 3rd Person. However, the love and concern that God the Father has for the believer is not so readily seen or experienced.

Thankfully, the Apostle Paul addressed this issue in his letter to the Church at Ephesus:

"Blessed be the God and Father of our Lord Jesus Christ, who hath blessed us with all spiritual blessings in heavenly places in Christ:

According as he hath chosen us in him before the foundation of the world, that we should be holy and without blame before him in love:

Having predestinated us unto the adoption of children by Jesus Christ to himself, according to the good pleasure of his will." Ephesians 1:3-5

In this passage of Scripture, Paul is explaining to believers that it was the 1st Person of the Trinity, God the Father, who both knew and loved us long before He had the worlds created by Jesus Christ. That it was of God the Father's original choosing that we have been brought into the household of faith.

Rather than being seemingly distant and uncaring, it is God the Father who initially planned the creation of, and eternal blessings for, all believers in Jesus Christ. Here in the book of Ephesians, we see that the love that God the Father has for the individual believer is both deep and personal. For the believer's very existence and future blessings have all come to us as a result of the loving Plan of God the Father.

Again, in any theological study which incorporates a wide range of subject matter, a certain redundancy of thoughts and/or examples can often occur. This occasional repetition of ideas however has been necessary in order to produce a more complete and better understanding within the individual studies.

Three appendixes have also been included in this work to reveal additional faulty paradigms that are more historical than theological in nature.

May God bless all who read this exposé on faulty paradigms, and may it serve to not only bring God glory, but also to bring the reader closer to each member of the Godhead through the experience of losing their own faulty misconceptions of Christian Theology. May the reading of this study truly be, a time of "Paradigms Tossed".

APPENDIXES

The Problem with the New Bible Versions

"The Modern Versions of the Bible are more accurate than the King James Version of the Bible because they are translated from older, and thus more reliable, manuscripts. In addition to this, the language of the King James Bible is archaic, and much harder to understand than modern English"

These are just some of the arguments that have been put forward to sell the modern translations of the Bible such as the RV, the NIV, the NASB, the Living Bible, the NKJV, and the host of other new Bible Translations that have been published since 1881. In order to better understand these attacks upon the traditional King James Bible, it is first necessary to give a brief history of the manuscripts used in the preparation of the various translations of the Bible.

A Brief History of Bible Manuscripts

The early manuscripts that have been used to translate the Bible for the most part fall under two separate categories, the Majority Texts, and the Minority Texts. The numerous sets of manuscripts that make up the Majority Texts, constitute over 80% of the written manuscripts, while the Minority Texts used in most Modern Bible translations constitute only about 1% of the other known Biblical manuscripts.

The Majority Text has come to us from numerous geographical locations, and while it is often referred to as the Textus Receptus, it is also typically called the Byzantine Text. This is because these manuscripts were prevalent during the Byzantine Period (A.D. 312 – 1453) of World History. These Greek texts were the texts of the Greek Church before the Reformation, and then the recognized Greek Text for the entire Christian Church for the immediate three centuries following the Reformation.

The manuscripts that make up the Minority Text come to us out of one geographical area, Alexandria, Egypt. For the most part, they fall under four different manuscript groups, Vaticanus (also known as B), Sinaiticus (Aleph), Bezae (D), and Papyrus 75. These groups not only disagree with the Majority Texts, but also with one another.

Regarding the faulty paradigm, "The Minority Texts are more accurate than the Majority Texts on the basis of their being older manuscripts", we can quickly and easily surmise that on a theological basis, this argument is fundamentally unsound. For the Bible tells us that there were those who were attempting to corrupt the Biblical texts of the New Testament, even as the New Testament was being written. In Paul's 2nd letter to the Corinthians, he writes:

"For we are not as many, which corrupt the word of God: but as of sincerity, but as of God, in the sight of God speak we in Christ." II Corinthians 2:17

In addition to the fact that, "Older is not necessarily better" with regard to Biblical manuscripts, we now know that the claim that the Alexandrian Minority Texts are older than the Majority Text's manuscripts is simply not true. The oldest of the Majority Text's manuscripts, P66, is now known to date back to A.D. 175, while the oldest manuscript from the Alexandrian Minority

Texts, Papyrus 75, is thought to date back to 200 A.D.

Regarding the other faulty paradigm, "That the Modern Versions of the Bible are "better" than the King James Version because the language employed in them is "easier to understand", we see that this argument also falls apart when held up to objective analyses. In a study led by the Grade-Level research company, Flesch-Kincaids, it was discovered that the King James Bible was easier to understand than the Modern Versions in over 88% of the passages that were analyzed. The researchers found that in their estimation, the King James Bible is typically easier to understand than the Modern Bible Versions largely because the King James Version commonly utilizes simple one or two syllable words, while the Modern Versions substitute this simplicity for multi-syllable words and phrases. In other words, the Modern Versions often employ a far more excessive and arduous language.

That the King James Bible's simplicity of speech translation is the better choice is affirmed by Paul in his second letter to the Corinthians:

"Seeing then that we have such hope, we use great plainness of speech." II Cor. 3:12, KJV

H. L. Mencken, arguably one of the most preeminent linguists of the 20th Century, made this statement about the King James Bible, when comparing it to the Modern Versions:

"An English Revised Version was published in 1885 and an American Revised Version in 1901, and since then many learned but misguided men have sought to produce translations that should be mathematically accurate, and in plain speech of every-day. But the Authorized Version has never yielded to any of them, for it is palpably and overwhelmingly better than they are.... Its English is extraordinarily simple, pure, eloquent, and lovely. It is a mine of lordly and incomparable poetry, at once the most stirring and the most touching ever heard of."

In addition to the language of the King James Bible being beautiful in and of itself, the Old English as employed in the King James Version is also a far more precise language than Modern English, and hence better suited for theological study. For example, in modern English, the distinction between singular and plural in pronouns is often blurred. As a case in point, in Modern English, the pronoun "you", can either be singular or plural. In the older English, the distinction between pronouns is precise. If a pronoun begins with a "T" (as in Thee, Thou, Thine, and Thy), then the pronoun is singular. If the pronoun begins with a "Y" (as in Ye or You), then the pronoun is plural. A prime example of the benefits of the precise nature of the Old English can be seen in Jesus' conversation with Nicodemus in the third chapter of the Gospel of John. Jesus said unto Nicodemus:

"Marvel not that I say unto thee, ye must be born again." John 3:7

When read in the Old English employed by the King James Version, what Jesus was saying to Nicodemus in essence was, "Marvel not that I say unto thee (specifically and singularly you) Nicodemus, Ye (both you and all of mankind) must be born again."

It should be noted that this exacting analyses of the verse is not possible using modern English pronouns.

So, we find that the stated arguments that were employed by the 19th Century translators in order to sell their new Modern Bible Versions, really do not stand up to honest scrutiny. Older is not necessarily better, especially regarding Bible manuscripts. Again, this is because there was corruption of the Biblical texts occurring even while the original manuscripts were being written. Even if older were better, the manuscripts that the Minority Texts are based upon are probably not older than the earliest existing manuscripts that were employed in the making of the King James Bible. In addition to this, apart from the fact that the modern-day reader of the Old English may have to familiarize himself with older style pronouns and spellings of certain words, the New Versions are really not easier to understand than the King James Bible due to the fact that they often employ "excessive verbiage." This in turn not only makes the Modern Translations harder to read, but also more difficult to memorize.

The fact that these Minority Text manuscripts which came to us out of Alexandria, Egypt are indeed the same manuscripts that had been rejected by Tertullian and other early Church Fathers as being "corrupted texts", should make today's Christian wary of these Modern Translations of the Bible. That these Alexandrian manuscripts have become the "go to texts" for modern Bible translators, begs the question, "How, and why on earth, did these discounted manuscripts that comprise the Minority Text, ever become the basis for the many new Modern Versions of the Bible?"

To answer this question, it is necessary to delve deeper into the history of the Minority Text.

The History of the Minority Text

The history of the Minority Texts traces back to the Philosophical School of Alexandria, Egypt, during the time that the Early Church was being established in the first three centuries of the modern era. Many scholars now contend that it was from this school that the newly written New Testament manuscripts had been corrupted. The person deemed most responsible for the altering of these manuscripts was Origen, who lived from 185 A.D to 254 A.D.

Origen, like the two preceding headmasters of the Alexandrian School, Pantaenus and Clement, was steeped in the philosophical constructs of Plato.

While most people believe that the great Greek philosophers

were only concerned with the realm of human reason, this is far from the truth. Plato's teacher, Socrates was deeply involved with the metaphysical world. He stated that, "A voice has been heard by me throughout my life... I call it a god or a daemon." Plato too was very conscious of the spiritual world. Unfortunately, many of his other worldly beliefs are diametrically opposed to the inspired Word of God as found in Scripture. Like Socrates, Plato too was interested in "oracles and daemons". He stated that the Universe contained "many beings more divine than man-daemons and gods, who are daemons of a superior order." Plato believed in a spiritual "hierarchy of beings". He also believed in the Biblically heretical concept of reincarnation. He wrote of mankind, "At their first embodiment, (they)... would be born a man... If he succeeds, he would pass to a home in his kindred star. If he failed at this, at his second birth, he would be a woman, next an animal."

Plato believed that the Universe was "subject to the laws of cyclic change," and that "God recreates the world over and over." Plato declared that God was not necessarily male or female but referred to God as "the One". He taught that, "The Universe is the thought of the universal mind or One." In homage to pantheism, he believed that the planet, "was endowed with life and reason".

On a more secular front, Plato was a humanist. He did not view mankind in the Biblical context of being a "sinner". He believed that man tends to "progressively grow". He referred to this growth of man as, "That which is always becoming." Plato believed that God made man as mortal creatures who would eventually become "Gods". This was picked up by Origen, who stated, "The end of life then ... is the progressive assimilation of man to God."

Plato also believed in an intellectual elitism and taught that in any society "the learned should rule", and "all religion and religious doctrine should be controlled by the state." He taught that the state should raise children from birth, "so that no parent knows his own child." In direct conflict with the Word of God,

Plato also believed that homosexual love was the highest form of love.

So, it can be clearly seen that the beliefs of Plato "fly into the face" of the beliefs and customs that are espoused by recognized Christian Doctrine. It is from this Platonic system of thought that Gnosticism would eventually blossom and grow. Gnosticism in part being the belief that man's freedom and salvation is to be found in knowledge. This knowledge, to the Gnostic, was often hidden, or esoteric. Again, the creed of the Gnostics flies in the face of Scripture, which warns of "Knowledge puffing up", and thereby serves to enhance man's sinful pride (I Corinthians 8:1).

What Origen and others from the Gnostic Alexandrian School attempted to do was to make the new Christian religion more palatable to their mystical, Gnostic way of thinking. Historical Greek scholar John Burgon, when commenting on the corruption of the Minority Texts, wrote:

"I am of the opinion that such deprivations of the text as found in Aleph and B (2 minority manuscript texts commonly used in Modern Bible versions), were in the first instance intentional. Origen may be regarded as the prime offender."

The early Church fathers recognized that these texts out of the Alexandria area of Egypt had been corrupted, so they were excluded from use in the early Church.

They also branded Origen a heretic due to the fact that he believed, amongst other things, that:

1) The sun, moon, and stars were living creatures.

2) That souls are pre-existent, and that Jesus took on a pre-existing soul.

3) That Jesus was not physically resurrected, and that man will not have a physical resurrection either.

301

4) That there will be no 2nd Coming of Jesus back to the earth.

5) That hell does not exist, and that Purgatory does exist.

6) That in the end, all, including Satan, will be reconciled to God.

7) That men should be emasculated.

We can see that it is with good reason that the Alexandrian Minority Texts that had been corrupted by Origen and others in the Alexandrian Schools, had been dismissed by Christendom and the historical Church for the better part of the history of the Church. It was not until the middle of the 19th Century, that these old "corrupted texts", were revived in England, and from there, into the Christian world. This was accomplished primarily through the efforts of two theologians from Cambridge University, Brooke Westcott and Fenton Hort.

Wolves in Sheep's Clothing

In the 7th chapter of Matthew's gospel, Jesus warned his disciples of "false prophets which come to you in sheep's clothing, but inwardly they are ravening wolves. Ye shall know them by their fruits" (Matthew 7:15,16).

Some would say that Brooke Westcott (1825-1901) and Fenton Hort (1828-1892) perfectly fit the bill for this warning from our Lord. For they came to the Christian community under the guise of religious pretense, as they were both ordained Priests in the Anglican Church. Their goal was to create a new Greek text for the formation of New Versions of the Bible. A new text that they claimed came from older and more reliable manuscripts. These manuscripts were however, the same aforementioned Minority Texts which had been corrupted by the Alexandrian School in Egypt. Again, texts that the early Church Fathers had rejected.

It has been contended by many that Westcott's and Hort's true intention in translating the old Alexandrian Minority Texts was that of injecting their Platonic beliefs into God's Word, thus undermining the traditional Christian values that God's Word inspires.

The list of Brooke Westcott's heretical beliefs is lengthy to the point of being voluminous.

1) Believed that Jesus' mother Mary was God in another form.

2) Believed that Jesus was just a man.

3) Did not believe that David in the Old Testament was an actual "chronological" person.

4) Did not believe in blood sacrifice. He believed that "the redemptive efficacy of Christ's work was to be found in his whole life."

5) Believed that Baptism, not the Blood of Christ brought man into a relationship with God.

6) Did not believe in the Deity of Christ ("Christ was and is a man.").

7) That Christians are co-equal with Christ ("Each Christian is in due measure a Christ").

8) Did not believe in the bodily resurrection of Christ, stating, "Socrates said, ... such as have purified themselves by philosophy live wholly without bodies for the future... The words are truly memorable."

9) Denounced the 2nd Coming of Jesus back to the earth, stating that there have been, "Many comings of Christ in the social forces."

10) Believed that Jesus, in essence, was a sinner.

11) Started many nefarious clubs, including "The Hermes Club" (Westcott's cohort Madame Blavatsky stated, "Satan or Hermes, are all one.").

12) Westcott did not believe in the Deity of Jesus Christ. He contended that, "Jesus never referred to himself as God", which of course is contrary to John 8:58, which states, "Before Abraham was, I Am.", and John 10:30, "I and my Father are one."

13) The various clubs that he either initiated or belonged to throughout his life (The Hermes Club, The Ghostly Guild, The Society for Psychical Research, The Eranus Club, The Apostle's, etc.) have all reportedly been involved with the sins of homosexuality, necromancy, and drug abuse, among others.

14) Believed that, The Apocrypha was "Divinely inspired".

There are many other facts about Westcott that should cause one to wonder, "How on earth could Brooke Westcott have been considered to be qualified by the Christian Theological community, to rewrite the New Testament? His religious beliefs were at best heretical, and all indications are such that he was more of a disciple of Plato and Origen than a follower of Jesus. In fact, Westcott's son stated that, "For many years, the writings of Origen were close to his hand, and he turned to them at every opportunity."

Westcott's devotion to Christianity can be seriously questioned due to the fact that his son also reported that it was Westcott's tradition at Christmas to tell the children, "Goblin stories".

The Christian should always heed the warning of the Lord, who stated in Matthew 7:20, "By their fruits, ye shall know them." One of the biggest red flags regarding Westcott's character and behavior is that he named the family dog, "Mephistopheles", which is the Greek equivalent for "devil" or Satan. Westcott had written to his son, "The dog is far more than a dog to me. He is a symbol."

Like many other intellectuals of the 19th Century (Sigmund Freud, Carl Jung, Lord Balfour, et al), Westcott devoted a substantial portion of his life to being obsessed with attempting to contact the spirit world. When one considers the fact that he was for the most part, "dumb" of speech (Many of his acquaintances stated that he was barely intelligible), in addition to his preoccupation with death (He formed the "Ghostly Guild" and belonged to many secretive clubs or groups that were obsessed with the paranormal, actively engaging in séances and necromancy), then one can question how much of his life was spent under the influence of "demonic forces". For two of the signs of demonic possession, as presented in the New Testament, are both "the inability to speak" (Matthew 9:32), and having, "a preoccupation with death" (Matthew 8:28).

Westcott's cohort, Fenton Hort, in earlier times, would also have likely been branded as a heretic, for Hort:

1) Did not believe in the Biblical concept of sacrificial atonement. Hort stated that, "The fact is, I do not see how God's justice can be satisfied without every man's suffering in his own person the full penalty for his sins."

2) Believed in purgatory, calling it, "A great and important truth."

3) Was a known necromancer who was deeply involved in "channeling." According to some historians, Hort may have indeed started the modern "New Age" channeling movement.

4) Described the King James Bible as being "villainous".

5) Referred to traditional evangelical Christians as being "dangerous", "unsound", "perverted", and "confused".

6) Claimed that America as an independent nation was "A standing menace to the whole civilization." In fact, Hort stated that he had a "deep hatred of democracy in all of its forms."

7) Was a big promoter of Root-Race Theory. The same theory of the advancement of the races that Adolph Hitler so notably based his actions upon.

8) Did not believe in the "Devil", or in an eternal "Hell".

9) Disavowed the existence of the Garden of Eden, stating, "I am inclined to believe that there is no such state as Eden..."

10) Believed that God was through with Israel, and believed in "Replacement Theology", the false doctrinal belief that the Church had permanently replaced Israel in God's Plan.

Hort was unabashedly devoted to his neo-Platonic beliefs during the 30 years that he and Westcott spent devising their Greek text (1851-1881). In a letter to the publisher of their New Greek text, A. MacMillan, Hort stated that during the time he and Westcott were working on revising the Greek text, that, "Plato was the center of my reading."

Inherent Problems with the New Bible Versions

The problems with the Modern Bible Versions that have been based upon the Westcott and Hort Greek translation are numerous and obvious. Included in the list of these new Bibles is The New International Version (NIV), The American Standard Version (NASB), Today's English Version (TEV), the New King James Version (NKJV), the Revised Standard Version (RSV), Good News For Modern Man, to name a few.

Listed below are just a small sampling of the many attacks on traditional Christianity that are to be found within the pages of the new Modern Bible translations.

The Deletion of Vast Amounts of Scripture

To the true man of God, every word found within Scripture is important. It is said of Samuel in the Old Testament, that he "did let none of His words fall to the ground" (I Samuel 3:19). Jesus said; "That man shall not live by bread alone, but by every word that proceedeth out of the mouth of God" (Matthew 4:4).

Scripture tells us of Satan's 3-fold modus operandi regarding the Word of God is to cause mankind to doubt God's Word (Genesis 3:1, "Hath God said"), to twist the meaning of the Word (Matthew 4:6 "If thou be the Son of God, cast thyself down, for it is written, He shall give His angels charge concerning thee"), and finally, to ultimately "steal" God's Word (Mark 4:15,"Satan taketh away the Word").

In the Modern Bible Versions, vast amounts of Scripture are simply deleted. It should be noted that the NIV Bible has 64,098 fewer words than the KJV. In developing their Greek text, Westcott and Hort oftentimes simply omitted many passages that did not fit into the Neoplatonic landscape that they were attempting to paint.

Dr. Gordon Fee of Wheaton College states that:

"The contemporary translations as a group have one thing in common: they tend to agree against the KJV... in omitting hundreds of words, phrases, and verses."

Modern Version Attacks Upon the Personages of the Triune Godhead

In numerous instances, the Modern Bible Versions refer to God, as the "One". According to author Gail Riplinger, in 800 instances in the NASB's Exhaustive Concordance, there is no Greek reference to allow for this change. So where does the idea of God being the "One", come from? Well from Plato, of course!

Plato did not believe in a specific God, nor did he believe that God was necessarily male or female, so he developed a gender-neutral name for God, "The One". Westcott and Hort, being the good disciples of Plato that they were, on many occasions felt obliged to change God's name to "The One", or simply "One".

For example, in John 12:45, in the King James Version of the Bible we read, "And he that seeth me seeth him who sent me." In the New American Standard Bible, this verse becomes:

"He who sees me sees the One who sent me".

Over and over again, in the Modern Bible Versions, God the Father becomes the "One". To what end one might ask? In the "Encyclopedia of Mysticism and Mystery Religions, "The term "One", is defined as, the

"Term for the Ultimate ..., in many mystery religions and philosophies."

So, we see that in the Modern Bible Versions, God often loses His particular individual Personage. He is no longer simply the "Lord GOD" or "Lord" (God the Father), or "LORD God" or "LORD" (God the Son), but in the New Bible Versions He often becomes "The One" or "One". In the Modern Bible Translations, God, as "The One", can become anything that you want Him to be; whether that be Buddha, Allah, Supreme Being, the Virgin Mary, or whichever God you may prefer on that particular day.

The Personage of Jesus also comes under attack in the Modern Bible Versions. In many instances, the pronouns, "You", "He", or "Him" are substituted for the specific name of Jesus (Matthew 4:18, Matthew 8:29, Mark 2:15, Mark 10:52, Luke 24:36) NASB NIV. Again, this is a subtle attack on the Personage of Jesus Christ.

Oftentimes the "Christ" of "Jesus Christ" (God our Savior), is also omitted in the Modern Versions (John 6:60, Acts 9:20,

Acts 19:4, I Corinthians 9:1, Hebrews 3:1, I John 1:7, Revelation 1:9, Revelation 12:17) NASB NIV. This of course downplays His role as the Savior of mankind. Interestingly, the Apostle John addresses this very issue:

"Who is a liar but he that denies that Jesus is the Christ." I John 2:22

Probably the most egregious assault upon the Person of Jesus, is the blurring of distinction between Jesus and Satan. In Revelation 22:16, Jesus is referred to as, the "morning star". It is one of the many different accepted names for the Lord Jesus. In the 14th Chapter of Isaiah, where Scripture chronicles the Devil's Fall, the traditional King James Text refers to Satan as "the son of the morning". The NIV however translates Isaiah 14:12:

"How have you fallen from heaven, "morning star", son of the dawn, you have been cast down to the earth, you who once laid low the nations."

So, in the NIV Version of the Bible, we now have Satan also becoming the "morning star". By simple inference, we can then logically assume that Satan and Jesus are both one and the same person! Such blasphemy.

In one of the many Pre-Incarnate appearances of Jesus in the Old Testament, that of His meeting with Shadrach, Meshach, and Abednego in Nebuchadnezzar's fiery furnace, the KJV in an obvious reference to Jesus Christ, proclaims Nebuchadnezzar stating, "... the form of the fourth (person) is like the Son of God." (Daniel 3:25). In the NIV and the NASB versions, the 2nd Person of the Trinity is removed, and the fourth person in the fire is now referred to as, "like a son of the gods".

The Modern Bible Versions also attack God the Holy Spirit. In traditional Scripture, the Holy Spirit is a close and personal God to the believer in Christ. Jesus often referred to Him as "the Comforter". The Holy Spirit was the Person who would come and intimately dwell within His disciples after Jesus had physically left the earth (John 14:16). In the Modern Bible translations, the personal "Comforter" of the KJV becomes either an impersonal "Helper" (NASB), or simply an "Advocate" (NIV), (John 14:14, John 14:26, John 15:26, and John 16:7).

In addition to each individual member of the Godhead coming under attack in the Modern Bible versions, we also see the Godhead itself assaulted. Neither Westcott nor Hort believed in the Trinity, so they opted to assault the great Trinitarian text of I John 5:7 as found in the King James Version of Scripture:

"For there are three that bear record in heaven, the Father, the Word (Jesus), and The Holy Ghost! And these three are one." I John 5:7 KJV

In the New International Version, again based upon the Westcott and Hort manuscript translation, the Three Personages of the Trinity are simply omitted:

"For there are three that testify: the Spirit, the water and the blood, and the three are in agreement." I John 5:7 NIV

Obviously, this rendering of the verse by the NIV effectively neutralizes the Biblical concept of the Trinity, as the only member of the Triune Godhead that is mentioned here is the "Spirit". So, we see that if one doesn't believe in, or like the idea of the Trinity, it's simple: You just write it out of the text!

"Doctrine as Opposed to Teachings"

In addition to the numerous attacks against the three members of the Godhead, we also find many other obvious and glaring areas where the Doctrines of the Church are also attacked. This starts with an attack on the concept of "Doctrine", itself.

Christianity is unique amongst the religions of the world in

310

that it maintains an exclusiveness when compared to all other religions. The God of Christianity claims to be the one and only God, and thereby does away with the validity of all other "religions":

"I am the Lord, and there is none else, there is no God beside me" (Isaiah 45:5). In addition to this, Christianity's method for man's salvation, is also exclusive:

"Jesus saith unto him, I am the way, the truth, and the life: no man cometh unto the Father but by me." John 14:6

Due to this exclusiveness that Christianity proclaims for itself, the tenets of its faith are never referred to as being simply "teachings", but rather, are termed as being, "Doctrine".

In numerous instances in Modern Bible translations however, the term "teachings", is substituted for "doctrine" (Matthew 7:28, 15:9, 16:12, 22:33, Mark 1:22, 1:27, 4:2, 7:7, 11:18, 12:38, Luke 4:32, John 7:16, 7:17, 18:19, Acts 2:42, 5:28, 13:12, 17:19, Romans 6:17, 16:17, I Corinthians 14:6, 14:26, I Timothy 1:10, 4:13, 4:16, 5:17, II Timothy 3:10, 3:16, II John1:9, Revelation 2:14, 2:15, 2:24) NIV and NASB et al.

By classifying the tenets of Scripture as mere "teachings", they become reduced in their significance to the level of the writings of other "teachers" such as Plato, Confucius, Mohammed, and Gandhi.

This attack on "Doctrine" is actually prophesied in the New Testament writings of Paul, who in his 2nd letter to Timothy wrote:

"For the time will come when they will not endure sound doctrine; but after their own lusts they shall heap to themselves teachers, having itching ears." II Timothy 4:3

The Removal of the Reality of Hell

Plato did not believe in a place of everlasting torment such as hell, and likewise, neither did Westcott or Hort. So we find that in the Modern Bible translations, that "hell" is often dismissed, and is often translated as either the "grave" (II Samuel 22:6, Job 11:8, Psalm 9:17, 16:10, 18:5, 55:15, 86:13 116:3, Proverbs 7:27, 15:24, Isaiah 5:14, 14:15, 28:15, Ezekiel 31:16, 31:17, 32:21, 32:27, Jonah 2:2, Habakkuk 2:5, Acts 2:27, 2:31) NIV, or simply as "death" (Deuteronomy 32:22, Job 26:6, Proverbs 23:14, 27:20, Isaiah 28:18, 57:9) NIV.

That the basic doctrines of Christendom should be hijacked by a pagan philosopher and his disciples, is a tragedy that defies description.

It should come as no surprise that Paul would warn the Colossian Church of the dangers of philosophy:

"Beware lest any man spoil you through philosophy and vain deceit, after the rudiments of the world, and not after Christ." Colossians 2:8

The Christian Becomes a Slave, and Hence God Becomes a Slave-Master

The Modern Versions can also be seen to denigrate the relationship of the Christian to his God. This is done by changing the concept of the Christian as being a "servant" of God, into a relationship where the Christian becomes a "slave" of God. This of course then transforms God into becoming a "slave-master". In the King James Version of John 15:20, we read:

"Remember the word that I said unto you, The servant is not greater than his lord. If they have persecuted Me, they will also persecute you."

In the New American Standard Version of the Bible, John 15:20 is rendered:

"Remember the word that I said to you, "A slave is not greater than his master", If they have persecuted me, they will also persecute you."

The change is subtle, but nonetheless insidious, for it creates a false dynamic regarding the relationship that exists between the Christian and his God.

This change of relationship for the Christian from being God's servant into becoming His slave, occurs numerous times as is evidenced in the New American Standard Bible (Mark 10:44, Luke 7:2, Luke 7:10, Luke 12:37, Luke 12:43, Luke 12:46, Luke 12:47, Luke 15:22, Luke 19:13, Luke 19:15, Luke 20:10, John 13:16, John 15:15, John 15:20, John 18:26, Acts 2:18, Romans 6:17, Romans 6:19, I Corinthians 7:21,21, Ephesians 6:5,6, Colossians 3:22, Colossians 4:1, I Timothy 6:1, II Peter 2:9, Revelation 6:15) NASB.

The Trashing of the Ten Commandments

Scripture is implicit in its warnings about the sin of idolatry. In Exodus 20:4, we read from the Ten Commandments:

"Thou shalt not make unto thee any graven image, or any likeness of anything that is in heaven above, or that is in the earth beneath, or that is in the water under the earth."

The history of Israel is a history of their being chastised by God for the worshipping of idols. The sin of idolatry however goes far beyond the overt act of worshipping physical objects. For anything that becomes more important to an individual other than God, is in fact, an idol. As an example, Jacob allowed his love for his son Joseph to get out of hand, and by so doing,

Joseph became an idol unto Jacob. This relational idolatry manifested itself by Jacob exhibiting favoritism towards Joseph over his brothers. This favoritism in turn caused his brothers to become jealous of Joseph, after which they subsequently sold him into slavery in Egypt, thus causing Jacob the pain of separation from his favorite son for an extensive length of time. So, we see that the sin of idolatry is quite serious in the eyes of God, and the repercussions for engaging in it can be quite severe.

Solomon too became a victim of idolatry by giving his many wives and concubines a more prominent place in his life than God. His lifelong struggle in finding true happiness apart from God is well chronicled in the Book of Ecclesiastes.

Much of the human misery found in the world in fact is a direct result of the sin of idolatry as mankind attempts to find ultimate happiness and fulfillment in this life through people, places, and things: and not in his Creator God.

In Paul's first letter to the Corinthians, he addresses the concern that the Corinthian Christians had about eating meats from the public markets, as a significant amount of those meats had been dedicated to the gods of that pagan city. Paul downplays the importance of abstaining from meats that had been ceremoniously offered to idols by writing, "an idol is nothing". Incredibly, in the New American Standard Bible, we find this declaration changed to:

"There is no such thing as an idol." I Corinthians 8:4 NASB

This rendering changes the entire meaning and intent of the verse, and of course, flies in the face of the totality of what Scripture has to say about idolatry. For, if there is "no such thing as an idol", then it logically follows that, "there is no such thing as idolatry". If there is no such thing as "idolatry", then effectively, there is no need for the 2nd Commandment!

Other Subtle Deceptions in Modern Translations

One of the most exhilarating things that a Christian can experience in the study of God's Word is the discovery of a hidden Scriptural truth that is buried beneath the surface of the text. An example of this can be found in the 20th Chapter of the Book of John, when Jesus appears to Mary Magdalene outside of His Garden tomb, soon after His resurrection. John writes:

"Jesus saith unto her, Touch me not; for I am not yet ascended to my Father: but go to my brethren, and say unto them, I ascend to my Father, and your Father; and to my God, and your God." John 20:17

At face value, it would seem that Jesus was being a little bit "persnickety" in His demand that Mary not touch Him. However, if we consider the fact that Jesus wore many hats, then the true connotations of John 20:17 comes to light. For Jesus is not only the King of Kings, the Lamb of God, and numerous other things to the Christian, but He also performs the role of the High Priest (Hebrews 7:17), in the Christian's life.

When we consider the Day of Atonement, when the High Priest was to bathe and cleanse himself, put on fresh linens, and was not to be touched by any human being before he entered the Holy of Holies to offer God the sacrifice of the blood of the lamb to atone for the sins of the people, it is then that the meaning of Jesus' request unto Mary to "not touch Him" becomes clear. At this point, Jesus was fulfilling the role of High Priest, and had yet to offer the sacrifice of His own Blood to the Father in the true Holy of Holies in Heaven. If Mary had touched Him, she would have ceremoniously defiled Him. We see this corroborated later, when after He had gone to heaven to offer His Blood in the true "Holy of Holies", and then reappeared unto the eleven remaining disciples, He then invited them to "handle" Him. This was a signification that His Blood sacrifice had been accepted by God the Father.

Again, Jesus' resurrection body apparently no longer had a need for blood, for He did not refer to Himself as having flesh and blood, but rather "flesh and bones" (Luke 24:39), thereby indicating that our resurrection bodies will be of a different nature, one which is no longer sustained by blood (I Cor. 15:50).

Now this fascinating reality of Scripture could be found out by the diligent student of the Authorized King James Text, but the same could not be said for someone reading today's Modern Bible Versions. For in them, the idea of Mary "not touching" Jesus, does not come into play. For the Modern Versions not only have Mary merely touching Him, but rather either "holding Him" (NIV), or "clinging to Him" (NASB):

"Jesus said to her, stop clinging to Me, for I have not yet ascended to the Father..." (John 20:17).

Obviously, this effectively obscures the reality of what was occurring between Jesus and Mary, and Jesus and the disciples, in these passages.

It can also be seen that Modern Bible Translations also omit many references to prayer (John 14:16, 17:9,17:15, 17:20, Luke 21:36, Acts 1:14, and James 5:16), and to fasting (Matthew 17:21, Mark 9:29, Acts 10:30, I Corinthians 7:5, II Corinthians 6:5, 11:27).

Tragically, vast portions of the Lord's Prayer are simply omitted in many Modern Versions of the Bible. In the NIV, in Luke 11:2, the words "Which art in heaven", and "Thy will be done, as in heaven, so in earth" are simply omitted. The same is true for, "but deliver us from evil" in Luke 11:4. Truly these are flagrant attacks on God's traditional Word.

Modern Bible versions are also very pro-Catholic in their treatment of Mary. Oftentimes Mary is given a capitalized title for her name and position, making her the "Virgin Mary". This occurs eleven times in the NIV, where the "virgin" of the

316

KJV becomes the "Virgin" in the NIV (II Kings 19:21, Isaiah 23:12, 37:22, 47:1, Jeremiah 18:13, 31:4, 31:21, 46:11, Lamentations 1:15, 2:13, Amos 5:2). This title implies of course that Mary was somehow above being merely human, that she was indeed Divine, a major tenet of the Catholic Church.

In addition, the word "begotten" is totally removed from the NIV, which in turn calls into question whether Jesus was begotten by, or sired, by God. This heresy is reinforced by the fact that the name "Joseph" in Luke 2:33 in the King James Version, is changed to "The child's father" in the NIV, or "his father", in the NASV and RSV. In Luke 2:43, the terms "Joseph and his mother" in the KJV are replaced by, "his parents", in the NIV and RSV. This of course obscures the fact that the true Father of Jesus, is God Himself, and not any human being.

There are numerous other deceptions and omissions in the Modern Versions of the Bible that go far beyond the scope of this study. For a more exhaustive listing of the numerous problems associated with the Modern Versions of the Bible, one should reference the many books that have been written on the subject, including, "New Age Bible Versions" by G. A. Riplinger, and "The New Athenians", by James H. Son.

Sadly, most of mainline Christendom unwittingly still promotes the use of these Modern Bible Versions. It seems that many have become caught up in this "spirit of unquestioning acceptance" of the Modern Bible Translations. This in turn begs the question, "How could so many seemingly intelligent and well-intentioned people be so wrong?"

The answer to the above question can probably best be understood in the excerpts from the following letter written by Dr. Frank Logsdon, who participated in the making of the New American Standard Bible. It was only after the translation was completed and published that Dr. Logsdon became fully aware of the many problems to be found within this Modern Translation of the Bible.

In this letter, Dr. Logsdon expresses his regret for his part in the making of the New American Standard Bible. Dr. Logsdon lays the blame for the many problems associated with the New American Standard Bible as the result of Satanic deception. In his letter of apology, Dr. Logsdon writes:

"I must under God renounce every attachment to the New American Standard. ... I'm afraid I'm in trouble with the Lord. ...We laid the groundwork; I wrote the format; I helped interview some of the translators; I sat with the translator; I wrote the preface. ... "

"I'm in trouble; I can't refute these arguments; it's wrong, it's terribly wrong; it's frighteningly wrong; and what am I going to do about it? ... I can no longer ignore these criticisms I am hearing and I can't refute them... "

"When questions began to reach me, at first I was quite offended. However, in attempting to answer, I began to sense that something was not right about the NASV. Upon investigation, I wrote my very dear friend, Mr. Lockman, explaining that I was forced to renounce all attachment to the NASV. ... The product is grievous to my heart and helps to complicate matters in these already troublous times. ... The deletions are absolutely frightening ... There are so many. ... Are we so naïve that we do not suspect Satanic deception in all of this? "

"I don't want anything to do with it... "

"The finest leaders that we have today ... haven't gone into it (the new version's use of a corrupted Greek text), just as I hadn't gone into it. ... That's how easy one can be deceived."

"... I'm going to talk to him (Dr. George Sweeting, then President of Moody Bible Institute) about these things ..."

"You can say the Authorized Version (KJV) is absolutely correct. How correct? 100% correct! ... If you must stand against everyone else, stand."

Dr. Frank Logsdon

The fact that one of the scholars responsible for the production of the New American Standard Bible could have been so deceived, and so regretful for his part in the undertaking, should give the present-day Christian cause for caution and concern when reading one of the Modern Translations of the Bible. For as a rule, all the Modern Biblical Versions utilize the same Westcott and Hort Greek Minority Text translation from which the NASB was created.

Conclusion

It is hard to deny the fact that the Modern Versions of the Bible contain not only subtle, but also overt attacks upon the essential Doctrines of traditional Christianity. That people with such dubious backgrounds and beliefs, such as possessed by Brooke Westcott and Fenton Hort, could have been given the power to produce the Greek Text upon which the Modern Bible Versions use as their primary source, defies logic. Especially when Westcott and Hort's text itself was based upon manuscripts that had been discredited since the time of the early Church, almost from the time they had originally been written.

For as much as both the Catholic Church and the Protestant affiliated denominations now utilize these same texts in their Biblical translations, this may very well be an indication of how these Modern Bible Versions could be the glue that will bring these two separate divisions within Christendom together for the formation of the Anti-Christ's Super Church at the end of the present age.

Meanwhile, it is this writer's opinion that today's Christian would do well to prayerfully consider whether he or she should be incorporating these Modern Bible Versions into their study of

God's Word. The evidence presented raises some serious questions as to whether today's Church has become a victim of wide scale deception regarding traditional Christian Doctrine through these Modern Translations of the Bible.

The True Origins of the Roman Catholic Church

"The Catholic Church originated in the 4th Century A.D., when Constantine made Christianity the official religion of the Roman Empire"

Most people are somewhat familiar with the "official story" as to the origin of the Roman Catholic Church. In the early 4th Century A.D., Constantine was busy quelling rebellions against his right to rule the Western portion of the Roman Empire. In 312 A.D., he fought a series of three battles against his Roman rival Maxentius. Before the start of the 3rd and decisive battle, which occurred at the Milvian Bridge in Rome, Constantine is said to have seen a vision from God. The vision was of a Christian Cross along with the words, "By this sign thou shalt conquer", written in Greek. While many scholars maintain that the severely outnumbered Constantine made up the vision in order to garner the support of the large local Christian population in the area, it remains a matter open for debate. We will never know this side of heaven whether Constantine's vision was real or not. What we do know is that after defeating the forces of Maxentius, Constantine did indeed start the process of making Christianity the official state religion of the Roman Empire in 313 A.D.

While some decry this act as being detrimental to the Church of Christ on the basis that the "Official Church" was now wedded to the government of Rome, the implications of Constantine's actions run much deeper than what most Christians could ever imagine. In order to better understand these implications, we must first examine some of the false religious systems of the Ancient World.

Babylon and the Mother/Son Religious Cult

After the Flood, the grandson of Ham, Nimrod, settled far away from the place where God had revealed himself to his great-grandfather Noah. It seems that he went as far as he deemed necessary from the light of God's Presence into the land of Shinar, and from there he led a growing community of people who would eventually give birth to the city known as Babylon. Nimrod may have inherited his propensity for spiritual darkness from his father Cush, whose name literally means, "blackened one." Apparently, Cush being of the black Hamitic race was not only dark in his physical appearance, but Cush's heart may also have been dark in his relationship with God.

Nimrod was known as a great hunter, which may have prompted his fellow men to choose him to be their leader. In Old Testament times, wild animals were a great danger to human populations. If we remember in the Book of Exodus that God had told the Hebrew people that he would not drive the inhabitants of the promised land out too quickly, "...lest the land become desolate, and the beast of the field multiply against thee" (Exodus 23:29). This sentiment is repeated in the Book of Deuteronomy:

"And the LORD thy God will put out those nations before thee little by little: thou mayest not consume them at once, lest the beasts of the field increase upon thee." Deuteronomy 7:22

It is easy to see how a person known to be a great hunter such as Nimrod would become a natural leader or protector of human populations. Nimrod in time would marry a woman known as Semerimus. This union between Nimrod and Semerimus would eventually give rise to the world's first recorded false religious system, the Babylonian Mother/Son Religious System. This is the false religious system that Scripture describes in the Book of Revelation as "...MYSTERY BABYLON, THE MOTHER OF HARLOTS..." (Revelation 17:5).

For it is from this post Flood religious system that the pre-ponderance of the false paganistic religious systems of the world have been initiated, including the religious system that has become to be known as the Roman Catholic Church.

Origins of the Mother/Son Religious System

Following the Flood, in the days of Noah's great-grandson Nimrod, there was no official written Word of God. The writing of God's Word would not occur until approximately 1,000 years later, when Moses penned the first five Books of the Bible, the Hebrew Torah. In Nimrod's day, the works and words of God were passed along largely by an oral tradition. Nimrod's wife Semerimus was more than aware of these oral traditions, especially of the promise that God had made in the Garden of Eden to Adam and Eve, that He would right the wrongs they had committed, through the "seed of the woman" (Genesis 3:15).

After the death of Nimrod, who by tradition is said to have died a violent death, Semerimus in her arrogance, declared herself to be this said woman, and that her son Tammuz, was the resultant "promised seed" who would bring blessings to the world. She claimed that she had become impregnated by the rays of the sun, thus making Tammuz a supernatural being, who was in fact, the reincarnation of Nimrod, the Protector or Shepherd King of the Babylonian people.

In this Babylonian religious system, Semerimus had declared herself to be the agent through whom the people could now approach God. This new religious system was symbolized by a mother holding her child in her arms.

In his book, "Prophecy for Today", J. Dwight Pentecost says of Semerimus and her religious system:

"She adopted the title of "the queen of heaven." She taught that salvation was administered through her by means of such

323

sacraments as the sprinkling of water and ceremonial cleansing. There was purgatorial cleansing after death. She originated the tradition that her son Tammuz on one occasion was out hunting, and that he was slain by a wild boar. All of the temple virgins who were set apart for the mother-child worship were called upon for a 40 day period of fasting. And at the end of that 40 day period, on the feast of Ishtar (Ishtar being another name for Semerimus or Ashteroth), Tammuz was resurrected. Therefore, the Feast of Ishtar was made an annual feast symbolizing the restoration of Tammuz from the dead. They set aside the egg as sacred to Tammuz, which was exchanged on the feast of Ishtar as the symbol of life out of death. The evergreen tree, the symbol of life, was made the symbol of Tammuz, and it was prominently displayed in mid-winter at the birthday celebration of Tammuz. The queen of heaven, as Semerimus was known, was worshipped by offering a round cake that was marked by the letter "T", which in the Babylonian and later in the Phoenician alphabet was a cross or an "X". And these crossed buns or cakes were offered to Tammuz and the mother of Tammuz on the yearly occasion of the feast of Ishtar."

The similarities of dogma between this Babylonian Church and the traditions and culture of our Christian Churches, both Catholic and Protestant, are obvious, and quite telling. Many of the traditional practices of the Christian Church, especially those concerning the celebrations of Christmas and of Easter, can clearly be seen to have derived from these early pagan traditions.

This Mother/Son religious system which was initiated by Semerimus would later spread into Phoenicia, where the mother's name was changed to Ashteroth, while Tammuz was still the name of the sacred son. It was in Phoenicia that the "son" worship of Tammuz became symbolized by the "sun", whose rays had impregnated Semerimus, and began to be referred to as Baal worship (Baal being an alternative name for Nimrod). After the overthrow of the Babylonian Kingdom, the Mother/Son Religion was instituted in Pergamos in Asia Minor.

This is the same Pergamos which Scripture declares to be,"the seat of Satan's Throne" (Revelation 2:13).

Later this religious system would reappear in Egypt, incorporating the names of Isis and Horus as the objects of worship. From Egypt the Mother/Sun religion would then emerge in Greece under the names of Aphrodite and Eros, after which it would make its final pre-Christian age appearance in Rome, where Venus and Cupid became the objects of worship.

Not only did this false religious system greatly affect much of the pre-Christian pagan world, but it also found its way into the world of God's chosen people Israel. Under the name of Baal Worship, this Mother/Son cult is often referenced throughout Israel's Old Testament historical record.

In the Book of Numbers, we find Balak bringing Balaam up to "the high places of Baal" (Numbers 22:41). It is interesting to note that just as in Babylon, which was known for its Tower, that the religious cult's place of worship was also in, "the high places." Many Biblical scholars believe that Nimrod's motivation for building the Tower of Babel was as an act of rebellion against God for His bringing about the destruction of the world excepting Noah and his family, by means of the Flood. That in Nimrod's mind, he believed that if he built a sufficiently high tower God would no longer be able to destroy mankind again by means of another Flood. Whatever may have been Nimrod's motivations, the resulting false religious system that was created at Babel continued to function in "the high places".

The worship of Baal in Israel's history is long and continuous. Again, Baal worship is just an extension of the original Babylonian Mother/Son religious cult. After the death of Joshua, we are told that Israel, "Forsook the Lord, and served Baal (the reincarnation of Nimrod as Tammuz) and Ashteroth (another name for Semerimus)" (Judges 2:13). In the days of the reign of Ahab and his wife Jezebel, we are told of Elijah's famous battle against the prophets of Baal (I Kings 18:19-40).

Later, Scripture refers to King Jehu's fight against Baal worship (II Kings 10:28), and how thereafter the high priest Jehoida had to once again destroy the house of Baal at the initiation of the reign of Joash (II Chronicles 23:17).

In the days of Jeremiah, Scripture informs us that Israel had again gone back to the Mother/Son religion of Baal:

"Therefore pray not thou for this people, neither lift up cry or prayer for them, neither make intercession to me; for I will not hear thee.

Seest thou not what they do in the cities of Judah and in the streets of Jerusalem?

The children gather wood, and the fathers kindle fire, and the women knead their dough, to make cakes to the queen of heaven, and to pour out drink offerings unto other Gods, that they may provoke me unto anger." Jeremiah 7:16-18

"Therefore thus saith the LORD; Behold, I will give this city into the hand of the Chaldeans, and into the hand of Nebuchadnezzar king of Babylon, and he shall take it:

And the Chaldeans, that fight against this city, shall come and set fire on this city, and burn it with the houses, upon whose roofs they have offered incense unto Baal, and poured out drink offerings unto other gods, to provoke me to anger." Jeremiah 32: 28,29

Later, in the days of Ezekiel, we find Israel again paying homage to the Mother/Son cult:

"Then he brought me to the door of the gate of the LORD's house which was toward the north; and, behold, there sat women weeping for Tammuz.

Then said he unto me, Hast thou seen this, O son of man?

turn thee yet again, and thou shalt see greater abominations than these.

And he brought me into the inner court of the LORD's house, and behold, at the door of the temple of the LORD, between the porch and the altar, were about five and twenty men, with their backs toward the temple of the LORD, and their faces toward the east; and they worshipped the sun toward the east." Ezekiel 8:14-16

In order to understand the degree of the severity of iniquity that was involved in Baal worship, we must first remind ourselves of the fact that Satan was and is the great counterfeiter of God. At the time of his personal falling away from God, he had made the following brazen declarations commonly referred to as, "The Five I Wills of Satan":

"How art thou fallen from heaven, O Lucifer, son of the morning! How art thou cut down to the ground, which didst weaken the nations!

For thou hast said in thine heart, I will ascend into heaven, I will exalt my throne above the stars of God: I will sit also upon the mount of the congregation, in the sides of the north:

"I will ascend above the heights of the clouds: I will be like the most High." Isaiah 14:12-14

Within these five "I Wills" of Satan, we find Satan declaring his intentions of becoming like God by mimicking God's place in the Universe, in essence by becoming a counterfeit version of God.

In the Old Testament sacrificial system, we must remember that God had the Hebrew priests eating the sacrifices of meat that had been offered unto Him in their worship ceremonies (Numbers 18:9,10). It should then come as no surprise that Satan would seek to copy this practice of God. He did it in a way that only an extremely evil and perverted being would devise; by demanding that the sacrifices made unto him should not be meat from animals, but rather from human beings.

In Baal worship, an iron statue of the satanic god Moloch was heated until it was red hot, at which time Hebrew babies were placed in Moloch's arms as an offering made unto him. This is referred to in the Book of Jeremiah:

"They have built also the high places of Baal, to burn their sons with fire for burnt offerings unto Baal, which I commanded not, nor spake it, neither came it into my mind." Jeremiah 19:5

"And they built the high places of Baal, which are in the valley of the son of Hinnom, to cause their sons and their daughters to pass through the fire unto Molech; which I commanded them not, neither came it into my mind, that they should do this abomination, to cause Judah to sin." Jeremiah 32:35

Just as the priests of the most high God were told to eat the meat that had been offered unto the Lord, so the priests of Lucifer were told to eat of the meat that had been offered unto Satan (Moloch).

It is of great interest to note the etymology of the English word "cannibal". In the Hebrew language, Cahn is a surname for priest. Cahn literally means "a priest", with the emphatic form of Cahn, Cahna, literally meaning, "the priest". Thus, "The Priest of Baal" is "Cahna-Bal", from which of course we derive the word "cannibal", loosely defined as, "one who eats human flesh". We can see that Baal worship in Israel was much worse than just an innocuous false religious practice.

The Babylonian System Comes to the Church

One of the primary reasons that Constantine married the Christian Church to the Mother/Son religious system of Rome was essentially, "because he could". For since the time of the

Caesars, every Roman Emperor had been crowned not only as Rome's secular ruler or "Emperor", but also as the kingdom's religious leader or, "Pontifex Maximus". The position of Emperor carried supreme authority in both the secular and sacred domains of the Roman Empire. It is of interest to note that the leader of the Roman Catholic Church, the Pope, to this day still maintains the sacred title of the Roman Emperor, that of, "Pontifex Maximus".

What Constantine did was not only replace Venus and Cupid in the Babylonian system with Jesus and Mary, but his actions also brought the paganistic rituals of Rome's version of the Mother/Son religion into the Christian Culture of the world. Thus, were the practices of the winter solstice celebration of the Son's birthday symbolized by the evergreen tree initiated, along with the 40-day observance of Lent, hot cross buns, Easter eggs symbolizing new life, and numerous other pagan beliefs and practices brought into the world of Christianity.

It has been said in describing the many nuances of the Roman Catholic Church that Roman Catholicism is:

1) Christian in name.

2) Roman in hierarchical structure.

3) Jewish in form, with its incorporation of the practice of a priestly go between, and lastly,

4) Pagan, in practice.

In order to better understand some of the theological errors, misconceptions, and paganistic practices that have been brought into the Christian Church and Culture through Roman Catholicism, it is best to hold them up to the light of Scripture. While this list is far from exhaustive, it will hopefully give the reader a sense of just how far "off base" the Roman Catholic Church is from Biblical Christianity.

Christian Commemorative Holiday Celebrations of the Birth of Jesus Christ

While the birth of Jesus is commonly celebrated throughout the world around the time of the Winter Solstice on December 25th in accordance with the celebration of the birth of Tammuz, we are not told within the pages of Scripture the actual date and year of the birth of our Lord Jesus into the world. While God certainly does have His Reasons for not revealing the exact day and year of Jesus' birth in His Word ("The secret things belong to the Lord." Deuteronomy 29:29), God does give the student of His Word many clear indications as to the approximate time when Jesus may have been born.

First, Jesus was most likely not born in the winter. We are told in the Book of Luke that at the time of Jesus' birth, the shepherds were out abiding with their flocks in the fields by night. Winters in Israel are cold and damp, making it highly unlikely that the shepherds would have been out in the fields with their flocks by night (Luke 2:8).

In addition to this, Luke also records that the decree was issued by Caesar for all to return to their hometowns to enroll to be taxed (Luke 2:1). Again, it is highly unlikely that such a decree would have been issued in the winter, as travel would have been extremely difficult to accomplish. This narrows our choice as to the time of year of Jesus' birth down to one of the other three seasons: spring, summer, or fall.

We know that God in His Word often aligns significant historical events with the three main Jewish Festivals of Passover, Pentecost, and Tabernacles. In the spring, we have the Passover Festival. Passover is associated with two events, first, the actual Passover of the Death Angel in Egypt, when God saved the firstborn of the Hebrew people when they covered their door with the blood of the sacrificial lamb, and secondly, with the

330

Crucifixion of Jesus Christ, when Jesus became the actual Passover Lamb.

The next Jewish Feast, that of Pentecost, is also in alignment with two significant historical events. First, Pentecost commemorates the actual Exodus of the Hebrew people out of Egypt to Mount Sinai, where the nation of Israel became God's representatives to the ancient world. In like manner, in New Testament times, Pentecost is also associated with the introduction and initiation of God's new representatives to the world, the Church.

The last major Jewish Feast, that of the Feast of Tabernacles, occurs somewhere between mid-September and the first week of October. To the Jewish people, Tabernacles is an acknowledgement of the visitation by God to the Hebrew people at Mount Sinai in the giving of the Ten Commandments. While the 12th Century A.D. Jewish rabbi Maimonides taught that the Law was given at the Feast of Pentecost, this idea is nowhere to be found either in Scripture or within ancient Jewish tradition. We are told in Exodus 19 that Moses ascended Mount Sinai soon after he and the Hebrew people arrived there at Sinai. Moses was on the mountain for 40 days, came down and broke the tablets, dealt with the people, and then went up the mountain again for another 40 days to receive the second set of tablets. The giving of the Law occurred over a time period that lasted from three to four months after Pentecost (Shavuot in Hebrew). This three to four month period of God's visitation to the Hebrew people is celebrated by the Hebrew people as the Feast of Tabernacles.

The Feast of Tabernacles therefore appears to be different than the other two major Jewish Festivals in that there does not appear to be a New Testament event that coincides with Tabernacles. This of course enters into the realm of speculative theology, but how appropriate would it be to have the Jewish Feast commemorating the visitation of God to His people in the giving of the Law in Old Testament times, to now be associated with a new visitation of God into the world in New Testament times, that being the birth of Jesus Christ who is the "completion of the Law": "For Christ is the end of the law for righteousness to every one that believeth." Romans 10:4

Again, this is speculative theology, but it certainly does fit in with a beautifully consistent story line or narrative of God's perfect sovereign control over world history.

Regarding the exact year of Jesus' birth, we are once again faced with uncertainty. For there is much disagreement amongst scholars as to the accuracy of the historical records of events around the time of the conversion from B.C. to A.D. on our calendars. While it is commonly believed that Jesus was born in the first year A.D., and that our calendars were set up to switch from B.C. to A.D. to commemorate this occasion, 1 A.D. may not be the true year of Jesus' birth.

Many astronomers have tried to determine the exact year of Jesus' birth through astronomical projections into the past. In so doing, they have tried to link the Star of Bethlehem which guided the three Wise Men, to the rare times that either Venus and Jupiter, or Saturn and Jupiter, have come close together in their orbits to create the appearance of a special star. These projections have never been commonly agreed upon however, and their astronomical estimations range anywhere from the year 2 B.C. to 7 B.C.

Perhaps the best way to determine the most likely year of Jesus' birth, is to work from an established historical date, and to use Scriptural principles in order to help us in our quest for the answer.

It is generally conceded that the Roman Emperor Titus destroyed Jerusalem in the historical year of 70 A.D. Theologians commonly agree that this event was a judgment upon the Nation Israel for their rejection of their Messiah. Knowing these two facts allows us to employ certain theological truths to more accurately determine the exact year of Jesus' birth.

1) The number 40 is listed 146 times in Scripture. While it is often associated with times of testing, it is also used to signify judgment, as in the case of the Judgment of the Flood, where we are told that "it rained for 40 days and 40 nights upon the earth" (Genesis 7:12). The number 40 can also denote "suspended judgment", as in the case of the 40 years of Wilderness wanderings endured by the Hebrew people, whereby the generation of believers who failed to trust the LORD all died off (Deuteronomy 1: 26-28, Psalm 95:6-11, Hebrews 3:8-11). In that God did not immediately judge the Jewish nation after the Crucifixion, we can surmise that the judgment of Jerusalem by Titus was somehow associated with 40 years of suspended judgment.

2) Jesus was about 30 years old when he began His ministry (Luke 3:23). His ministry lasted three years, so we know that Jesus was likely 33 years old when He died.

3) In the parable of the barren fig tree in the Book of Luke, we read:

"He spake also this parable; A certain man had a fig tree planted in his vineyard; and he came and sought fruit thereon, and found none.

Then said he unto the dresser of the vineyard, Behold, these three years I come seeking fruit on this fig tree, and find none: cut it down; why cumbereth it the ground?

And he answering said unto him, Lord let it alone this year also, till I dig about it and dung it:

And if it bear fruit, well: and if not, then after that thou shalt cut it down." Luke 13:6-9

If we consider that this parable is likely teaching that the suspended judgment brought upon Israel probably did not start at the conclusion of Jesus' three-year ministry and Crucifixion, but rather was delayed for an additional year to give the Hebrew people time to reflect upon what they had done in crucifying their Messiah Jesus. We can then surmise that the Nation of Israel's rejection of their Messiah was not complete until the time of their rejection of the message given to them by Stephen as recorded in the Book of Acts (7:1-60).

This event occurred approximately one year after the Crucifixion, at the time that Stephen had given the High Priest and the other Jewish rulers a recounting of the history of the Nation of Israel, and of how they as a nation had rejected their true Messiah. When Stephen had concluded his history lesson to the Jewish rulers, they had cast him out of the city and stoned him (Acts 7:58). It was at this time that the fate of the nation was now sealed. God in His grace had given the Jewish people an extra year to consider what had recently transpired, and they had now once again rejected their Messiah.

If we now subtract the 40 years of suspended judgment from the destruction of Jerusalem in 70 A.D., then we can surmise that Stephen was most likely stoned to death in the year 30 A.D. If we then subtract the added year of grace that God had provided to the nation Israel to repent for their rejection of the Messiah, we know that the Crucifixion probably occurred in the year 29 A.D. Finally, if we then subtract the 33 years of the length of Jesus' life, we can probably conclude that Jesus was most likely born in late September, or early October, of the year 4 B.C.

The time of the Savior's birth can be seen to be connected not to the Sun and the Winter Solstice, as the false Mother/Son religious cult would have us to believe, but rather most likely to the time of the Jewish Feasts. For as in the words of Jesus, "Salvation is of the Jews" (John 4:22).

It should therefore be recognized that the association of the celebration of the birth of Jesus at the time of the Winter Solstice is not Biblical, but rather comes to us directly from Babylon, where the celebration was a Holy Day to honor the birthday of Tammuz.

334

The Celebration of the Death and Resurrection of Jesus Christ Known as Easter (The Feast of Ishtar)

While the seasonal timing of the celebration of the death and resurrection of Jesus in conjunction with the Jewish Passover is accurate, many of the traditions of the celebration known as Easter have also regrettably come to us from Babylon.

The idea of a 40-day Lenten period of abstinence comes to us directly from Paganistic Babylon, from the Festal Virgins praying 40 days for Tammuz to come back from the dead. In like manner, so do the Semerimus and Tammuz honoring symbolisms of hot cakes and eggs come to our Easter traditions directly from Babylon. These practices are nowhere to be found within the pages of Scripture.

Even the name of the celebration, Easter (Ishtar), has its origins from within the Babylonian Mother/Son Religious Cult. The Christian tradition of eating ham at Easter time (we must remember that Tammuz was reportedly killed by a wild boar) is also a tradition borne out of the false Babylonian Religious System.

Christian Doctrinal Issues within Roman Catholicism

There are numerous doctrinal issues between Biblical Christianity and Roman Catholicism that go far beyond the celebrations of Christmas and Easter. The following list is by no means exhaustive but is given to show just how far Roman Catholic Dogma deviates from Biblical Christianity.

The Veneration of Mary

In keeping with the Babylonian tradition established by Semerimus, Mary is given the status of being an intermediary

335

between God and man within the Roman Catholic Church. In speaking for the Catholic Church, St. Bernard (1090-1153) declared that, "Mary was crowned "Queen of Heaven" (the same title given to Semerimus in Babylon) by God the Father, and that she currently sits upon a Throne in heaven making intercession for Christians." Scripture however informs us that, "there is only one mediator between God and man, that being the man Jesus Christ" (I Timothy 2:5).

It is common practice within the Catholic Church to pray to Mary, such as in the prayers of the rosary. Nowhere in Scripture is the Christian ever told to pray to Mary, or for that matter, to any of the departed souls from this earth. This practice is known as necromancy and is strictly forbidden within the pages of God's Word (Deuteronomy 18:10-12).

It should be of interest to note that Mary played no significant role within the early Church, and that in Acts 1:14, we are told that the disciples prayed "with" Mary, and certainly never "to" her.

Not only does the Catholic Church regard Mary as an inter-cessor for Christians, but since the time of the Middle Ages and up to and through the time of Vatican Council II (1962-65), there has been a movement within the Catholic Church to grant Mary the blasphemous title of "Co-Redeemer", although this title has never become official Catholic Dogma.

While the Catholic Church exalts Mary and gives her special status as the Mother of God, this was an idea that was foreign to our Lord Jesus Christ. In fact, throughout recorded Scripture, Jesus never refers to Mary as "mother". On two instances he referred to her as "woman", both times in an apparent mild rebuke to Mary for her not understanding the ways of God:

"Jesus saith unto her, Woman, what have I to do with thee? Mine hour is not yet come." John 2:4

"When Jesus therefore saw his mother, and the disciple standing by, whom he loved, he saith unto his mother, Woman behold thy son." John 19:26

While it is commonly believed by many that the Catholic Doctrine of the Immaculate Conception is in reference to the Virgin Birth, this too is far from the truth. For the doctrine of "The Immaculate Conception" within the Catholic Church states that, "The Virgin Mary was free from original sin from the moment of her conception." This was adopted as official Roman Catholic Dogma in 1854 under the papacy of Pope Pius IX. This heretical belief also flies right into the face of Holy Scripture, for the Bible clearly states:

"As it is written, There is none righteous, no not one:

There is none that understandeth, there is none that seeketh after God." Romans 3:10,11

"For all have sinned, and come short of the glory of God." Romans 3:23

Christian Priesthood

The Roman Catholic Church's veneration of an earthly priesthood to stand as intermediaries or "go-betweens" between God and man, is also a concept that is not found within Scripture. To the Christian, there is only one High Priest, that being the LORD Jesus Christ. The Book of Hebrews tells us:

"Wherefore Holy brethren, partakers of the heavenly calling, consider the Apostle and High Priest of our profession, Jesus Christ." Hebrews 3:1

"Seeing then that we have a great high priest that is passed into the heavens, Jesus the Son of God, let us hold fast our profession.

For we have not an high priest which cannot be touched with the feeling of our infirmities; but was in all points tempted like as we are, yet without sin." Hebrews 4:14,15

The Christian is taught in Scripture that all Christians have the status of priesthood, and that they have no need for an intermediary between them and their Savior.

"Ye also, as lively stones, are built up a spiritual house, an holy priesthood, to offer up spiritual sacrifices, acceptable to God by Jesus Christ." I Peter 2:5

"But you are a chosen generation, a royal priesthood, an holy nation, a peculiar people; that ye should show forth the praises of him who hath called you out of darkness into his marvelous light." I Peter 2:9

In addition to this, at no place in either the Old or the New Testaments do we find support for the Roman Catholic hierarchical structure of popes, cardinals, bishops, monks, nuns, brothers, and sisters. These offices and functions have their origins in the religious/political systems of Babylon and Rome. They are nowhere to be found within the written Word of God.

The Worship of Idols

It is common to find statues of saints, and numerous other physical objects or idols, within the confines of Catholic places of worship. At the Catholic Council of Trent which was held between 1545 and 1563, it was declared that, "It is lawful to have images in the Church and to give honor and worship unto them." This of course is in strict contradiction to the legal foundation of the Christian Religion, the Ten Commandments:

"Thou shalt not make unto thee any graven image, or any likeness of any thing that is in heaven above, or that is in the earth beneath, or that is in the water under the earth:

Thou shalt not bow down thyself to them, nor serve them: for I the LORD thy God am a jealous God, visiting the iniquity of the fathers upon the children unto the third and the fourth generation of them that hate me." Exodus 20:4,5

It is of interest to note that God in His Word calls special attention to the sin of idolatry. In the first tablet of Moses, idolatry is the only sin mentioned that carries a message of warning of an ongoing punishment for those who violate this individual commandment. This of course is God's way of telling the believer to be particularly wary of the sin of idolatry.

In ancient Babylon, there were many symbols of idol worship, including the mother holding the child in her arms, along with various figures of the sun in honor of Tammuz. Another obscure idol that came out of Babylon that has been adopted by the Catholic Church is the Crosier, or shepherd's hook. It was a symbol for Nimrod, for he was not only known as the "Great Hunter" but was also known as the protector of the people, or "The Shepherd". The Crosier represents Nimrod in his role as the Shepherd. Abydenus, a student of Aristotle, who recorded the works of the 3rd-4th Century B.C. Babylonian priest Berosus, tells us that Nimrod was the first world ruler to bear the title of "Shepherd-King".

It is of interest to note that the ancient Chaldean language is similar to the Hebrew language, and in Hebrew, "Nimrod the Shepherd", is written as, "Nimrod Heroe". In other words, Nimrod was not only the world's first "Shepherd-King", but in so doing, he was also the world's first false human idol, or "Hero".

An idol is anything that we place in our hearts as a priority that comes before God. While modern day man smirks at the thought of the adherents of ancient paganistic religions carving out or forming figures of the sun, animals, or other mythological figures as meaningless idols, he has no problem spending large amounts of money (sometimes more than a day's wages) on a sports jersey with the name of his favorite sport's "hero" prominently displayed on the back.

For the Roman Catholic Church to openly put its stamp of approval on the use of idols in their cathedrals and worship ceremonies, is in direct defiance of the Word of God, and goes beyond any form of reason that one could possibly imagine. Yet the incorporation of idols and relics in Catholicism remains to this day an important part of Catholic Dogma.

Purgatory

The Catholic Church also adopted from Babylon the concept of Purgatory. The F&W Dictionary describes purgatory as, "Any place or state of temporary banishment, suffering, or punishment." In terms of Roman Catholic Theology, purgatory is "a state or place where the souls of those who have died penitent are made fit for paradise by expiating venial sins and undergoing any punishment remaining for previous unforgiven sins."

The concept of purgatory is found within the numerous false Babylonian Systems of the World. In Greece, we find Plato opining that before man's final deliverance from the wrongs that he has committed in this world, that "some must first proceed to a subterranean place of judgment, where they shall sustain the punishment they have deserved." In like manner, the Catholic Church believes that a person's soul must burn in hell until their sins have been purged. Catholicism has also taught in the past that in order to speed up this process, a person may give money to a priest who will then create special masses for the individual, and thereby speed up the purgatorial process. In the Middle Ages, these corrupt monetary payments were known as "indulgences".

The concept of purgatory flies straight into the face of what God's Word teaches on the matter of the forgiveness of sins, and of the sufficiency of the sufferings of Jesus while on the Cross.

Scripture clearly teaches that the penalty for all of the believer's sins were paid for on the Cross by the LORD Jesus Christ:

"Verily, verily, I say unto you, He that heareth my word, and believeth on Him that sent me, hath everlasting life, and shall not come into condemnation; but is passed from death to life." John 5:24

"There is therefore no condemnation to them which are in Christ Jesus, who walk not after the flesh, but after the Spirit." Romans 8:1

"Who his own self bare our sins in his own body on the tree, that we, being dead to sins, should live unto righteousness: by whose stripes ye were healed." I Peter 2:24

Scripture also informs us that for there to be any forgiveness or remission of sins, there must first be the "shedding of blood", which is far beyond the realm of the Catholic Mass or Indulgences, making the concept of Purgatory and its remedies by the Catholic Church irrelevant:

"And almost all things are by the law purged with blood; and without shedding of blood is no remission." Hebrews 9:22

Communion

God's Word teaches us that communion is a sacred rite to be performed as a memorial to the Crucifixion. Our Lord instituted the first Christian communion with His disciples, where he declared, "This do in remembrance of me" (Luke 22:19).

The Catholic Mass is a perversion of the rite of Holy Communion. In the Catholic Mass, we find the performance of a continual bloodless sacrifice of Jesus, as if the Cross itself was not sufficient. This of course is blasphemy of the highest order. Scripture states categorically that the sacrifice of Jesus Christ was

341

both totally sufficient and complete:

"For Christ also hath "once" suffered for sins, the just for the unjust, that he might bring us to God, being put to death in the flesh, but quickened by the Spirit." I Peter 3:18

In addition to this, the round wafer that is used in Catholic Communion also originated in the Babylonian Mother/Sun Religious System. It is a symbol for the Sun, in honor of Tammuz. While the Catholic Church maintains that the letters on the wafer "IHS" stand for "Iesus Hominum Salvador" ("Jesus the Savior of Men"), Alexander Hislop in "The Two Babylons" states that the "IHS" letters originally came out of the Egyptian Mother/Sun System, and that the letters were a designation of the Egyptian Trinity of "Isis" (Mother), "Horus" (Child), and "Seb" (Father).

It should come as no surprise then to learn that the Catholic practice of the waving of the hand both horizontally and vertically to symbolize the Sign of the Cross, also originated out of Babylon, where Hislop informs us that it was used to signify a "T", to show honor and obeisance to Tammuz.

Salvation by Grace

Roman Catholicism believes in a non-specific system of works in order to gain the approbation of God and to acquire salvation. Catholicism teaches that salvation is attained through the doing of good works such as being baptized, praying to Mary, keeping sacraments, going to Mass, and attending confession, amongst other things.

This idea of salvation by works also originated in Babylonian Doctrine. It was symbolized in the Egyptian Mother/Son System by the "Scales of Anubis". In this system, the good and the bad deeds of every individual were weighed on a balance of two separate scales, and judgment was pronounced according to the balance that was struck between the two scales. In Roman Catholicism, these scales of Justice or Judgment are not administered by Anubis, but rather by Saint Michael the Archangel, with the balancing of one's good deeds versus his bad deeds determining if one should receive justification or condemnation.

It is interesting to note how the God of the Bible makes mockery of this Babylonian system of "justification by works" through the incorporation of the Babylonian scales of judgment in the Book of Daniel. In the fifth Chapter of the Book of Daniel, we find Daniel chastising the Babylonian King Belshazzar for his insolence towards the God of Heaven:

"And thou his son, O Belshazzar, hast not humbled thine heart, though thou knewest all this;
But hast lifted up thyself against the Lord of Heaven....and the God in whose hand thy breath is, and whose are all thy ways, hast thou not glorified." Daniel 5:22,23

The sovereign Lord God of Heaven then went on to have a Hand appear in the room, which wrote on the wall:

"MENE, MENE, TEKEL, UPHARSIN", of which the word TEKEL is translated as: "...Thou art weighed in the balances, and art found wanting." Daniel 5:27

So here we have God addressing the Babylonian king in terms appropriate to the king's faulty religious understanding. The Lord then exhibits His sense of humor by making this disparaging remark to King Belshazzar that not only chastises him, but also makes a mockery of the Babylonian Religious System's heretical Scales of Justice ("Thou art weighed in the balances and art found wanting!").

In contrast to the Babylonian paganistic justification by works doctrine that has been adopted by the Catholic Church, Holy Scripture declares that man's salvation is dependent upon faith alone, and not through works:

"Therefore we conclude that a man is justified by faith without the deeds of the law." Romans 3:28

"For what saith the scripture? Abraham believed God, and it was counted unto him for righteousness." Romans 4:3

"For by grace are ye saved through faith; and that not of yourselves: it is the gift of God:

Not of works, lest any man should boast." Ephesians 2:8,9

Celibacy and the Monastic Life

The Catholic Church is well known for its demands for celibacy amongst its leaders of the faith. For Catholic Priests, Nuns, and other Church hierarchy are forbidden to marry. This practice also originated in Babylon. Semerimus, in her hypocrisy (unless of course one believes that she was impregnated by the rays of the sun), was the world's first religious leader to have demanded celibacy of her priesthood. Apparently, her husband Nimrod had been dead for quite some time when Tammuz was born, so her demand of virginity and celibacy of her Festal Virgins was likely made in order to make her claim of being impregnated by the sun seem to be more palatable. The practice of celibacy for the priesthood was carried on in many of the subsequent Mother/Sun religious cults in Western Civilization, most notably in the Roman Empire.

Not only was the monastic lifestyle adopted by the Mother/Son cults of Western Civilization, but it also spread from the Babylonian "cradle of civilization" into the Far East at the time that mankind migrated to all parts of the world after the "confusion of speech" that God brought about at the Tower of Babel (Genesis 11:6-9).

In India, the adherents of Hinduism also adopted the Babylonian celibate monastic priestly lifestyle, as did the later adherents of Buddhism in both China and Japan. We see that the influences of the Babylonian System have indeed spread throughout the whole world, and that she is truly what Scripture proclaims her to be, "The Mother of Harlots", or false religious systems (Revelation 17:4-5).

The idea of a celibate priesthood is nowhere to be found in Scripture. The Old Testament Hebrew priests were free to marry or not marry as they chose.

God's Holy Word clearly foretold of this coming apostacy of the Roman Catholic Church, which brought in the Mother/Son cult's paganistic practice of priestly celibacy into the Church. In the Book of Timothy, we read:

"Now the Spirit speaketh expressly, that in the latter times some shall depart from the faith, giving heed to seducing spirits, and doctrines of devils;

Speaking lies in hypocrisy; having their conscience seared with a hot iron;

Forbidding to marry, and commanding to abstain from meats, which God hath created to be received with thanksgiving of them which believe and know the truth.

For every creature of God is good, and nothing to be refused, if it be received with thanksgiving." I Timothy 4:1-4

Here we see God's Word not only prophesying the Catholic Church's future establishment of a celibate priesthood, but also of its coming injunction of "forbidding to eat meat on Fridays".

In practice, the idea of a "celibate priesthood" has often proven to be a fallacy wherever it has been implemented. Hislop states, "The records of all nations where priestly celibacy has been introduced have proved that, instead of ministering to the purity of those condemned to it, it has only plunged them in the deepest pollution."

Dave Hunt, in his monumental work on the history of Roman Catholicism, "A Woman Rides the Beast", addressed the issue of Roman Catholic celibacy thusly:

"History is replete with sayings that mocked the church's false claim to celibacy and revealed the truth: "The holiest hermit has his whore", and, "Rome has more prostitutes than any other city because she has the most celibates", are prime examples.

So rampant was the internal corruption of the city of Rome, that Pope Pius II (1458-1464) declared that Rome was "the only city run by bastards" (sons of popes and cardinals)."

Hunt then goes on to quote Catholic historian Peter de Rosa, himself a former Jesuit: "Popes had mistresses of fifteen years of age, were guilty of incest and sexual perversions of every sort, had innumerable children, were murdered in the very act of adultery (Pope John II was killed by a jealous husband who found him in bed with his wife). ...In the old Catholic phrase, why be holier than the pope?"

Dr. Angelo Rappoport in his book, "The Love Affairs of the Vatican", wrote:

"In 1490 there were not less than 6,800 prostitutes in Rome. They enjoyed the protection of the Holy Church, and were known under the designation of Cortegiane, which means, "an honest courtesan" (meretrix honesta).

These indiscretions of the Roman Catholic clergy were not confined to the men within the Roman Catholic hierarchy. Anselm of Bisate, an 11th Century cleric, proclaimed that the nuns were no less promiscuous than the priests."

Rappoport goes on to state that, "This scandalous life of the nuns became so notorious that special laws had to be issued by

346

the Carolingians (Frankish descendants of Charlemagne) as well as by the Church."

Due to the political intrigue that the Roman Catholic Church constantly found itself engaging in, the Papacy was temporarily moved out of Rome to Avignon, France in the 14th Century (1309-1376). In so doing, the Papacy exported the widespread corruption that they had injected into the social fabric of Rome, into the nation of France. Dr. Rappoport again writes:

"With the entry of the Papal Court in France, corruption, immorality, and debauchery entered the country. The Holy See taught the French people all sorts of crimes, of excesses, and luxury, not to forget the art of poison. Such is the blessing which the holy fathers are bringing, a blessing which is best of all noticeable in holy Rome itself."

The French poet scholar Petrarch called Avignon, "The modern Babylon on the banks of the Rhone. All that people say of the ancient city of Babylon is nought compared to Avignon, for here one sees the personification of that debauchery and immorality related in ancient myths and legends of the gods of pagan antiquity."

To this day, the Roman Catholic Church remains plagued by many sexual scandals revolving around homosexuality and pedophilia, whereby it must silently pay off its many victims with untold millions of dollars in hush money. Sadly, the priests who are guilty of these crimes are never removed from their positions within the church, they are just transferred to another unsuspecting parish.

Ironically, it seems that the only way for one to be removed from the Roman Catholic priesthood, is to commit the only unforgiveable sin of the priesthood, that being the "sin of marriage" (I Timothy 4:3). For in the Roman Catholic "Code of Canon Law", it is considered "a scandal" for a priest to marry. How unfortunate that the sexual sins of the Catholic clergy are not considered to be "scandalous" and grounds for dismissal within the Roman Catholic Church.

Monastic Priesthood "Shaving of the Head"

With the establishment of the celibate monastic priesthood, also came the development of other priestly practices which directly tie the Roman Catholic Church to the Babylonian Religious System. Hislop tells us that, "In the Church of Rome the heads of the ordinary priests are only clipped, the heads of the monks or the regular clergy are shaven, but both alike, at their consecration, receive the circular tonsure (haircut or shave) ...." In other words, the Catholic clergy receive a symbolic circular haircut or shaving at the time they are consecrated.

In the Chaldean culture, the circle represented either "zero", "seed", or "the sun". In the Babylonian Mother/Son Religious System, the circle is used as a symbol for Tammuz on two fronts. For Tammuz was said to have been born from:

1) "The seed" of his mother Semerimus (from her claim that she was the woman who had provided "the seed" of Genesis 3:15).

In addition to:

2) The physical "Sun" (whose rays Semerimus had claimed had physically impregnated her).

We see that this circular shaving of the head for the priesthood is a practice that originated out of Babylon to show honor to Tammuz and is practiced to this day by many of the various adherents to the Babylonian Religious System.

Again, these practices are an afront to Scriptural Doctrine. In the Old Testament Levitical Priesthood, the act of shaving one's head was strictly forbidden by God. It is in the Book of Leviticus that God delivered His specific instructions for the Priesthood to

Moses:

"They shall not make baldness upon their head, neither shall they shave off the corner of their beard, nor make any cuttings in their flesh." Leviticus 21:5

Sunday Worship

The practice of worshipping on Sundays also comes to us from the Babylonian System. In Babylon, the first day of the week was designated as the Sun's day, or simply Sunday, in honor of the Sun. For after all, the Sun was the father of the beloved Tammuz, who in turn was the reincarnation of Babylon's Great Protector and Hero, Nimrod. In the Old Testament, the designated day of worship was Saturday, the sabbath, the last day of the week:

"Remember the sabbath day, to keep it holy.
 Six days shalt thou labor, and do all thy work.
 But the seventh day is the sabbath of the LORD thy God: in it thou shalt not do any work, thou, nor thy son, nor thy daughter, thy manservant, nor thy maidservant, nor thy cattle, nor thy stranger that is within thy gates:

For in six days the LORD made heaven and earth, the sea, and all that in them is, and rested the seventh day: wherefore the LORD blessed the sabbath day, and hallowed it." Exodus 20:8-11

"Ye shall keep my sabbaths, and reverence my sanctuary: I am the LORD." Leviticus 26:2

The changing of the Christian day of worship from Saturday to Sunday was initiated by Constantine. Again, it was his right to do so, because after all, he was not only the Emperor but also the Pontifex Maximus or Pope. This is all consistent with the Book of Daniel's prophecy about the coming Anti-Christ, of whom Scripture states:

"And he shall speak great words against the most High, and shall wear out the saints of the most High, and think to change times and laws: and they shall be given into his hand until a time and times and dividing of times." Daniel 7:25

Constantine's changing of the Christian day of worship was just a precursor to the changes that will one day be instituted by the coming Anti-Christ, who will be the Devil Incarnate. Scripture alludes to the fact that this coming world dictator will be propped up by the "False Prophet" (Revelation 19:20), who many Bible Scholars believe to be none other than the head of the Babylonian Mother/Son Religion, the "Roman Catholic Pope".

The fact that it was at the behest of the Catholic Church that Christian worship was changed from Saturday to Sunday was acknowledged by James Gibbons in "The Catholic Mirror", where he stated:

"The Catholic Church...By virtue of her divine mission, changed the day (of worship) from Saturday to Sunday." From the Catholic publication, "Our Sunday Visitor" (February 5, 1950) we read:

"Protestants do not realize that by observing Sunday, that they accept the authority of the spokesperson of the Church, the Pope."

So here we once again see the contention that has been stirred up by the Church of Rome by its attacks on the Word of God. Whether a Christian chooses to worship on Saturday or Sunday is likely of little significance to God, for it is now a strong societal cultural tradition within the world, and God still, "looks not on the outward appearance, but rather upon the heart" of those who are engaged in worshipping Him (I Samuel 16:7).

The changing of worship from Saturday to Sunday should simply be viewed for what it is, another attack on God's Word initiated by the world's current representative of the Babylonian

Mother/Son Religious System, the Catholic Church.

The Rosary

The Rosary is a system of repetitive prayer that is incorporated by the Catholic Church as a daily prayer schedule. The Catholic faithful employ a string of Rosary Beads in order to keep track of where they are in their repeating of the prayer cycle of the Rosary. There are ten small beads which are followed by a singular large bead in the rosaries string of beads. The two chief prayers that are recited while praying the Rosary are the "Hail Mary" prayers, and the Lord's Prayer. The Hail Mary prayer is said on each of the ten small beads, and the Lord's Prayer is spoken only on the singular large bead which occurs before and after each group of ten small beads.

The Lord's Prayer aspect of the Rosary is essentially the same prayer that Jesus taught his disciples in the Book of Matthew:

"After this manner therefore pray ye: Our Father which art in heaven, Hallowed be thy name.

Thy kingdom come. Thy will be done in earth as it is in heaven.
 Give us this day our daily bread
 And forgive us our debts as we forgive our debtors.
 And lead us not into temptation, but deliver us from evil:
For thine is the kingdom, and the power, and the glory forever. Amen." Matthew 6:9-13

The "Hail Mary" aspect of the Rosary is not based upon God's written Word and is recited as follows:

"Hail Mary full of grace, the Lord is with thee. Blessed art thou amongst women, and blessed is the fruit of thy womb, Jesus. Holy Mary, Mother of God, pray for us sinners, now and at the hour of our death. Amen."

Some Rosaries are known as "single decade (group of ten) rosaries". They consist of only ten beads which are often accompanied by a cross or a medal. The larger rosaries incorporate numerous decades of small beads which are separated by a singular large bead.

The Roman Church has 20 mysteries which are reflected upon in the Rosary, they are divided into:

5 Joyful Mysteries - spoken on Monday and Saturday
5 Luminous Mysteries - spoken on Thursday
5 Sorrowful Mysteries - spoken on Tuesday and Friday
5 Glorious Mysteries - spoken on Wednesday and Sunday

This incorporation of the concept of spiritual "Mysteries" regarding the praying of the Rosary, serves to solidify the association between the Roman Catholic Church and the false One World Religious System that will emerge directly preceding the return of Jesus Christ back to the earth to initiate His Millennial Kingdom. For its name is "...Mystery, Babylon The Great,.." (Revelation 17:5).

The Catholic Rosary's incorporation of sacred beads accompanied by ritualistic repetitive prayers did not start with the Church of Rome. For the beads are found among many of the pagan nations of the ancient world, not only in the peoples of both the West and Far East, but also in the New World, within the religious artifacts of ancient Mexico.

Hislop in "The Two Babylons" documents that these sacred beads were not merely necklaces that hung from one's neck as in the Grecian statue of Diana, but in India were held in one's hand, in China often hung from one's wrist, and in ancient Rome, just as in the Catholic Church, were hung from one's breast.

The etymology of the word "rosary" goes all the way back to Babylon itself. In Chaldee, the word "ro" is equated with "thought", while "shareh" is the Chaldean word for "director".

So, in the English form, the beads are equated with, "aiding or directing one's thoughts".

Given the fact that in the reciting of the Rosary, the Hail Mary prayers are spoken on a 10 to 1 ratio to the Lord's Prayer, it should be quite obvious, even to the casual observer, that the Veneration of Mary is of far greater importance and significance in the Mother/Sun Roman Catholic Religious System than the proper acknowledgment of either God the Father, or God the Son, or God the Holy Spirit.

Of even greater significance for the Christian when considering the Roman Catholic rite of reciting the Rosary, is the fact that Scripture condemns the use of "repetitious prayer". In the Book of Matthew, we read:

"But when ye pray, use not vain repetitions, as the heathen do: for they think that they shall be heard for their much speaking.

Be not ye therefore like unto them: for your Father knoweth what things ye have need of, before ye ask him." Matthew 6:7,8

Here we have the Lord likening the practice of repetitious prayer to a religious rite that is reserved for those who are "outside of the faith", whom He refers to as, "the heathen".

It is of great interest to note that this condemnation of repetitious prayer, occurs immediately before the Lord taught His disciples the Lord's Prayer (Matthew 6:9-13). The irony here is overwhelming. First, we have Jesus condemning the use of repetitious prayer, after which he then teaches His disciples the Lord's Prayer as an antidote to paganistic repetitive ritual. The Roman Catholic Church, which purports to follow Jesus, then takes this same Lord's Prayer, and incorporates it into an ancient heathenistic religious rite, where it too now becomes, "vainly repeated"! As the saying goes, "You can't make this stuff up"!

Papal Infallibility

Few doctrines in the Roman Catholic faith are as controversial as that of Papal Infallibility. We shall see however that this heresy too had its origins from within the Babylonian System.

The Encyclopedia Brittanica describes the doctrine of Papal Infallibility as: "The doctrine that the Pope, acting as supreme teacher and under certain conditions, cannot err when he teaches in matters of faith or morals."

Papal Infallibility when considered in terms of Roman Catholic Dogma states:

"That by virtue of the promise of Jesus to Peter, the Pope when appealing to his highest authority is preserved from the possibility of error on doctrine initially given to the Apostolic Church and handed down in Scripture and tradition". (Wikipedia)

The whole idea of the Pope being infallible due to his place in the Apostolic Succession that started with Peter as the Head of the Church, is based upon numerous gross misinterpretations of Scripture. In the Book of Matthew, we read:

"He (Jesus) saith unto them, But whom say ye that I am?

And Simon Peter answered and said, Thou art the Christ, the Son of the living God.

And Jesus answered and said unto him, Blessed art thou, Simon Barjona: for flesh and blood hath not revealed it unto thee, but my father which is In heaven.

And I say also unto thee, That thou art Peter (in Greek petros), and upon this rock (in Greek petra) I will build my church; and the gates of hell shall not prevail against it." Matthew 16:15-18

354

Here we have Jesus telling Peter that he is blessed because God the Father in Heaven had revealed to Peter the identity of who Jesus really was. Jesus then tells Peter that his name is petros (signifying a small stone or pebble), and then goes on to say, "upon this petra (referring to himself, a massive rock) I will build my church." Matthew Henry states that a more common and perhaps easier to understand translation of Matthew 16:18 reads as follows:

"Thou art Peter, thou hast the name of a stone, but upon this rock (perhaps pointing to himself), I will build my Church."

In the Old Testament, it is the Creator God Jesus (John 1:10) who is the true Rock of our Salvation:

"... He (Jeshurun) forsook God who made him, and lightly esteemed the Rock of his salvation." Deuteronomy 32:15

"Of the Rock that begat thee thou art unmindful, and hast forgotten God that formed thee." Deuteronomy 32:18

The Apostle Paul reminds us that it is Jesus, and Jesus alone, who is the foundational rock of our faith:

"For other foundation can no man lay than that is laid, which is Jesus Christ." I Corinthians 3:11

"And did all drink the same spiritual drink: for they drank of that spiritual Rock that followed them: and that Rock was Christ." I Corinthians 10:4

Ironically, it is Peter himself who declares that within the Church, all believers are merely (small) lively stones who have as their foundation, the chief cornerstone, the Lord Jesus Christ:

"Ye also as lively stones, are built up a spiritual house, an holy priesthood, offer up spiritual sacrifices, acceptable to God by Jesus Christ.

Wherefore also it is contained in the Scripture, Behold, I lay in Zion a chief cornerstone, elect, precious: and he that believeth on him shall not be confounded." I Peter 2:5,6

We see that not only is Jesus the true foundational Rock upon which the Church is built, but the concept of an Apostolic Succession starting with Peter is nowhere to be found within Scripture.

Many theologians believe that the Word of God teaches that there are "twelve Apostles" (Matthew 10:2-4), and only twelve. After the demise of Judas, the remaining apostles drew lots and chose Matthias to replace Judas (Acts 1:26). But this choice was of man's choosing and methodology, and not of God's. God chose rather to have Paul replace Judas as one being "born out of due time" (I Corinthians 15:8).

Paul also stated that in order to be an Apostle one had to have seen the risen Christ (I Corinthians 9:1). This fact alone appears to disqualify any of the subsequent Popes from being a part of any Apostolic Succession.

The doctrine of Papal Infallibility did not become Official Roman Catholic Church Doctrine until the 1st Vatican Council in 1870. Prior to this, the Roman Church taught that it was indeed infallible based not only upon their misinterpretation of Matthew 16:18, but also on Jesus' prayer for Peter in the Book of Luke, "But I have prayed for thee, that thy faith fail not: ..." (Luke 22:32).

Prior to Vatican 1, the Catholic Church had never specified whether this implied infallibility belonged specifically to the Pope, or to the Bishops in Council underneath the headship of the Pope. Vatican 1 merely assigned infallibility to the Pope alone.

There are many scholars who believe that the issue of Papal Infallibility was brought up at Vatican I for the purpose of re-establishing Papal power amongst the secular governments of the world, and not to resolve any issue regarding the infallibility of Bishops.

Again, this supposed ecclesiastical authority of Papal Infallibility seems to originate from the Roman System, where the Emperor was head of both the political and religious systems. In the Ancient World, this too appears to be the case.

In the book "Nineveh and its Remains", we are told by Layard that the kings of Egypt and Assyria (of which Babylon was part), were also the "head of both the religion and the state." As such, the rulers of the Ancient world, as Sovereign Pontiffs, were revered and treated as if they were "God's direct representatives in the world."

The revering of the Pope is most poignantly illustrated in the Catholic ritual of the Cardinals "kissing of the Pope's feet", a rite which is merely an extension of a practice which originated in Babylon. Francois Gaussen, in "The Prophet Daniel Explained", informs us that, "the kings of Chaldea wore on their feet slippers which the kings they conquered used to kiss."

This reverence for rulers comes to us directly from the Babylonian Religious System, where Semerimus' claims of being married to God, as evidenced by her becoming impregnated by the sun's rays, were a part of official Babylonian Dogma. Not only was Semerimus considered to be a Divinity, but by virtue of God being his direct father, the reincarnated Nimrod in the person of Tammuz was also considered to be Divine. This idea of Divine ties to rulers was not unique to Babylon. We are told by Diodorus Siculus, a first century B.C. Greek historian, that in Egypt, the kings were also regarded to be, "partakers of the divine nature".

It is easy to see that by the dictates of the Babylonian paganistic tradition, the idea of Papal Infallibility could be born. This of course should never be used as a consideration by any Christian for the reverencing of any person other than the Lord Jesus Christ. This is a clear dictate of Scripture. Even the reverence and love that one has for his own parents is to become secondary in the life of the true follower of Jesus Christ; "He that loveth father or mother more than me is not worthy of me..." (Matthew 10:37).

It is the clear message of God's Word that becoming the head of an organization or bureaucracy doesn't make the new leader perfect in any way, especially in one's decision making or moral abilities. Consider the case of Saul, who at the time of the initiation of his reign as the King of Israel, there was not to be found in all of Israel "a goodlier person than he." (I Samuel 9:2). His kingship however was marked by a degradation of not only his own personal moral fiber, but also by a litany of foolish decisions and errors:

"...behold, I have played the fool, and have erred exceedingly." I Samuel 26:21

The overriding Scriptural lesson to be learned from the life of Saul is, "with power comes corruption". As Lord Acton (1834-1902) stated, "Power tends to corrupt, and absolute power corrupts absolutely." Becoming the head of an organization as large as the Roman Catholic Church should in no way signify that this person, the Pope, should now be free from corruption. In fact, Scripture teaches that the opposite is true. Positions of leadership are typically filled "by the basest of men" (Daniel 4:17).

To make Peter as an example of infallibility regarding the doctrines of the Church, when considered in the light of Scripture, is also a ludicrous assertion. Scripture reveals to us that Peter did not know the first thing about the ways of God regarding salvation. When Jesus had told his disciples that he must suffer great things from the religious rulers and then be killed, Peter rebuked him. Jesus then informed Peter that his remarks indicated that he was being used by Satan as a tool to promote theological heresy, for the cross must come before the crown:

"But he turned, and said unto Peter, Get thee behind me,

Satan: thou art an offense unto me: for thou savorest not the things that be of God, but those that be of men." Matthew 16:23

God the Father would also have to correct Peter for his lack of understanding of Scriptural truths. At the Transfiguration, Peter told Jesus that they should make three booths, one for Jesus, one for Moses, and one for Elijah (Matthew 17:4). God the Father then intervened, and informed Peter that what they had just witnessed was not about Moses or Elijah, but solely about the Lord Jesus:

"While he yet spake, behold a bright cloud overshadowed them: and behold a voice out of the cloud, which said, This is my beloved Son, in whom I am well pleased; hear ye him." Matthew 17:5

Later, after Peter had "put the icing on his theological cake" by denying Jesus three times (Mark 14:72), it would appear that the Roman Catholic Church's first Pope was anything but infallible in either his decrees or his actions.

Perhaps the greatest example of the absurdity of the Roman Catholic Doctrine of Papal Infallibility is to be found in the historical case of Joan of Arc. On May 30, 1431, Joan was burned at the stake as a heretic and cross dresser, after a much publicized trial conducted by the Catholic Church, which was at the time under the domain of Pope Eugenius IV. In 1456, Pope Calixtus III ordered a re-examination of the trial that pronounced Joan was innocent, and declared that she was indeed a martyr.

In 1909, we find Joan being beatified by then Pope Pius X, and then later canonized by Pope Benedict XV in 1920, making her a "full-fledged saint" in the Catholic world. We must remember that this is the same world that had previously (1431) declared her to be a "full-fledged heretic". So much for Papal Infallibility.

The above listed Roman Catholic Doctrinal issues are again, by no means exhaustive. They are presented to exhibit a sense of just how far the Roman Catholic faith differs from traditional Biblical Doctrine, and to show just how closely the Roman Catholic Church is allied not with the Word of God, but rather with the tenets of the Babylonian Mother/Son Religious System.

The Babylonian Mother/Sun Religious System and the Far East

We have largely focused on the effects of the Babylonian Religious System within our Western Culture throughout the ages, especially its influences on the Roman Catholic Church. It should also be recognized that the influences of Babylon also extend to the major religions of the Far East, especially in India and China, where two of the largest religions of the world, Hindu and Buddhism, co-exist.

In India, while the Hindu religion now worships a multitude of Gods, this was not the case early in its history. Initially Hindus worshipped the gods Krishna and Brahm. From Moor's "Pantheon", we find the following statement from the early Hindu texts which is attributed to Krishna:

"The great Brahm is my womb, and in it I place my fetus, and from it is the procreation of all nature. The great Brahm is the womb of all the various forms which are conceived in every natural womb."

It is quite easy to see the similarities between early Hindu worship and the religion of Babylon. They both contain a certain duality incorporating male and female gods. Like Babylon, the Hindus also incorporate the worship of the Sun (Surya) within their religious system. As in Babylon, the Hindus also believe the soul to be eternal, and upon death can be reincarnated to the physical realm in a new body, just as Nimrod supposedly did in Babylon, when he returned to the world as Tammuz.

China's main religion is Buddhism. The Buddhist Religion originated in Hindu India. It was started by Guatama Buddha, who lived from approximately 563 to 483 B.C.

In the Hindu caste system into which Buddha was born, we know that Buddha was by birthright slated to be a Hindu Brahmana ruler. In an apparent effort to exhibit his idea of "moral superiority", Buddha renounced his right to rule on the basis of his birthright, and began to teach that the status of attaining Brahmana leadership should not be by birthright, but by both doing great deeds and by not engaging in sinful acts.

Buddha then left his hometown to spread his new gospel to the world at large, leaving behind his wife and child ("so much for Buddha's moral superiority"), and settled in China. From there the Buddhist Religion took shape, eventually becoming one of the largest religions of the world.

In Buddhism, as in Babylonianism and Hinduism, we again find both Sun worship and a belief in reincarnation. The Buddhist belief in reincarnation takes a different form from that found in Hinduism and Babylonianism, for the Buddhist believes that "rebirth does not necessarily take place by becoming another human being, but rather as an existence in one of the six Gati (realms), which the Buddhists call Bhavachakra.

Given the numerous similarities between the ancient paganistic religious systems of both Western Civilization and the Far East, it is easy to see why the Babylonian Religious System is referred to in Scripture as the "Mother of Harlots" (Revelation 17:5). For out of Babylon, all of the major Paganistic religious systems of the world can be seen to have had their origin.

The Post Constantinian History of the Roman Catholic Church

Since the time of its marriage into the Roman governmental structure in the days of Constantine, the Catholic Church's involvement within the political intrigue of the nations of Europe has been well documented. These attempts by the Roman Catholic Church to politically create a "heaven on earth" however, fly straight into the face of Scripture. For the Church's primary function is to call out to the lost, and according to the Great Commission, to educate all the people of the world in the ways of God, not to politically "rule over them." In the Book of Matthew, we read:

"Go ye therefore, and teach all nations, baptizing them in the name of the Father, and of the Son, and of the Holy Ghost:

Teaching them to observe all things whatsoever I have commanded you: and, lo, I am with you always, even unto the end of the world." Matthew 28:19,20

While Scripture tells the believer to be subject to the "higher powers" (Romans 13:1), and to "render unto Caesar the things that are Caesars" (Matthew 22:21), Jesus specifically told his disciples that His Kingdom "was not of this world" (John 18:36). The spiritual goal of the true believer should never be that of "ruling the world", but rather of "teaching the world" about the Love of God, and of His provisions for the forgiveness of our sins.

The Catholic Mother/Son Religion and the Rise of Islam

Not long after Constantine united the Church to the State, and in so doing forever politicizing the Church, we find forces working in the world towards the creation of a new religious system. This religion was the Religion of Islam, which was founded by Muhammad in the 7th Century A.D., a religion that now in the 21st Century, has become the 2nd largest religious affiliation in the world.

362

While Islam developed largely as a result of the familial feud between the descendants of Abraham's children, Ishmael and Isaac, the Babylonian and now Catholic Mother/Son religion also played a significant role in the development of its doctrinal structure. This of course is in keeping with what the Bible describes as the Babylonian System's role as the initiator of the false religious systems of the world, or "The Mother of Harlots" (Revelation 17:5). For right from its inception, we find within Islam the same exultation and veneration of the Catholic's "Mother Mary".

In Islam, we find Mary highly regarded and holding a "singularly exalted place", as she is mentioned at least 70 times within the pages of Islam's sacred book, the Quran. In fact, Mary is venerated to such a degree in the Islamic faith, that she is the only woman specifically mentioned within the pages of the Quran. It is also of great interest to note that Mary is mentioned more times in the Quran than she is mentioned within the pages of the Bible's entire New Testament.

In the Quran's Surah 3:42, we read:

"...O Mary! Behold Allah has chosen you, and made you pure, and exalted you above all the women in the world."

Here we find the Quran essentially referring to Mary as being, "the greatest woman of the world". This of course is the same degree of exultation that was originally bestowed upon the originator of the Mother/Son religious system, Semerimus, in Babylon.

The Quran is also careful to point out the fact that Jesus, while regarded as a Prophet in Islam, was perhaps more importantly viewed as, "The Son of Mary" (Surah 3:45), further adding to the status of Mary within the new religion of Islam.

On numerous occasions, Muhammad in the Hadith (sayings of the Prophet), referred to Mary as being, "the Master of the women in Paradise." This status of Mary granted from within

Islam is obviously in keeping with the traditions of the Babylonian Mother/Son Religious System.

Further Abuses of the Roman Catholic Church

Just as the abuses of Babylonian Baal worship in Israel led to the murder of untold numbers of Israel's children through Satanic sacrifice in Old Testament times, so too did the abuses of the Babylonian Roman Catholic Church lead to numerous deaths in the period of time known as the Inquisition. For in the Catholic Inquisition, a vast unknown number of followers of Jesus Christ in addition to numerous Jewish and Muslim peoples of the world were needlessly slaughtered.

In the 12th Century A.D., the Roman Catholic Church initiated the "Office of the Holy Inquisition". The function of this new office was to "root out religious heresy in the world". The primary targets of the "Holy Inquisition" being non-Catholic Christians, Jews, and Muslims.

The "Holy Inquisition" started in France in 1184 A.D. and continued there until the 14th Century.

From the History Channel, we are told that during the Inquisition, the Roman Catholic hierarchy would dispatch Inquisitors to a town, "...and announce their presence, giving citizens a chance to admit to heresy. Those who confessed received a punishment ranging from a pilgrimage to a whipping. Those accused of heresy were forced to testify. If the heretic did not confess, torture and execution were inescapable. Heretics were not allowed to face accusers, received no counsel, and were often victims of false accusations."

This system of course is in direct conflict with the standards of our Western Legal Tradition, and obviously fraught with built in tendencies and potentialities for abuse to anyone unfortunate enough to have been caught up within its jurisdiction.

The worst abuses occurred during the period of the Spanish Inquisition (1478-1834). Not only did it ravage the people of Spain, but it was also exported to the Spanish New World where we find the Inquisitors burning Lutherans at the stake in Mexico in 1574, and from there continuing on down to Peru, where numerous other Protestants were tortured and/or burned alive.

After conquering Spain in 1808, Napoleon abolished the Spanish Inquisition, but it re-emerged after Napoleon's defeat in 1814. The Inquisition was not openly terminated until 1834. Officially however, the "Supreme Sacred Congregation of the Roman and Universal Inquisition" has never ceased from within the official dogma of the Roman Catholic Church. It continues to this day under the name of, "The Congregation for the Doctrine of the Faith".

Nobody truly knows the accurate number of how many people were killed by the horrific Crusade against humanity known as "The Inquisition", as the numbers range anywhere from a few thousand (from pro-Catholic sources), to anywhere up to 68 million (W.C. Brownlee, an anti-Jesuit 19th Century Protestant Clergyman). By most accounts, the number of Christians and Jews killed during the Catholic Inquisition can conservatively be estimated to be an amount totaling in the millions of people. This is far more than the number of Christians who were killed in the Coliseum by the secular government in Rome in the first three centuries of the modern age. How ironic that Rome's secular government should be more gracious in its dealings with perceived dissidents than Rome's ecclesiastical government, the Catholic Church.

Whatever the actual number of deaths caused by the Inquisition truly are, it is apparently a number which can only be known by God. When coupled with the 1 to 3 million deaths that occurred as a result of the Roman Catholic inspired Crusades against Islam and the peoples of the Holy Land (1096-1271 A.D.), it is obvious that the Roman Catholic Church has a lot of blood on its hands.

As in the atrocities of torturing and then burning dissidents at the stake in the Inquisition, so too was the cruelty of the Roman Catholic Church against the inhabitants of the Holy Land during the Crusades. Dave Hunt writes in "A Woman Rides the Beast":

"In 1096 Pope Urban II inspired the first crusade to retake Jerusalem from the Muslims. With the cross on their shields and armor, the Crusaders massacred Jews across Europe on the way to the Holy Land. Almost their first act upon taking Jerusalem "for Holy Mother Church" was to herd all of the Jews into the synagogue and set it ablaze."

The Roman Catholic Church and Human Freedom

The Babylonian Mother/Son religious system of Semerimus and Tammuz demanded strict obedience of its subjects in both the secular and sacred realms of life. The idea of personal human freedom, or individual "God given rights", that now permeates much of our secular Western Culture, had seldom been given much consideration in the cultures in which the Babylonian System held control in the Ancient World. It should therefore come as no surprise that when the Magna Carta, a legal document which granted English citizens basic democratic human rights, was issued on June 15th, 1215, that it would immediately come under attack by the Roman Catholic Church. Although the Magna Carta would one day be termed, "the mother of European Constitutions", Pope Innocent III (1198-1216) was quick to condemn it, and to pronounce this document, "null and void", upon its arrival.

It seems that the Roman Catholic Church has never been as much concerned with the happiness, dignity, and well-being of its subjects as it has been with the wielding of, "absolute power", on both the secular and sacred levels. It is a well-documented historical fact that the Roman Catholic Church has throughout its existence backed numerous ruthless totalitarian governments. This has repeatedly occurred not only up to and through the Middle Ages, but also in the Post Reformation world, including the malevolent governments of Mussolini and Hitler in the 20th Century, which were fully supported by the Roman Catholic Church's hierarchy.

It is also evident that in the Roman Catholic mindset "dictatorial religious systems" operate best alongside "dictatorial secular governments".

The Future of the Roman Catholic Church

Not only has the official Roman Catholic Church had a well-documented and sordid history regarding political intrigue and corruption, but according to Biblical Prophecy, its worst moments may still be yet to come. It is generally agreed upon by most Biblical scholars that the Beast that will rule the world in the last days mentioned in the Book of Revelation (Revelation 17:3) is the Anti-Christ, or Devil Incarnate. The Book of Revelation also mentions a 2nd Beast, and it is this 2nd Beast who will help bring the 1st Beast to power:

"And I beheld another beast come up out of the earth; and he had two horns like a lamb, and he spake as a dragon.

And he exerciseth all of the power of the first beast before him, and causeth the earth and them which dwell therein to worship the first beast ..." Revelation 13:11,12

Many students of Biblical prophecy claim that the 2nd beast mentioned in the Book of Revelation will be none other than a future Pope of the Catholic Church. This 2nd Beast appears to work in conjunction with a Woman who is said to "ride the first Beast", the Anti-Christ:

367

"... and I saw a Woman sit upon a scarlet coloured Beast, full of names of Blasphemy, having seven heads and ten horns." Revelation 17:3

This Woman is described by the Apostle John as being, "a great whore who sits upon many waters" (Revelation 17:1). Many students of Bible prophecy believe that this woman is a representation of none other than the Roman Catholic Church. There are numerous reasons for this assumption:

1) In that this Woman is described as a "whore", we know that she is a "false bride". Scripture is careful to point out that the "true bride" of Jesus Christ consists of born again believers (Revelation 19:7, 21:9), and does not come exclusively out of any particular religious sect or denomination.

2) This Woman is also said to "sit upon many waters", so we know that her influence is worldwide, a characteristic that is also shared by the Roman Catholic Church. As we have noted, the influence of the Roman Papacy has spread far and wide over the face of the whole earth during the past two millenniums.

Scripture is quick to point out that this influential Woman is also to be equated with a great influential city: "And the Woman which thou sawest is that great city, which reigneth over the kings of the earth." Revelation 17:18

The only city that can be said to have wielded worldwide influence over the past 2,000 years would be the City of Rome.

3) John goes on to write that this Woman is also tied directly to the false Babylonian Religious System:

"And upon her forehead was a name written, MYSTERY, BABYLON THE GREAT, THE MOTHER OF HARLOTS AND ABOMINATIONS OF THE EARTH." Revelation 17:5

Ironically, the person who equates the Roman Catholic Church with Ancient Babylon, is the Apostle Peter himself. The people of the 1st Century A.D. were not devoid of having a knowledge of world history. In Peter's day, there was an awareness of how the Roman life and culture had originated in ancient Babylon, so much so, that the city of Rome was on occasion referred to as, and considered to be, synonymous with Babylon. Evidence of this fact can be seen in Peter's first Epistle, which is well known within theological circles to have been written by Peter from the city of Rome. In his closing salutations, Peter writes:

"The church that is at Babylon, elected together with you, saluteth you; and so does Marcus my son." I Peter 5:13

Here we see this clear illustration of Peter making the association between Ancient Babylon with his present whereabouts, the city of Rome. There was no functioning city of Babylon at the time of the writing of Peter's epistle, having been abandoned in the 2nd Century B.C., so here we find Peter clearly equating Rome as being synonymous with Ancient Babylon.

4) John, the writer of the Book of Revelation, then goes on to inform us of the location of the city wherein the great whore resides. For we are told that this city, sits upon seven mountains or hills (Revelation 17:9). While there may be more than one of the world's modern-day cities that are located on seven hills, only one of them can be said to have been influential on a worldwide scale for over two millenia, that being the city of Rome.

5) A further indication as to the identity of this Woman is to be found within her symbolic colors. John tells us that in his vision, the woman he sees was clothed in purple and scarlet colors (Revelation 17:4). From the Biblical account of the Crucifixion, we know that purple and scarlet were the official royal colors of the Roman Empire, as Jesus was openly mocked by the Roman soldiers, who had put upon Him a purple and scarlet robe (Matthew 28:28, John 19:2,5). Interestingly, the Roman Catholic Church to this day incorporates the symbolic use of purple and scarlet, its Bishops being adorned in purple, its Cardinals arrayed in scarlet vestments.

The Woman and the Beast

This Woman is said to ride atop a scarlet Beast (Revelation 17:3). This Beast, the Anti-Christ, is evidently controlled to some degree by the Woman (the Roman Catholic Church) and the 2nd Beast (the Pope). This is at the time of the initiation of Satan's reign over the earth during the time of the Great Tribulation period, which immediately precedes the return of Jesus Christ back to the earth to set up His Millennial Kingdom.

We are told in Scripture that the Anti-Christ will rule over an earth that is divided into ten separate Kingdoms:

"And the ten horns which thou sawest are ten kings, which have received no Kingdom as yet; but receive power as kings one hour with the Beast." Revelation 17:12

It is interesting to note that in 1973 the Club of Rome divided the world into ten separate economic trading blocs. These ten Regions which are recognized by the European Commission may indeed be the ten separate kingdoms over which the Anti-Christ wields his control.

Scripture goes on to indicate that this one-world system will grow tired of being under the control of the Woman, and will work to bring about her destruction, thus giving the Anti-Christ full control over the earth:

"And the ten horns which thou sawest upon the beast, these shall hate the Whore, and shall make her desolate and naked, and shall eat her flesh, and burn her with fire.
 For God hath put in their hearts to fulfill His will, and to agree, and give their Kingdom unto the Beast, until the words of God shall be fulfilled.
 And the Woman which thou sawest is that great city, which reigneth over the kings of the earth." Revelation 17:16-18

The efforts of these ten kings or rulers to finally remove the power of the Babylonian inspired Roman Catholic Church by bringing about its destruction is then deemed to be successful:

".... Babylon the great is fallen, is fallen, and is become the habitation of devils, and the hold of every foul spirit, and a cage of every unclean and hateful bird.

For all nations have drunk of the wine of the wrath of her fornication, and the kings of the earth have committed fornication with her, and the merchants of the earth are waxed rich through the abundance of her delicacies.

And I heard another voice from heaven, saying, Come out of her, my people, that ye be not partaker of her sins, and that ye receive not of her plagues.

For her sins have reached unto heaven, and God hath remembered her iniquities." Revelation 18:2-5

Thus, we see the end of the Roman Catholic Church, and with it, the end of the reign of terror upon the peoples of the earth by the Babylonian Mother/Son Religious System.

A Caveat

It must be stated that this paper has not been written as a condemnation of those who practice the Catholic faith. Some of the finest people of the world are those who attend Catholic Churches. Their contributions to the good of the societies in which they live is typically without measure, as is their discipline in attempting to follow the edicts of Christ. Sadly, many of them will never know the assurance of salvation that comes with entering into a personal relationship with Jesus Christ.

Thankfully, there are numerous Catholics who do indeed belong to the true Church of God, who have been "born again" by the Spirit of God, and who will eventually occupy God's Eternal Kingdom.

While Scripture gives a firm general command for believers to abandon this Whore of Babylon (Revelation 18:4), for reasons known only to God, He has seen fit for many born-again Catholics to grow in their faith not within Protestant, Evangelical, or other Gospel preaching Churches, but within the place where they had originally been planted, the Catholic Church.

There will be no such apology made to the Roman Catholic hierarchy however, for as we have seen, it is a part of a system dating back to Ancient Babylon that aligns its practices more with Semerimus and Tammuz than it does to the true God of Heaven, and His Son Jesus Christ.

The hierarchical history of the Roman Catholic Church is not one of being "the salt of the earth", but rather is a history associated with totalitarian governmental authority, gross sexual immorality, the displacement of whole human populations, and the persecution, torture, and murder of those who dare disagree with the Paganistic Tenets of the Roman Catholic faith.

Conclusion

Clearly, the origins of the Roman Catholic Church far predate the time when Constantine made Christianity the state religion of the Roman Empire in the 4th Century A.D. As we have learned, the Roman Catholic Church had its true beginning in the Mother/Sun Religious System of Ancient Babylon.

The influence of the Babylonian Mother/Sun Religious System has literally spread itself across the entire face of the earth. It has proven itself to be exactly what Scripture declares her to be, the seed from which the false religious systems of the world have grown, the "Mother of Harlots" (Revelation 17:5).

372

The Prophet Jeremiah clearly envisioned this paganistic monstrosity in the days of the Old Testament, where he testified:

"Babylon hath been a golden cup in the LORD's hand, that made all the earth drunken: the nations have drunken of her wine; therefore the nations are mad." Jeremiah 51:7

Soon after the birth of Christianity into the world, we find this same Babylonian System infecting the true Church of God, creating what has come to be known as the Roman Catholic Church. While the world at large views Catholicism as being representative of the "Universal Christian Church", nothing could be farther from the truth. Ironically, while the word "catholic" does mean "universal", the Roman Catholic Church in truth and practice does not represent "Universal Christianity" at all. Instead, it is representative of "Universal Paganism", for its creeds, practices, and dogma are tied directly to the ancient Babylonian Mother/Son Religious System, the Mother of all false religious systems.

When at last the real Bride of Christ is raptured and taken out of this world, the Roman Catholic Church and its Pope will then finish its last appointed task, that of uniting the world into a single religious system, the prophesied One World Babylonian Super Church.

It is easy to see how apostate Protestantism will unite with Catholicism in the coming ecumenical movement to form the One World Religion due to their many cultural similarities. The Babylonian glue that will hold Islam together with Catholicism in the coming Super Church will be their mutual "Veneration of Mary", while the adherents of the Hindu and Buddhist religions will also easily join ship with Roman Catholicism due to the many similarities between their monastic priesthoods.

After the establishment of this One World Super Religious System, which of course is merely another extension of the Babylonian System, the reigning Pope will cause the whole world to worship the Anti-Christ (Satan Incarnate) as God, under penalty of death for all who refuse to do so (Revelation 13:11-15).

This Babylonian Whore, who through the ages has so faithfully served her master Lucifer, will eventually be cast off as a menstruous cloth by Satan once she has accomplished her purpose of bringing him into the position of being worshipped as God (Revelation 18:2).

This of course should serve as a stern warning to all who would join league with Satan, for he has no problem with turning on his own followers in order to accomplish his own selfish desires. It is also a strong vindication of Scripture, for in God's Word we find the sharp contrast between the character of Satan, and that of the LORD:

"The thief (the devil) cometh not, but for to steal, and to kill, and to destroy: I am come that they might have life, and that they might have it more abundantly." John 10:10

"All that the Father giveth me shall come to me; and him that cometh to me I will in no wise cast out." John 6:37

Even so, "come quickly Lord Jesus." Revelation 22:20

Paradigms Tossed - Appendix Faulty Paradigm 3-1

Faulty Prophetic Paradigm #1

The Millennial Day Aspects of Prophecy - "Christians should never attempt to predict the historical time of Jesus Christ's 2nd Coming, for Scripture clearly states, "But of that date and hour knoweth no man, no, not the angels of heaven, but my Father only"(Matthew 24:36)

The pages of the history of the Church are littered with failed attempts at predicting the time of the 2nd Coming of Jesus back to the earth, when He returns to set up His Millennial Kingdom. Of the early Church Fathers, Irenaeus (130-202 A.D.) predicted that the 2nd Coming would occur in 500 A.D., while Pope Sylvester II (946-1003) would later predict that Jesus would return to the earth on January 1, 1000 A.D.

Throughout the more recent history of the Church there have also been numerous failed attempts at predicting the time of Christ's 2nd Coming. Among them is the Italian mystic Joachim De Fiore (1135-1202), who stated that the Millennium would begin somewhere between 1200 and 1260 A.D. Later John Mason (1646-1694) would claim that the Millennial reign of Christ would be initiated in the year 1694. The renowned scientist Sir Isaac Newton (1643-1727) also threw his name into the prognosticator's hat, and stated that the Millennium would start in the year 2000 A.D. The noted evangelist John Wesley 1703-1791) maintained that Jesus would return in the year 1836, while the Catholic Apostolic Church erroneously claimed that Jesus would return in the year of 1901. New Ager Benjamin Crème would later predict that Jesus would arrive back on planet earth on June 21, 1982. The list of those who have attempted to ascertain the time of the 2nd Coming of Jesus Christ is seemingly endless.

With the many false predictions that have been made through-out the history of the Church, one might think that this alone is ample evidence to indicate that the Christian should not be seeking to know the time of Jesus' return to the earth to set up His Millennial Kingdom. This of course begs the question, "If Jesus did not want us to know the time of His 2nd Coming, then why did He go to such great lengths to inform us of what would be historically occurring at the time of His return in Matthew 24, and in other Biblical passages"?

The key to understanding this conundrum can be found in the wording of Matthew 24:36. Notice that when Jesus said, "But of that day and hour knoweth no man", He did not mention the words, "week, month, or year". In other words, what Jesus may have been alluding to in Matthew 24:36 was that although the exact day and time of His return may not be known by mankind, the general time frame of His 2nd Coming could certainly be understood. In fact, the Word of God clearly indicates that the Christian should be attempting to discern the time of Jesus' 2nd Coming. In the 21st Chapter of the Book of Luke, we read:

"And when these things begin to come to pass, then look up, and lift up your heads; for your redemption draweth nigh." Luke 21:28

When we consider the fact that the three wise men, the aged Simeon, and the prophetess Anna had obviously understood the time frame of Jesus' First Coming into the world (Matthew 2:1,2, Luke 2:25,38), it seems that the Church Age believer could likewise be able to discern the approximate historical time frame of Jesus' 2nd Coming back to the earth.

Regarding the numerous aforementioned false predictions made over the past 2,000 years of Church History, it seems apparent from the Book of Daniel that the believers in Christ would not know the time of His 2nd Coming until the very end of the Church Age. For Daniel states that up until the very time of Christ's 2nd Coming, the knowledge of the actual time frame would be hidden or "sealed" from man's understanding.

"But thou, O Daniel, shut up the words, and seal the book, even to the time of the end: many shall run to and fro, and knowledge shall be increased." Daniel 12:4

In this passage of Scripture, Daniel also teaches that this time period would be a time of massive travel throughout the earth, and a time of a great explosion of knowledge. These indicators seem to describe the world of the 20th and 21st Centuries, the world in which we now live.

The Multiple Aspects of the Second Coming

The 2nd Coming itself is not an event that occurs on a single day in time, but rather is a "program" that unfolds over a specific time period. This is not a unique occurrence in Scripture. For example, when we consider the various aspects of "The Resurrection", the rising from the dead with a new body, we see that this too occurs over an expanse of time and is not confined to a single day.

Regarding the Resurrection, we are told that Jesus Christ was the "first fruits" (I Corinthians 15:20). Later we are told by Paul that the departed Church Age believers would be resurrected at the time of the invisible return of Christ to the earth, at the Rapture of the Church (I Thessalonians 4:16). Next, a resurrection of the Old Testaments' saints will then occur at the visible 2nd Coming of Jesus back to the earth (II Timothy 4:1). Finally, there will be a resurrection of the remaining dead at the time of the Great White Throne Judgment (Revelation 20: 12,13). Therefore, we can ascertain that the "Resurrection" is not a single event, but rather a "program" that is carried out over numerous years.

In like manner, the 2nd Coming of Jesus Christ back to the earth is also a program that occurs over a period of years. In the initial phase of the 2nd Coming, we find Jesus leaving His throne in heaven and invisibly returning to the earth to receive his Bride, the Church, at the time of the Rapture:

"For the Lord himself shall descend from heaven with a shout, with the voice of the archangel, and with the trump of God: and the dead in Christ shall rise first:

Then we which are alive and remain shall be caught up together with them in the clouds, to meet the Lord in the air: and so shall we ever be with the Lord." I Thessalonians 4:16,17

Soon after the Rapture of the Church, the world will experience the wrath of a 7-year tyrannical reign over the earth by Satan's emissary, the Anti-Christ (Daniel 9:24-27, Revelation 13:7).

At the conclusion of this time period which is known as "the time of Jacob's trouble" (Jeremiah 30:7), Jesus Christ shall visibly appear in the air with his saints and holy angels (I Thessalonians 3:13, Matthew 24:30,31). At this phase of the 2nd Coming, we are told that every eye shall see him:

"Behold he cometh with clouds; and every eye shall see him, and they also which pierced him: and all kindreds of the earth shall wail because of him." Revelation 1:7

Scripture indicates that the conditions upon the earth will be very different at the opening phase of God's program for the Second Coming, when Jesus returns invisibly to Rapture the Church, than what they will be at the conclusion of the Second Coming, when Jesus returns visibly approximately seven years later.

In the Book of Matthew, Jesus describes the condition of the earth at the time of His invisible return to the earth to receive His Bride the Church. It is a time where life on earth is going on pretty much in its usual normal fashion:

"But as the days of Noah were, so shall also the coming of the son of man be.

For as in the days that were before the Flood they were eating and drinking, marrying and giving in marriage, until the day that Noah entered into the ark.

And knew not until the Flood came, and took them all away; so shall also the coming of the son of man be." Matthew 24:37-39

Conversely, in the later phase of the Second Coming, when Jesus visibly returns to the earth, Scripture tells us that the earth will be enveloped in extreme chaos and suffering:

"And there shall be signs in the sun, and in the moon, and in the stars; and upon the earth distress of nations, with perplexity; the sea and the waves roaring;

Men's hearts failing them for fear, and for looking after those things which are coming on the earth: for the powers of heaven shall be shaken.

And then shall they see the Son of man coming in a cloud with power and great glory." Luke 21:25-27

The world has often experienced many of the same signs that Jesus had stated would immediately precede His 2nd Coming. The common verses that are typically cited to indicate the timing of the 2nd Coming are from the 24th chapter of the Book of Matthew, "You shall hear of wars and rumors of wars", and "Nation shall rise against nation, and kingdom against kingdom: and there shall be famines, and pestilences, and earthquakes, in diverse places." (Matthew 24:6,7). These verses however refer to events that occur "after" the initiation of the program of the Second Coming, that is, after the time of the Rapture of the Church, and do not refer to the timing of Christ's physical appearance at the end of the period known as the Second Coming. The time of Jesus' physical reappearance at the end of

379

the 2nd Coming will be very predictable, as Scripture clearly indicates that it occurs at the end of a specific 7-year time period commonly known as "The Tribulation", the missing seven years from Daniel's prophecy (Daniel 9: 24-27). This 7-year time period is initiated when the Anti-Christ signs a peace treaty with the Nation of Israel (Daniel 9:27).

This of course prompts us to ask the question, "How can one know when the approximate time period in which the Rapture of the Church occurs?" For according to Jesus, the condition of the world at the time of the Rapture will be such that life is going on in a manner that is pretty much,"business as usual" (Matthew 24:37,38).

One way in which the approximate time of the Rapture of the Church can be ascertained is through the study of the Millennial Day aspects of Biblical types and prophecy.

Millennial Day Aspects of Prophecy

While the attempt to better understand the historical time frame of the Rapture of the Church through the study of the Millennial Day approach to prophecy should be considered as "speculative theology", it is not an endeavor that is condemned by Scripture. Rather, it can be argued that such attempts appear to be encouraged by God's Word:

"It is the glory of God to conceal a thing: but the honor of kings is to search out a matter." Proverbs 25:2

God's Week of Creation and Man's Week of Work upon the Earth

In the first two chapters of the Book of Genesis, we are given an account of God creating the heavens and earth over a period of six days, which is then followed by a seventh day in which it is said that God rested (Genesis 2:2). This account shows God accomplishing His work over a time period of one literal week. In like manner, many theologians have argued that it would therefore make perfect sense to have the period of "man's work" on planet earth also be accomplished start to finish in a period of one week. We know from world history that mankind has obviously been working and struggling upon the earth for literally thousands upon thousands of weeks and years, so we can conclude that man's prophetic workweek could not possibly consist of literal days.

In the prophetic Book of Daniel, we are given a prophecy which consists of 70 seven-year weeks, or an expanse of time which lasts 490 years (Daniel 9:24-27). From this we can ascertain that in Scripture, a week does not always consist of seven literal days, for as we see here in the Book of Daniel, the length of time in one of Daniel's weeks consisted of seven literal years.

If we want to speculate as to the most likely time frame for the week of "man's work" upon the earth, we need look no further than God's Holy Word. For in both the Old and New Testaments, we are told that one day with God is equivalent to a thousand years for man:

"For a thousand years in thy sight are but as yesterday when it is past, and as a watch in the night." Psalm 90:4

"But beloved, be not ignorant of this one thing, that one day is with the Lord as a thousand years, and a thousand years as one day." II Peter 3:8

It is therefore likely that the prophetic week for the completion of "man's work" upon the earth would logically consist of seven 1,000-year days, making a total of 7,000 years for the completion of "man's work" upon the earth from start to finish. In theological circles, this method of study is often referred to as the "Millennial Day" or "Sabbath Millennial Day" perspective of Biblical prophecy.   381

There is a problem however with giving mankind a 7,000-year time frame in order to accomplish his work. That problem being the fact that the numbers simply do not add up. The Archbishop of Ussher (1581-1656) and many others, have calculated that according to the Biblical record, Adam was created in the year 4004 B.C. This would mean that the initiation of man's seventh day, the Millennium or 1,000-year reign of Christ over the earth in which he is to be given rest, would had to have occurred no later than the year 1996 A.D. This is a year that has obviously come and gone at the time of this writing (2021 A.D.).

This brings us to a point where in order to establish a defensible millennial time frame for Biblical prophecy, we need to consider the millennial aspect of Biblical prophecy from other avenues of approach than the one currently employed, that being, an analyses of Millennial Day Prophecy in which man's "week" of work starts in the year 4004 B.C.

We know from the prophetical word in Scripture that there would be an historical time in which God would cut off Israel for a certain length of time before He would revive and restore them as His primary messenger to the world. In the Book of Hosea we read:

"Come and let us return unto the LORD: for he hath torn, and he will heal us; he hath smitten, and he will bind us up.

After two days will he revive us: in the third day he will raise us up, and we shall live in his sight." Hosea 6:1,2.

In this passage of Scripture, we find Hosea prophesying of a future time in which God would set Israel aside for a period of two "days", after which He would restore them back into fellowship with Him in the third day. Now if these prophetical "days" were actually periods of 1,000 years each, it would seem that by discovering the year in which Israel was cut off, that we could also ascertain the other millennial time frames of mankind's history.

The Cutting Off of Israel

We know from Appendix 2 of this study, that Jesus was probably not born at the time of the conversion of the calendar from B.C. to A.D. Rather, He was more likely born in the year 4 B.C. We arrived at this date by calculating backwards from a generally known and accepted historical date, that being 70 A.D., the year Titus sacked and burned Jerusalem. By using Biblical principles, we understand that in Scripture the number 40 represents both judgment and suspended judgment. By subtracting 40 from 70 A.D., we come to the year 30 A.D. as being the likely year that Israel was cut off and set aside by God for His purposes. From the parable of the unfruitful fig tree (Luke 13:6-9), we then allowed for the fact that God had granted Israel one year to repent for their sin of crucifying Jesus. This places 29 A.D. as the likely year of the Crucifixion. We know from other Scripture that Jesus was thirty years old when He began His ministry (Luke 3:23), and that His ministry lasted three years, so we can surmise that Jesus was approximately 33½ years old at the time of His death, which gives us 4 B.C. as the likely year of His birth.

If we use the year 30 A.D. as the time that God cut off Israel as prophesied by Hosea, and then allow for the days of Hosea's prophesy to be two periods of 1,000 years each, we then arrive at a date of 2030 A.D. for the time of the completion of Israel's two days of being set aside in the plan of God. These 2,000 years would then be followed by a period of 1,000 years in which Israel would be restored to a place of prominence in God's interactions with the world. This 1,000-year period would be man's seventh day on earth, a period when the curse will be taken away from the earth, and man will in a sense rest from his labors, just as God is said to have rested after the six days of creation. This period of 1,000 years is commonly referred to as the Millennium, a time on earth where Christ shall rule for 1,000 years (Revelation 20:4). This gives us a time for the completion of the Millennium to be 3030 A.D.

This line of reckoning Biblical timelines gives us an accounting for the last three days (3,000 years) of man's seven-day (7,000 years) week of work on earth. If we then go back to 30 A.D. and subtract four days, or 4,000 years, we arrive at a date of 3970 B.C. This is necessary in order to accurately establish a 7,000-year analogous timeline for "man's work" upon earth. This would make the timeline for the week of "man's work" on earth to begin in 3970 B.C., and then conclude after 7,000-years in the year 3030 A.D.

The problem with establishing this timeline, is that to my knowledge, there are no major historical events that have been known to have occurred in the year 3970 B.C.

Through using Biblical principles and types, we must now seek to understand what may indeed have occurred in the year 3970 B.C. that is of special spiritual significance.

Man's Week of Work Begins with Man's Sin

When Adam was created, it can hardly be said that the countdown for man's 7,000-year work on earth had begun. For at the time of his creation, Adam was in a state of sinless perfection. He was both acknowledging in, and living under, God's rule over his life. His every need was provided for him without any toil on his part. It is therefore quite likely that the timeline for man's work on earth, did not start with man's creation, but rather with his fall into sin.

Although most students of Scripture surmise that Adam fell into sin almost immediately after he was created, this belief is not supported anywhere within the pages of the Word of God. The expanse of time between Adam's creation and the Fall is a fact that is known only to God. Just as Scripture is silent on matters such as many of the unknown events of Jesus' early childhood, and the location of Moses' grave, so too is it silent on the matter of how long Adam lived in a state of perfect obedience to God.

Adam and the Last Adam

From our study on Jesus Christ being the Last Adam in Chapter 11 of this work, we know that Adam as created, was a unique human being. For Eve was not created separately. She was formed from the rib that was taken out of Adam (Genesis 2:21,22). Thus, it can be said that Adam as created was the true representative head of the whole human race. The total attributes of humanity, both male and female, the unique talents of all three races (Semitic, Hamitic, and Japhetic), were all present within Adam as created. Within Adam is to be found the total potential talents and abilities that humanity would ever display. In Adam as created, we have the intellectual, the scientist, the poet, the philosopher, the craftsman, the artist, the musician, the manager, the nurturer, and the athlete. Eve and each one of Adam and Eve's offspring are merely fragments of the totality of human life and potential that originally existed in Adam.

Likewise, Jesus Christ as the last Adam was a total and complete human being, possessing both male and female personality types, and the full expression of human potential. Jesus would have possessed the intellectual capabilities of Einstein, the artistic flair of Michelangelo, and the athletic capabilities of Michael Jordan. We see in both Adam and Jesus, the only true "Renaissance Men" who have ever existed. All other men and women who have ever been born into this world have been merely fragments of Adam as originally created.

That Jesus should be a similitude of the First Adam was necessary in order for Jesus to die judiciously for the whole human race. This is why Scripture is careful to refer to Jesus as the "Last Adam" (I Corinthians 15:45). Just as Adam as created possessed all the human talent and abilities that have ever existed, and therefore representative of all mankind, so too was Jesus complete in His humanity. If Jesus had not possessed the full realm of human capabilities (both male and female, red and yellow, black, and white) as did Adam, then under the Biblical principle of "an eye for an eye and a tooth for a tooth" (Exodus 21:24), Jesus could have only died for one other person, and not for all of humanity. Hence both Jesus and Adam as originally created, were both similar and unique in terms of their humanity.

If Jesus was a similitude or "type" of Adam, would it not make sense for Adam in certain ways to have also been a "type" of Christ? We are not talking in terms of being a "savior" here, but rather in sharing similarities in the outworking of their individual lives.

In Jesus' life, we know that he lived 33½ years without sinning. Could it be possible that the First Adam had also lived a total of 33½ years before he sinned? This would most certainly solidify Jesus' title in His role as the "Last Adam" and in further establishing His credentials in making Him uniquely qualified to die on behalf of the entire human race!

The most amazing thing about the possibility of Adam living under God's complete control for 33½ years before he sinned, is the fact that when we add 33½ years going forward from the year of Adam's creation in 4004 B.C., we come up with the year 3970 B.C.

If 3970 B.C. marks the year in which man's millennial work week starts, then amazingly, when we add the first four days (4,000 years) to the year 3970 B.C., we then arrive at the exact year that Israel was cut off in Hosea's prophesy, 30 A.D.!

This effectively lines up with God's setting aside of Israel in 30 A.D. as prophesied by the prophet Hosea, and reveals a millennial time frame for man's week of work on earth (7,000 years) to initiate in 3970 B.C., and end in the year 3030 A.D.!!!

"O the depth of the riches both of the wisdom and knowledge of God! How unsearchable are his judgments, and his ways past finding out!

For who hath known the mind of the Lord? Or who hath been his counsellor?

Or who hath first given to him, and it shall be recompensed unto him again?

For of him, and through him, and to him are all things: to whom be glory forever. Amen." Romans 11:33-36

That the first Adam could have lived 33½ years without sinning, and then while standing underneath a tree became a sinner, should then be followed by the Last Adam (Jesus), who also lived 33½ years without sinning, who would then "become sin" after being nailed to a tree, speaks volumes of both the beauty and magnificence of the Plan of God!!! (II Corinthians 5:21).

God's Timelines

Again, if we take the start of man's week as initiating with the Fall of Adam in 3970 B.C. and go ahead in the future to the setting aside of the nation of Israel as God's messengers to the world in 30 A.D., we have an elapsed time of 4,000 years. If we then add the two days or 2,000 years signifying the return of Israel into God's favor, we arrive at the year 2030 A.D. Next, if we add the last or seventh day onto the millennial time clock (1,000 years), we arrive at the end of the Millennial Kingdom in the year 3030 A.D. At this time man's week on earth would be complete, and according to Biblical prophecy, God will then destroy the heavens and earth by fire:

"But the day of the Lord will come as a thief in the night; in the which the heavens shall pass away with a great noise, and the elements shall melt with fervent heat, the earth also and the works that are therein shall be burned up." II Peter 3:10

It is at this time that God will then create a new heavens and earth:"For, behold, I create new heavens and a new earth: and the former shall not be remembered, nor come into mind." Isaiah 65:17

"And I saw a new heaven and a new earth: for the first heaven and the first earth were passed away; and there was no more sea." Revelation 21:1

If this prophetic millennial timeline is accurate, that would indicate that each of the timelines of man's history could be known except one, that being the time of the Rapture of the Church. If the Millennial Kingdom is initiated in 2030, then we know that the completion of the 7-year Tribulation Period would also be in the year 2030 A.D., which would make the start of the 7-year Tribulation to occur in the year 2023 A.D.

Scripture does not indicate a specific duration of time between the Rapture of the Church and the covenant that the Anti-Christ will make with the Nation of Israel which will signify the start of the 7-year time period known as the Tribulation (Daniel 9:27). Therefore, if this millennial interpretation of Biblical prophecy is correct, then one could likely expect the Rapture of the Church to occur at any time between now and the year 2023 A.D.

Another possible end time scenario would be for the Tribulation Period to start in the year 2030, at the end of and not during Israel's 2,000 years of being set aside by God. This however seems to be less likely, for it would necessitate a 7007 year time frame for the history of man's salvation in order to have Jesus' Millennial reign last a full 1,000 years.

Either way, time will soon tell if these speculations of the millennial aspects of Biblical prophecy which links the initiation of man's week of work with the possible time of Adam's Fall in the year 3970 B.C. will prove to be true, for the first six days of man's work on earth will soon be concluded.

If not, we do know from Scripture that Jesus' eventual 2nd Coming will be soon. For in speaking of His return, Jesus had said, "Surely I come quickly" (Revelation 22:20). When we consider this statement from Jesus' perspective, he was in essence saying, "Though it took 4,000 years for me to appear on earth as the Savior at my First Coming, my reappearance at the Second Coming will not take anywhere near as long of an expanse of time" (As an interesting aside, Jesus' birth in 4 B.C. was exactly 4,000 years after the original creation of Adam in 4,004 B.C.).

It is this belief in the imminent and soon return of Jesus back to the earth at His 2nd Coming that has been the glorious hope and expectation of the Church over the course of the past 2,000 years.

"He that testifieth these things saith, Surely I come quickly. Amen. Even so, come, Lord Jesus." Revelation 22:20

MANKIND'S POSSIBLE 7,000 YEAR TIMETABLE FROM

THE FALL THROUGH THE MILLENNIUM

Adam's Creation	The Fall	Jesus' Birth	The Crucifixion	Israel cutoff	Rapture & Tribulation	2nd Coming	Millennial Kingdom
I	I	I	I	I	I	I	I
4004 BC	3970 BC	4 BC	29	30	2023	2030	3030

Faulty Prophetic Paradigm #2

The Shortening of Days - "The correct interpretation of Matthew 24:22, where Jesus states,"Except those days be shortened, no flesh would survive", will not be known until after the completion of the Tribulation Period"

Through the years, theologians have disagreed as to what Scripture means regarding "the shortening of days" mentioned in the 24th chapter of the Book of Matthew.

The verse in question reads as follows:

"And except those days should be shortened, there should no flesh be saved: but for the elect's sakes those days shall be shortened." Matthew 24:22

While some theologians argue that this verse is to be interpreted as, God will make the literal 24 hour days during the Seven Year Tribulation Period to last a shorter expanse of time (say 23 hour days for example instead of the customary 24), others contend that, "If Almighty God permitted those days to go beyond their allotted time frame, no flesh would be saved", or more simply, "The trouble of these days will not be allowed to get to the point of destroying everyone" (Bible Resources).

Throughout the history of the Church, this "shortening of days" is seldom definitively defined and has often been considered to be an aspect of Scripture that will not be totally understood until after the time that it has actually occurred.

In order for us to better understand this "shortening of days" regarding the last 7 years of Daniel's Prophecy, it may be useful to put the 490-year expanse of time of Daniel's Prophecy within its proper historical time frame.

Daniel's Prophetical Message

One of the preeminent end time prophetical messages was delivered to the prophet Daniel by the Angel Gabriel during the time of Israel's Babylonian Captivity in the 6th Century B.C. In the Book of Daniel we read:

"Yea whiles I was speaking in prayer, even the man Gabriel, whom I had seen in the vision at the beginning, being caused to fly swiftly, touched me about the time of the evening oblation.

And he informed me, and talked with me, and said, O Daniel, I am now come forth to give thee skill and understanding.

At the beginning of thy supplications, the commandment came forth, and I am come to show thee; for thou art greatly beloved: therefore understand the matter, and consider the vision.

Seventy weeks are determined upon thy people and upon thy holy city, to finish the transgression, and to make an end to sins, and to make reconciliation for iniquity, and to bring in everlasting righteousness, and to seal up the vision and prophecy, and to anoint the most Holy.

Know therefore and understand, that from the going forth of the commandment to restore and to build Jerusalem unto the Messiah the Prince shall be seven weeks, and threescore and two weeks: the street shall be built again, and the wall, even in troublous times.

And after threescore and two weeks shall Messiah be cut off, but not for himself: and the people of the prince that shall come shall destroy the city and the sanctuary, and the end thereof shall be with a flood, and unto the end of the war desolations are determined.

And he shall confirm the covenant with many for one week: and in the midst of the week he shall cause the sacrifice and the oblation to cease, and for the overspreading of abominations he shall make it desolate, even until the consummation, and that determined shall be poured upon the desolate." Daniel 9:21-27

In this Scripture passage from the ninth chapter of the Book of Daniel, we are told of a vision given to Daniel by the Angel Gabriel concerning the prophetical time frame which would occur regarding:

1) The appearance of Israel's Messiah on the world stage.

2) The consummation of man's self-rule on earth before the initiation of the Millennial Kingdom, the time often referred to as the Great Tribulation, the Seven Year Tribulation Period, or the Time of Jacob's Trouble.

The vision that was given to Daniel concerned a time frame that totaled 70 weeks of time. These weeks we now know to be periods of 7 years per week, which makes the total time frame of Daniel's vision to take place over 490 years. Within Daniel's vision we are also told that there would be a division of these 490 years into two separate blocks of time, the first block consisting of 69 weeks or 483 years (Daniel 9:25), and the second time period being one week, or seven years (Daniel 9:27). Daniel was told that the initiation of the first block of time would be "the commandment to restore and build Jerusalem", and would end with the appearance of the Messiah (Daniel 9:25). After this, Daniel was told that the Messiah would be "cut off " (Daniel 9:26)

The second block of time would commence when Satan's representative the Anti-Christ, would appear on the world stage and sign a seven-year peace treaty with the Nation of Israel, thus "confirming the covenant with many for one week" (Daniel 9:27).

This seven-year period of time would also be divided into two periods of time consisting of 42 months each. The first period of 42 months being a time of relative peace, while during the second period the world would go through the greatest troubles it has ever experienced. It is this last period of time which had prompted the prophetical proclamation given by Jesus that we are now examining, that "except those days be shortened, there should no flesh be saved" (Matthew 24:22).

The Initiation of the First 69 Weeks

When we seek to determine the time of the initiation of the first 69-week (483 year) time period, we run into a conundrum. For there were three such proclamations made that were recorded in the Book of Ezra. The first proclamation was made by Cyrus in the year 538 B.C., the second by Darius in 518 B.C., and the third by Artaxerxes in 457 B.C.

The answer to this riddle lies in the fact that the Book of Daniel states that this proclamation would be made to not only rebuild the Temple, but to "restore and build Jerusalem." (Daniel 9:25). In the proclamation given by Cyrus, we find that his decree concerned only the rebuilding of the Temple (Ezra 1;1-3). In the decree sent forth by Darius, we find an order to rebuild and restore the Temple, but a release of only some Jewish elders to do so. It is not until the decree of Artaxerxes in 457 B.C. that we find a release of the Jewish people in general who were willing to return to the land, thereby allowing for not only the rebuilding and restoration of the Temple, but also for the reformation of the City of Jerusalem itself, the true restoration and rebuilding prophesied by Daniel.

When we then add the 483 years of Daniel's prophecy on to the year 457 B.C., we arrive at the year 26 A.D. To this we must now ask ourselves the question, "What significant historical event occurred in the year 26 A.D.? When we refer to Appendix 3-1,

394

"The Millennial Day Aspects of Prophecy" in this study, we know that Jesus was likely born in the year 4 B.C., and that the Crucifixion occurred in 29 A.D., which then brought about the setting aside of the Jewish people by God in the year 30 A.D. at the time of the Jewish authorities stoning of Stephen, the Church's first martyr.

In that we know that Jesus' ministry lasted for a period of three years, we can surmise that the initiation of His ministry had to have occurred in the year 26 A.D. To this we must ask the question, "Are there any Scripture verses that serve to corroborate the fact that the initiation of Jesus' public ministry is indeed the completion of the 483 years of Daniel's prophecy? The answer is an emphatic, "Yes!"

In the Book of Mark, we find Jesus declaring that the public initiation of His Ministry in 26 A.D. is indeed the presentation of their true Messiah to the nation of Israel. For here Jesus states:

"...The time is fulfilled, and the kingdom of God is at hand: repent ye, and believe the gospel." Mark 1:15

The "time" that Jesus is referring to here, is a direct reference to the completion of the 483 years of Daniel's prophesy. For in this passage, we find Jesus categorically stating, "the time is now fulfilled."

The Last Seven Years of Daniel's Prophecy

An interesting phenomenon occurs during the second block of time mentioned in Daniel's prophecy. For in this last week of seven years, time is not reckoned in the same manner as it was in the first block of time. For in the first 69 weeks (483 years), time is reckoned using solar years, which consist of 365 days per year. In the last week of seven years however, we find time divided into two 3½ year periods of 1,260 days each (Revelation 11:3, 12:6). This form of time reckoning is known as lunar or "prophetic years". Each solar year therefore has five more days in it than a lunar or prophetic year. Therefore, during the last seven years of Daniel's prophecy, the elapsed time will have 35 fewer days in it than if God had continued to reckon time in the same manner as He had during the first 69 weeks.

Here we now see the true "shortening of days" that Jesus mentioned in Matthew 24:22. It is now quite evident that what Jesus was saying in this passage in Matthew could be paraphrased as such:

"That if the length of those years had been reckoned in the same manner as the years had been reckoned during the first 69 weeks of Daniel's Prophecy, that is for an additional 35 days, then no flesh would have survived." Matthew 24:22

We see that this "shortening of days" is neither mystical, nor impossible to figure out. It is just another example of God in His Great Omniscience knowing all "potential history", and then making the necessary allowances for it in His Plan. To Him be the Glory forever and ever! Amen.

POSSIBLE TIMETABLE FOR DANIEL'S 70 PROPHETIC WEEKS
TOTALING 490 YEARS

Initial 69 Weeks			70th Week		
483 solar years			7 lunar years		
I_____I			I_____I		
Artaxerxes	Initiation of	Messiah	Start of the	Millennial	Eternal
Decree	Jesus' Ministry	Cut-Off	7 year Tribulation	Kingdom	State
I_____	I_____	I_____	I_____	I_____	I____
457 BC	26 AD	29	2023	2030	3030

Paradigms Tossed - Appendix Faulty Paradigm 3-3

Faulty Prophetic Paradigm #3

Prophetic Implications of the Jewish Feasts - "There is little to be learned from the Old Testament Feasts in understanding Biblical Prophecy"

While it is common for students of Biblical prophecy to immediately turn to the Books of Daniel and Revelation when studying prophecy, there is also much wisdom and understanding to be garnered from examining the Old Testament Jewish Feasts and their relationship to the prophetic Word. There are numerous insights to be gained from these Feasts in our study of Biblical Prophecy.

The 7 Major Jewish Feasts

As in other numerical aspects of God's Word and Creation, it is no accident that there are 7 major Jewish Feasts found in Scripture, for the number seven represents "completeness" in things pertaining to God. Of the seven Feasts, the first three are considered to be the "spring feasts" which carry on into summer with the Feast of Pentecost, and the last three are known as the "fall feasts". They are as follows:

1) The Feast of Passover

2) The Feast of Unleavened Bread

3) The Feast of Firstfruits

4) The Feast of Pentecost

5) The Feast of Trumpets

6) The Feast of Atonement

7) The Feast of Tabernacles

While it is common to tie the three major Feasts of Passover, Pentecost, and Tabernacles respectively to the Crucifixion, Birth of the Church, and 1st and 2nd Comings of Christ, the other four feasts are also duly representative of actual historical prophetic events that either have already occurred or are about to occur in the future. We shall see that God in His Sovereign control over history has ordained that these 7 Feasts would find their ultimate prophetic fulfillment in the same time frame within the year as the original event that had initially prompted the celebration of the Feast.

Each one of the first four spring and on into summer feasts have already found their prophetic fulfillment in historical Biblical events:

The Feast of Passover

The Feast of Passover takes place on the 14th day of the first month of the Jewish year. It was initiated by the Hebrew people's killing of the Passover Lamb at the time of their Exodus from Egypt. Like all of the Jewish Feasts, it was a foreshadowing of future events, and was prophetically fulfilled in 29 A.D. with the Crucifixion of our Lord Jesus Christ at the time of the Feast of Passover of that year.

The Feast of Unleavened Bread

The Feast of Unleavened Bread originated with the Hebrews being told to make unleavened bread for their quick flight out of Egypt one day after Passover (Leviticus 23:6). In God's Word, leaven is symbolic of sin (Exodus 12:15, Leviticus 2:11, Luke 12:1).

This feast occurs one day after the Passover Feast and was later to be fulfilled by the burial of Jesus, the true sinless Bread of Life, whom God the Father made to be sin for us, who knew no sin, that we might be made the righteousness of God in him (II Corinthians 5:21). Through his death on the cross, Jesus overcame the effects of sin for all who by faith, would come to believe in Him:

"Therefore we are buried with him by baptism into death: that like as Christ was raised up from the dead by the glory of the Father, even so we also should walk in newness of life.

For if we have been planted together in the likeness of his death, we shall be also in the likeness of his resurrection:

Knowing this, that our old man is crucified with him, that the body of sin might be destroyed, that henceforth we should not serve sin." Romans 6:4-6

In preparation for the Feasts of Passover and Unleavened Bread, the Jewish people thoroughly swept their houses so that there would be no leaven found in them during the times of the Feasts of Passover and of Unleavened Bread. This was done in obedience to the direct command made by God to remove all leaven out of their houses prior to the Feast of Unleavened Bread (Exodus 12:15). Very interestingly, this Jewish practice of thoroughly sweeping one's house to remove any possible leaven contained therein has morphed into the common secular practice of "spring cleaning" found throughout much of Western Civilization.

This same aspect of cleaning one's house before the Feast of Unleavened Bread was dutifully performed by Jesus immediately prior to the first Passover of His earthly ministry, when He made a whip and physically removed the "sinful element" or "leaven" of the money changers out of His own Father's House (John 2:18). Scripture also tells us that Jesus once again swept the leaven out of His Father's House for the Feast of Passover/Unleavened Bread by overturning the tables of the money changers, and stopping the carrying of merchandise into the Temple, at the time of the Passover that preceded His Crucifixion (Mark 11:15,16).

Jesus told His disciples that He was the "true bread" that had come down from heaven, and that the bread that Moses had supplied to their forefathers in the Wilderness was just a fore-shadowing of things to come:

"Then Jesus said unto them, Verily, verily, I say unto you, Moses gave you not that bread from heaven; but my Father giveth you the true bread from heaven.

For the bread of God is he which cometh down from heaven, and giveth life unto the world." John 6:32,33

In the Church's first communion, which we commonly refer to as the "Last Supper", Jesus took the bread, broke it, and declared it to be "his body" (Luke 22:19).

In the Jewish Passover/Unleavened Bread's Seder ceremony, 3 pieces of unleavened bread were placed in a linen bag. This unleavened bread had stripes (char burns) and was punctured. The leader of the ceremony would take the middle piece of unleavened bread (matzah) and remove it from the linen bag. He would then break this piece of bread into 2 pieces, and place one of the pieces back into the bag. He would then wrap the other piece in a linen cloth, which was then hidden somewhere within the house. This piece was known as the afikomen. It remained hidden in the house until the children of the house were told to search for it. The child who found the afikomen was rewarded with a gift. The afikomen was then broken into many pieces and was eaten by all who were taking part in the ceremony.

In this ceremony, we see that the 3 pieces of unleavened bread would come to symbolize the 3 members of the Godhead, while the second piece of bread which was removed from the bag represented the 2nd Person of the Trinity, Jesus Christ. Just as the matzah was broken into two pieces, so too was Jesus broken at the Cross. As the piece of matzah was both pierced and striped, so too was Jesus not only pierced (Zechariah 12:10), but Scripture also tells us that Pilate had Jesus whipped (Matthew 27:26), and that it is by His stripes that we are healed (Isaiah 53:5). As this broken piece of matzah was wrapped in linen, so too was Jesus wrapped in linen for His burial (Mark 15:46). Just as the child who found the matzah is rewarded with a gift, so too is the child of God who finds salvation in Jesus, for these children of God are given the gift of the Holy Spirit (Acts 2:38).

The Feast of Firstfruits

The Feast of First Fruits commenced at the time when Israel first came into the Promised Land after their Exodus from Egypt and had reaped the harvest of the first fruits thereof (Leviticus 23:10). It takes place during the week long Passover Celebration on the first day after the Sabbath that occurs in the midst of the week. The Feast of Firstfruits ends 50 days later at the time of the Feast of Pentecost. The Feast of First Fruits found its historic prophetic fulfillment in the Resurrection of Jesus, who represented the "firstfruits" of God's harvest of souls for the Eternal State.

The Feast of Pentecost

The Feast of Pentecost, which is also known as the "Feast of Weeks" or the "Festival of Harvests", occurs 50 days after the Sabbath of Firstfruits, and commemorates the harvest of the land. It coincides with the arrival of the Hebrew people at Mount Sinai 50 days after they had left Egypt. It was symbolic of God's provision of sustenance for His representatives to the world, the Nation of Israel.

The Feast of Pentecost was prophetically historically fulfilled

401

in New Testament times with the giving of the Holy Spirit on the day of Pentecost. This giving of the Holy Spirit was for the sustenance and equipping of the Church in its role as God's new representatives to the world (Acts 2:1-4).

The Church is now living in the time interval between the Feast of Pentecost and the Feast of Trumpets, with the last 3 historical prophetic fulfillments of the 3 remaining Jewish Feasts yet to be fulfilled.

The Feast of Trumpets

The Feast of Trumpets, also known as Rosh Hashana, starts on the first day of the Jewish New Year and continues for ten days until the Day of Atonement or Yom Kippur. It marked the period of 10 days of consecration and repentance before God in which the Jewish people were to do no servile work (Leviticus 23: 24-25).

The Feast of Trumpets occurred over a period of two full days in which there were 100 trumpet blows. This was accomplished by 9 sets of 11 trumpet blows, which were then followed by a single long and loud blow to complete the 100th blow. It was this "last blow" or "last trump" which Paul referred to in his first letter to the Corinthian Church, which many believe to represent the future time of the Rapture of the Church:

"Behold, I show you a mystery; we shall not all sleep, but we shall all be changed.

In a moment, in the twinkling of an eye, at the last trump: for the trumpet shall sound, and the dead shall be raised incorruptible, and we shall be changed." I Corinthians 15:51,52

The Feast of Trumpets represented many things to the Jewish people, who referred to the feast itself by many different names. It is of great interest to note that most of these names can also be associated with the Rapture of the Church, which also causes many in Christendom to believe that the Feast of Trumpets represents the foreshadowing of this future historical prophetic event.

One of these synonymous Jewish names for the Feast of Trumpets is "Yom Teruah", which means, the "day of blowing", or the "day of the awakening blast". It is often believed that this "awakening blast" refers to the time when the dead in Christ shall be figuratively "awakened" to be caught up in the air, soon to be followed by those who are alive, to forever be with the LORD at the time of the Rapture of the Church (I Thessalonians 4: 16,17).

"Yom Teruah" also refers to "judgment". Immediately after the Rapture of the Church, Christians will be judged at the "Judgment Seat of Christ" to receive rewards for their faithful service in this life (II Corinthians 5:10).

Another Jewish name for the Feast of Trumpets is "The Wedding Day of the Messiah". It should be dutifully noted that in the same time frame that the Judgment Seat of Christ occurs in the Heavens, so too does the marriage of the Messiah to His Bride, the Church occur. Scripture refers to this event as "The Marriage Supper of the Lamb" (Revelation 19:9).

In the Jewish culture, when the Jewish Groom was to become betrothed to his future bride, he would take the "bride price" from his father's house and bring it to the house of the father of his future bride. They would then have an engagement party and a glass of wine together in order to "seal the deal". After this ceremonial drink, the future groom would vow to not drink wine again until the day of the future wedding. At this time, the groom would then return to his father's house and build an addition onto his own father's house in which he and his bride would then live after their marriage ceremony. This of course also holds special symbolic significance to the Christian.

At the Biblical event which unfortunately has been termed by

Christendom as being "The Last Supper", we find Jesus making the same vow, "to not imbibe of the fruit of the vine again until he drinks it new with the disciples in His Father's Kingdom" (Matthew 26:29).

This is an obvious reference to the Jewish betrothal ceremony. For here at the supper party, we observe Jesus talking to His future bride regarding His role as the future Groom of the Church. Another interesting aspect of this is that after Judas had left the dinner party in order to betray Him, that Jesus had told the remaining disciples that He would soon be leaving them, and that He would be going back to His Father's House to prepare individual mansions for them (John 14:2,3). This too is an obvious reference to the Jewish betrothal process.

In this regard, what we mistakenly refer to in Christendom as being "The Last Supper", could and should be more appropriately called, "The Betrothal Dinner of the Lamb."

The Feast of Atonement

The Feast of Atonement (Day of Atonement /Yom Kippur) is considered by many to be the most important of the Jewish Feasts. It occurs on the 10th day of the 7th month, following the Feast of Trumpets. It is a solemn day for the reckoning of sin in which no work was to be done (Leviticus 23:28).

In the prophetic historical future, the Jewish people will have their final reckoning for sin (Atonement) at the time of the 2nd Coming of Jesus back to the earth. The Book of Zechariah states that at the 2nd Coming, the remnant of the Jewish people will "have the spirit of grace and supplication poured out on them, and they shall look upon him who they have pierced, and they shall mourn for him, as one mourneth for his only son" (Zechariah 12:10).

The Feast of Tabernacles

The last Jewish feast, the Feast of Tabernacles, signifies the dwelling of God with man. It lasts for a period of one week and starts with the collection of palm and willow branches for outdoor booths, which the people were commanded to camp out in before the Lord for a period of one whole week (Leviticus 23:40). This was done so that future generations of Jewish people would be reminded that God had their ancestors dwell in booths after He had brought them out of the land of Egypt in acknowledgment of their great deliverance (Leviticus 23:43). The Feast of Tabernacles not only represented God's Presence with the Jewish people but was also meant to signify the giving of the Law at Sinai, for every seven years at the Feast, the Law was to be read to the people (Deuteronomy 31:10,11).

In the prophetic historical future, the Feast of Tabernacles is to signify the dwelling of God with man, as it is referred to by Zechariah of the time that mankind will either tabernacle with God or be removed from the Earth. It is the time of the Millennial Rule of Christ over all the Earth (Zechariah 14: 9, 16,17).

It is significant that Jesus may have indeed been born at the time of the Feast of Tabernacles, thus signifying His initial dwelling with man. It is also significant that many of the Jewish people recognized Jesus as their Messiah, as is evidenced by their putting palm branches at His feet at the time that He road into Jerusalem on a donkey on Palm Sunday. The Book of John tells us that they:

"Took branches of palm trees, and went forth to meet him, and cried, Hosanna: Blessed is the King of Israel that cometh in the name of the Lord." John 12:13

By laying down palm branches at the feet of Jesus and His donkey, the Jewish people were symbolically showing Him that they recognized Him as being their Messiah, and that they were ready for Him to Tabernacle with them and rule over them in His Kingdom. This of course is typical of the ways of man. **405**

For it is mankind's natural desire to receive a crown without having to experience a cross (Luke 9:23).

Fortunately for the Redeemed, Jesus chose His Father's will in the matter (Luke 22:42), and thereby chose the way of the "Cross before the Crown" in order to secure the redemption of those who, by faith, would come to Him for salvation.

"For as the heavens are higher than the earth, so are my ways higher than your ways, and my thoughts than your thoughts." Isaiah 55:9

In conclusion, there are obviously many prophetic and general theological ramifications to be found with the 7 major Feasts of the Jewish people. In that the historical prophetic fulfillment of the first four feasts occurred on the same calendar days that coincided with the actual feasts themselves, it is entirely logical and probable that God would have the three remaining major eschatological occurrences of the Rapture, 2nd Coming, and Initiation of the Millennial Rule of Christ to also coincide with the actual dates of the Feast of Trumpets, Atonement, and Tabernacles.

Again, while Jesus stated that "no man knoweth the date or the hour" of His return, He did not say a word about either the month or the year (Matthew 24:36). At the time of the writing of this treatise in the Fall of 2021, this allows for some interesting speculation regarding future possible time frames for the Rapture, 2nd Coming, and Millennial Kingdom. This would especially hold true if God were to indeed base His time frame of future eschatological events on a Millennial Day time frame, which would allow for 6,000 years of man's self-rule followed by 1,000 years of rest from self-rule during the Millennial Kingdom of Christ.

The Jewish Feast of Trumpets is a two-day event, the start of which is based upon changing lunar cycles. Due to the fact that the Jewish day begins at sundown, the Feast of Trumpets occurs over a 3-day period. In the year 2022, the Feast of Trumpets will occur on September 26-28. In the year 2023, the Feast of

Trumpets will occur on September 16-18. If the Millennial aspects of prophecy contained in the three prophetic papers which constitute Appendix 3 of this treatise prove to be true, then it is quite possible that the Rapture of the Church could indeed occur during the above-mentioned time frames in September of the years 2022 or 2023.

If Israel was truly cut-off in the year 30 A.D., then their national two-day (2,000 year) hiatus from God would end in the year, 3030 A.D. (Hosea 6:2). This would make the likely time of the 2nd Coming of Jesus back to the Earth to occur October 6-7 in the year 2030, at the time of Yom Kippur or the Feast (Day) of Atonement of that year. By working backwards from October 6th or 7th of the year 2030 and subtracting 2520 days (the length of the 7-year Tribulation Period or "last week" of Daniel's prophecy, Revelation 11:2,3; 12:6), it then follows that one should arrive at the date in 2023 that the Anti-Christ would sign his historic peace treaty with the Nation of Israel (Daniel 9:27).

Again, the three parts of Appendix 3 are to be considered "speculative theology". The author stands by the assertions presented in the preceding appendixes and chapters of this book as being valid and thoughtful interpretations of both Biblical Doctrine and/or History, and are meant in no way to be speculative, unless otherwise stated.

If one should find themselves reading these three parts of Appendix 3 in the year 2024 and there has been no Rapture of the Church or initiation of the 7-year Tribulation Period, then one should surmise that either God has not planned His outline for the history of mankind within a Millennial time frame, or that the author has made some mistakes in his interpretations of how the Lord's Millennial 7,000 year history of mankind's life in a sinful state is to be calculated.

It must also be remembered that man's history is often couched in two different systems of reckoning of time, lunar and solar years. This too can obviously cause some difficulties in calculating specific dates, times, or time periods. The purpose the author has in mind for proposing these dates or times is not for the sake of predicting the exact times, but rather to give the reader the real sense of urgency that the time of the return of the Lord back to the Earth may indeed be near.

One thing that can be categorically stated in matters concerning the 2nd Coming of Jesus back to the earth is that it will likely happen during the Fall Feasts of Israel, and that He is not going to take as long in accomplishing His 2nd Coming as He did in the 4,000 years it took for Him to appear at His 1st Coming to the earth (4004 B.C. to 4 B.C.). For from His "Big Picture" time frame reference, Jesus had promised His followers that His 2nd Coming would not take anywhere near as long to occur as had the first, for He stated to them… "Behold I come quickly" (Revelation 22:7). To this, the Apostle John added, "Even so, come Lord Jesus" (Revelation 22:20).

This of course has been the blessed hope of the Church since the time of its inception!

All honor, praise, and glory be unto God!

Made in the USA
Las Vegas, NV
21 June 2023

73665902R00233